D1325531

GETTING
SKILLED

BOOKS BY TOM HEBERT AND JOHN COYNE

THIS WAY OUT: *Alternatives to College*
BY HAND: *A Guide to Schools and Careers in Crafts*
GETTING SKILLED: *A Guide to Private Trade and Technical Schools*

207841

A Guide to
Private Trade and
Technical Schools

TOM HEBERT
and
JOHN COYNE

LC1045
H35
1976

A Sunrise Book

E. P. DUTTON

NEW YORK

Library of Congress Cataloging in Publication Data

Hebert, Tom.
Getting skilled.

"A Sunrise book."
Bibliography: p.
1. Vocational education—United States.   2. Vocational
education—United States—Directories.   3. Technical education—
United States.   4. Technical education—United States—
Directories.   I. Coyne, John, joint author.   II. Title.
LC1045.H35   1976   374.8'73   75–33053

Dutton-Sunrise, Inc., a subsidiary of E. P. Dutton
Copyright © 1976 by Tom Hebert and John Coyne
All rights reserved. Printed in the U.S.A.

10   9   8   7   6   5   4   3

No part of this publication may be reproduced or transmitted in any form
or by any means, electronic or mechanical, including photocopy, recording,
or any information storage and retrieval system now known or to be invented,
without permission in writing from the publisher, except by a reviewer who
wishes to quote brief passages in connection with a review written for inclu-
sion in a magazine, newspaper or broadcast.

Published simultaneously in Canada by Clarke, Irwin & Company Limited,
Toronto and Vancouver
ISBN: 0-87690-183-6 (cloth)
        0-87690-202-6 (paper)

Designed by The Etheredges

*To the school owners
and their students—
they couldn't believe a book was
being written about them.*

CONTENTS

ACKNOWLEDGMENTS

We would like to thank the following people who helped us move through the world of private trade and technical schools. At the National Association of Trade and Technical Schools (NATTS): President Leo Kogan, Counsel Bernard Ehrlich, Phil Taylor, Dan Finn, Ron Blakely, Nancy Admams, Bob Stephens, Jackie Joyner, Louise Goddard, Alberta Bertuzzi, Johnnie Farrar, Bob Gleason, Cynthia Hairston, and Executive Director Bill Goddard. Phyllis Shaughnessy provided useful editorial assistance.

Officials at two other private school associations helped us at important points. At the National Home Study Council: Bill Fowler, Mike Lambert, and Cordelia Richards. At the Association of Independent Colleges and Schools (private business schools): Mary Wine.

We owe special thanks to the students who took time to answer such questions as "What are you doing here?" as we prowled about their schools.

■ xiii

Higher Education has discovered proprietary (profit-seeking) education and has studied its mechanisms and effectiveness. Many of these "establishment" people shared their thoughts and research with us and suffered many telephone interruptions of their working day. Guidebook writers depend upon such people: Alexander Astin, American Council on Education; Harvey Belitsky, Upjohn Institute; Louis Bender, Florida State University; August Bolino, Catholic University, Washington, D.C.; Thomas Corcoran, Educational Policy Research Center, Syracuse; Jill Holland and Judy Morris, Ohio State Center for Research and Development in Vocational and Technical Education; John Holland, Center for Social Organization of Schools, Johns Hopkins University; Kenneth Hoyt, University of Maryland Counseling Department; William Hyde, University of Chicago, Comparative Education Center; Homer Kempfer, Institute of Independent Study, Richmond; Elwood Shoemaker, Catholic University; and Wellford Wilms, Center for Research and Development in Higher Education, University of California, Berkeley. The Bibliography contains the references to their work.

The librarians at the American Council on Education and the American Personnel and Guidance Association found what we needed every time. The ERIC Clearing House on Higher Education is friendly and its system works very well.

At the American Association of Higher Education: Ken Fisher and Jane Lichtman. At the College Entrance Examination Board in New York: Solomon Arbeiter and Pat Bell. At the Brookings Institution: George Arnstein and Dick Graham. At the Institute for Policy Studies in Washington, D.C.: Karl Hess and Arthur Waskow. At the B'Nai B'Rith Career and Counseling Service: Norman Feingold. At the AFL-CIO education department: Jack Sessions.

All facts, opinions, and reports find a natural home in Washington, D.C. Without exception, the following people have been in the "finest tradition of government service," i.e., they have taken the time to explain things. At the U.S. Office of Education: David Bayer, Office of Guaranteed Student Loans; Leroy Cornelson; Bob Calvert, National Center for Educational Statistics. Over at the National Institute of Education, our special informed source: Mary Ann Millsaps.

At the Federal Trade Commission: Henry Cabell and Brian Hampton. At the Department of Labor: Harry Leiberman; and at the Bureau of Labor Statistics: Kopp Michelotti. At the Office of Economic Opportunity: Charles Stallford. At the General Accounting Office: Rosemary Mylecraine. On the Hill: Joe Luman, Staff Director of the House Special Studies Subcommittee.

At the now packed-up-and-gone National Commission on the Financing of Postsecondary Education: George Weathersby and Ted Youn.

At the Federal Aviation Administration: Irving Birnbaum, Dr. Oliver Lane, and Mervin Stricker.

The state offices of education that oversee the school industry are the most knowledgeable observers. Three state officials were very helpful to us: Frank Albanese, executive secretary of the Ohio State Board of School and College Registration; Charles Conlon, Maryland Specialist in Accreditation; Jim Manning, Virginia Supervisor of the Proprietary School Service in the State Department of Education.

The following educators own or direct schools. They gave us the run of their schools and answered the tough questions: Noel Adams, Alfiero Alfieri, John Benanti, Manny Bloch, Mary Borsky, Gene Bremers, Phil Chosky, Warren Davies, Dick Diggs, Lou Dimasi, Al Dreyfus, Don Finch, Michael Freedland, Mo Gaebe, John Griffin, Lou Hernandez, Charles Janssen, Morris Kirshenbaum, Les Klein, Virginia Marti, Carl McDonald, Edward and Anna Lee Porter, Marlo Ratsvog, Mr. and Mrs. George Thatcher, Jack Tolbert, Lew Warner, and John Wilson.

There are fifteen more: Ron Baillie, Jack Bisblingoff, Mrs. Boldt, John Cowan, Mrs. Frank, Frank Gale, Bill Hart, Fred Hirsch, John Johns, H. V. Leslie, Adrian Marcuse, Booker T. Thomas, the man from Teller Training Institute, Douglas Wagner, and Mary Wise.

If depending on all of the above wasn't enough, we have special friends and associates who deserve recognition for sticking with us: Dr. Janie Beers, who was there at the discovery of this educational underground, and Gerald Allan Schwinn, who contributed much to our analysis of the school industry. Michael Prewitt, Fred Raab, Peter Noterman, Shirley Porro, Uncle Don Currie, Elene Hebert, Lee Baxandall, and John Hanrahan were essential members of the expedition.

Dear people who took us in while we wrote: Pat Bell, Terry Guilliams, the Warren Dewars, Bill Brookes, Ginna and Harold Fleming of No-name Farm, and Bill and Jane Brown of the Penland School of Crafts, Penland, North Carolina.

. . . *He was an expert sack-sewer, and six dollars a day and board was the lowest wages he ever looked at. The way to get ahead of this short-stake labor game was to learn some kind of work that people were likeliest to be short of, and then instead of having to beg and kiss people's tails for a job, you made them beg you. The thing to do was to sell your work, not your complexion or politics or church membership or ability to do sleight-of-hand tricks for the girls after working-hours.*

—H. L. DAVIS, *Honey in the Horn,* 1935

GETTING SKILLED

ONE

INTRODUCTION: ARE YOU SPECIALTY ORIENTED?

The tall girl was a community college dropout. We met her in a midtown Manhattan private medical-dental assisting school. Her course was about forty weeks long; she was paying for it herself. We asked her how she was doing. "Good . . . I feel special now. I am learning something special for something special. We feel needed, special. . . . Doctors and patients need us."

By now that girl has completed her course of training and is working as a medical assistant. She may have gotten the job on her own, but there is a very good chance that she and her employer discovered each other through the school's job placement officer. At any given moment, 150,000 people like her are getting skilled in schools accredited by the National Association of Trade and Technical Schools (NATTS), with 90,000 graduating each

year. Many hundreds of thousands more are attending good unaccredited schools. They are young, old; male and female; black
and white. Some have been to college; most are high school
graduates. They have all made the decision to get skilled in a
school specially designed for skill training and job placement.
The decision was the hardest part.

Turn to the black separator in the back of this book. The
NATTS *Directory of Accredited Private Trade and Technical
Schools* begins there, on page 149. These 421 schools belong to
the National Association of Trade and Technical Schools. The
listings are arranged in two different groups: in the first, schools
are listed by the training they offer; in the second, by the states
they are located in.

DO YOU WANT TO LEARN A SPECIFIC OCCUPATIONAL SKILL?

This book is meant to be flipped through and thumbed. Scan
the NATTS Directory from the acting school (Laurence Merrick
Theatre Academy, Hollywood) to the X-ray technician school
(Medical Training Institute, California); from the Herzing Institute in Alabama (computer training) to the Wyoming Technical Institute (a school for automotive and diesel technicians).
The Directory lists for you the finest vocational schools in the
United States. The rest of the book explains how they work, and
your role in selecting and attending one.

Look through the schools that interest you—the ones that
offer courses in skills you've dreamed of possessing, or now realize you need. The Directory is a kind of career-counseling device.
It allows you to pick up on which skills are taught in specialty
schools. Knowing what is out there is important; the Directory
is a list of over one hundred occupational alternatives.

WHY GET SKILLED?

In the early stages of researching this book we talked to tall,
intense Marshall Palley, Director of the New Vocations Center of

the American Friends Service Committee in San Francisco. We told him we wanted to do a book about learning skills and getting jobs. Marshall shot out of the chair. "Here is what I tell young people these days. Pick a vocation and stick with it. Generalization will come naturally, as you feel the need to expand the job to keep it from becoming dead. If you don't specialize, it's difficult for you to do *anything*. You have no defined context within which to work. The liberal arts education that college students get today brings them no closer to knowing what they want to do than when they graduated from high school. It's important to provide training or apprenticeships in specific vocations rather than more generalized education."

Having definite working skills (a specialty) allows one to survive—and survive in some style. A skill gives:

personal confidence,
good working habits,
employability,
independence, and
a base for learning new skills.

Further, basic skills don't change much over time; they are more stable than jobs. A skilled person can be flexible in changing job situations. The girl who was learning to be a medical assistant was also learning the basic skills of how to work with people, how to manage an office, and how to work in a laboratory. Her future career can, and will, go in many directions.

Similarly, a person who attends a broadcasting school will learn the operation of a radio station at the same time that he is increasing his employability in sales management and public relations. He will learn copywriting, editing, small business management, and sales presentations. After an initial period in a small or rural station, graduates of broadcasting schools are often hired away by sponsors, who can use the graduates' reputations and basic communications skills in their businesses. Other training follows the same pattern. People use their training in unpredictable ways.

Skilled people are in demand. Look in tonight's paper. There will be columns and columns of help wanted ads for skilled people—not college people, *skilled* people.

In January 1975, Ernest B. Furgurson reported in his column for the *Baltimore Sun:*

> I checked the Baltimore paper. It had no less than 65 columns of help wanted, which means about 1,800 jobs. . . . What the ads show most clearly is the demand for trained help in nearly every field. In all of those hundreds of ads, there was not a single call for a plain unskilled laborer. But there were columns of opportunities for people with such a basic qualification as typing. . . . It reaffirms something working parents have been trying to drum into their young for centuries: If you get yourself a skill, a trade, you have something nobody can take away. If you have none, you are just so much filler material in the job market.

We used to have conveyor-belt careers. A kid was picked up at one end, put through school, oriented to a job or profession, put to work, worked and moved around for thirty years, and finally dropped off the belt when he reached old age. No more. The U.S. Census Bureau reports that on the average we change basic jobs every five years; that's six to eight mini-careers in a lifetime.

There is no more job security. Early on one should nail down one's basic talents—the type of work one likes and does best—and then get the skills involved.

These trade and technical schools teach skills, not jobs. This book is about skills, not salaries. Skills come first. A school owner told us, "We give students basic knowledge to compete."

"One of Maudslay's fellow-workmen bore testimony to the qualities of his art: 'It was a pleasure to see him handle a tool of any kind, but he was *quite splendid* with an eighteen-inch file.'"
—LEWIS MUMFORD, *The Myth of the Machine*, 1970

THE SCHOOLS THEMSELVES

Trade and technical schools are all around us; they exist in communities throughout the country. Yet they are generally unknown, except to their students and their students' families. There is perhaps a vague community awareness—people see the signs on buses, or read advertisements, but never connect them with the kid next door who is about to start studying at one of these schools. They constitute an important, effective sector of education in the United States. But because they are so little understood, trade and technical schools rarely spring to mind as a worthwhile alternative, even to those people who could profit from them most.

Private trade and technical schools are independent, small, job-oriented, practical, intensive, and student-centered. They are often called "proprietary schools," which means they are privately owned and operated, in hopes of making a profit. They advertise and they use salespersons. They enroll thousands of students who are satisfied with their training. After studying these schools closely for two and a half years, we are still amazed at how well they work. Although public school officials habitually scorn them as profit seekers, we have found more integrity in proprietary school owners than we ever expected to see in educators. They do what they promise to do. This is small business America. This is what it is like.

▪ The proprietary school has been common since the 1880s. It is a very traditional sort of business, usually owned by small entrepreneurs. These profit-seeking schools are not supported by taxes.

▪ The schools sell a product: training. They provide a service: job placement.

▪ The basis of proprietary school training is the *performance contract* that is signed by both the student consumer and the school. The school agrees to give the training if the student abides by the fee schedule and the school rules. Both sides have to live up to the contract.

■ The schools are small, averaging fewer than three hundred students. They are usually friendly, personal places. Staffs are small, too. There is a president or director; a chief of instruction who also teaches; a bookkeeper; a job placement officer. The school usually occupies rented office space downtown and space is likely to be limited. "Take your average university president's office and board room, divide by two, and you get the size of the average proprietary school," one owner told us. Given this simple structure, these schools—unlike community colleges—are not *confusing*. A couple of offices and a couple of courses.

■ Because of their low visibility, the best schools have vigorous recruiting campaigns and use well-trained salespeople to seek out and talk with prospective students. Salespeople give the prospective student a chance to get all his questions answered. From their own end, they size up the student to see if he's likely to be a success at the school.

■ Schools also depend on their graduates to recruit new students. The reputation of the school—which is based primarily on how many of its graduates find and keep the jobs they want—is very important to school owners. The majority of new enrollments come through student referrals, one to another. School owners know from bitter experience that a few unhappy students can poison the recruiting pot. The result is that it is not in the interest of these schools to hustle an unpromising student into enrolling; he will only drop out and criticize the school. Once a student *is* enrolled, however, these schools aim to keep their part of the bargain. As the owner of an electronics school put it, "If a student is unhappy or not doing as well as he can, we've probably made a mistake somewhere. I hear about it and move on it." *These schools do their best to give students what they pay for.*

■ Proprietary schools are student-centered in another way. School owners have a *belief* in students that we've rarely encountered on college campuses.

▪ The school is out to create an "employable personality." "I know what employers are looking for," the owner of one secretarial school told us, "and I don't have any hangups about changing my students' attitudes or behavior if it will get them a better job." To that end, his female students are required to wear dresses to school, and all students are forbidden to smoke.

▪ Many schools still take for granted certain sex roles. Women are just beginning to show up in the automotive, electronics, and welding schools. Men are applying for fashion merchandising and medical assisting programs that they ignored before. A few of the more conservative schools will try to dissuade applicants of either sex if they have not dealt with that sex before. Be pushy. You have a right to the training you want. We feel that the private school industry will have solved its sex-bias problems before the rest of the education establishment.

▪ Schools accredited by NATTS are integrated. Blacks and whites study in proprietary schools with little or no friction. As one school owner pointed out, "Working-class people judge one another by how well a person holds up his end."

▪ The fly-by-night, here-today, gone-tomorrow schools are a myth nowadays. A school that skips with prepaid tuitions and leaves untrained students behind is very rare. When a school does close, nearby schools team up to "train out" the remaining students. The typical rate of closure per year is about 15 percent, a figure that is matched in any sector of small business.

▪ These schools are more education oriented than profit oriented. The reputation of a school and the value of a particular course can be easily checked by prospective students. Schools that put profits ahead of good training go out of business quickly. You can't fool students long.

"We get them to do things they have never done before. . . . We just keep a wrench in their hands. . . . A kid comes back every day if he is learning."

—AN AUTO REPAIR SCHOOL

THE STUDENTS

Most of the students we've met in private trade and technical schools seem to enjoy having finally taken root somewhere. Their futures for the next few years are fairly clear to them, or else they aren't worried because the process of training and their probable job placement create confidence. That may be the most striking thing about these students: their confidence and savvy about who they are and where they're going.

Most students pay their own tuition. A quarter of the students in trade and technical schools are veterans and another 35 percent have Guaranteed Student Loans that they will repay later. About 15 percent of the students are on various other subsidized government programs. Students are proud that they have been able to shoulder a one- or two-thousand-dollar debt. For many, it is their first step into adulthood.

Having paid that much money, they carefully watch their investment. They are consumer-minded and do not hesitate to complain about anything inferior in a school. We want to emphasize this important phenomenon. Students are willing to pay large amounts of money for quality training, but they want their money's worth. (See Appendix E, #7)

Debbie Billet was the first woman student to enroll in the thirty-six-week Automotive Technology course at Lincoln Technical Institute, outside Washington, D.C.

I've always been interested in mechanical type stuff and it's what I've always enjoyed doing the most. I needed to be able to do something to survive. And just the whole general orientation with women has been non-mechanical and it's hard to be able to do all these things on your own unless you get some kind of formal training. Most men from the time they're young have always been directed and interested in working on their cars and everything and I never had any background in it and so I needed to get the formal training.

It's just really hard to take yourself seriously unless you know what you're doing, 'cause guys tend to think being a girl, you just don't know what you're talking about. Like for example bleeding brakes, you always end up being the one that pumps the brakes and there's nothing to it, anybody can do it. It's just good to be able to know that you know what you're doing.

THE TRAINING

▪ To be good, training must be up-to-date. The teachers have had years of experience out in the field. Those who have just come from active employment are prepared to teach new skills and requirements.

School administrators want the courses they offer to be up-to-date. Trade journals, discussions, personal involvement in the field—all contribute to their awareness of the quality of what they are selling.

▪ Most schools offer both long and short courses. Some are comprehensive and some specialized. For example, one school might offer a two-week course in sewing dresses, whereas another would provide complete tailoring, which would require sixty weeks.

▪ The *average* course today is 1,200 hours, or forty weeks. Classes generally meet six hours per day, five days a week. Most schools offer the alternative of evening classes as well.

▪ The training is "hands-on" the actual equipment used in the field, almost from the very first day. The theory end is foreshortened and the practical emphasized. Structurally, private school training is *problem-solving* and *modular* (segmented into small learning units) to enable the teachers to evaluate student progress weekly and catch problems early. This also allows for a flexible curriculum; units can be added or dropped without disturbing the whole cycle.

▪ The short, intensive nature of private school training means that more information can be applied on the first day of work. Students have studied the fundamentals and the applied skills just recently and are not apt to have forgotten as much as in long courses. One machinist school we visited can place graduates successfully after only *one month* of training. That month is spent on a crash trigonometry course and daily use of five machines until competence is acquired. Everything is fresh in the mind that first morning on the job.

■ Students who want to study a certain skill but are afraid of some supposed math or science requirement should talk to someone at the school. Chances are, they have found a way of getting around the bad high school experience many of us had in those subjects. We have heard this statement often: "Oh, I was scared about the math. I mean, I thought I was just dumb in it. But after they explained how it was used and taught us these few shortcuts, I found out I could do it."

■ Dr. Harvey Belitsky, author of *Proprietary Vocational Schools and Their Students,* reports that 41 percent of each day at a NATTS school is spent in "concrete institutional settings." That means that almost half the time is spent in joblike situations, the rest in classes.

■ Proprietary schools are not intrinsically competitive. They are *achievement oriented.* The employers determine what will constitute "entry-level" skills—the minimum skills needed to get a job in a given field. The schools contract to bring the student to that level of competence. Each student repeats a unit of work until *he* or *she* is good at it.

■ Typically, a *buddy system* is used. A student who has "taken hold" is seated near a person who is having problems with a unit. Peer education can't be surpassed.

■ *All* schools provide remedial work and tutorial assistance if it is needed.

■ A student rarely has to wait more than a month or two for a class to start in the subject he's interested in.

■ The great strength of private school training is the *roller coaster effect.* Once you begin, the training carries you along, easing you over the bumps and around the sharp curves, with mounting involvement leading to a fast finish.

"One feature of a tough admissions policy which bears special mention is what we call our Bad News Sheet, which is given to every applicant, and which lists all the negative aspects of this career. Our first goal with every man is to put him in touch with reality."

—A WELDING SCHOOL

HOW GOOD ARE THEY?

Most schools do what they promise to do: train for the best possible job in the shortest amount of time. How good are they?

▪ Students are well satisfied. In one large study, conducted by the American Institutes for Research, more than 80 percent of all students surveyed said that their schools "provide good job training, practical skills emphasis, good teaching and equipment needed for learning." This has been our impression as well.

▪ Most students complete their training. In six- to twelve-month courses, for example, 65–75 percent will graduate.

▪ Sixty to 80 percent will get jobs directly relating to their training. That's high, considering that in any group of young people some don't want to go immediately to work, some blow interviews every time, and some have just barely passed the course and therefore have minimal skills.

If you are in a hard-working school and you work hard, you'll learn the skill and can most likely get a job where you'll be using it.

▪ Proprietary schools are closely scrutinized by many private and government groups: the National Association of Trade and Technical Schools; the Association of Independent Colleges and Schools (business schools); the National Home Study Council; the Federal Trade Commission; the United States Office of Education; state licensing boards; the Internal Revenue Service; consumer protection groups; and the media. Under such heavy surveillance, school owners tend to keep their standards high.

"We hold our teachers accountable for how well our students do out there."

—A BROADCASTING SCHOOL

For years one horse was pulling the plow while another got the oats: the private schools trained and placed millions of young people while the public schools got approval, higher status, the funding for elaborate facilities.

This picture has changed.

Costs have soared in the public schools, while their enrollments and popularity have fallen; meanwhile, legislators, educators, and government officials have finally visited the private schools to see if they work. At last, kind words and testimonials have started to come.

From a pamphlet, "Good Training, Good Jobs," published by the U.S. Office of Education in 1970:

> Private business, trade and technical schools are able to offer a solid, but specialized, educational background and supplementary training to equip their students for responsible and worthwhile careers after a relatively brief period of study. This is because the private school student may concentrate only on those courses pertaining specifically to the job for which he is training.

> Other advantages of private schools: the students can usually begin classes almost immediately after enrollment; completion of the entire program generally can be accomplished within a brief period of time—usually less than a year and often under 6 months; the curriculum is so flexibly stuctured that it may be entirely skill-oriented; and most private schools offer job placement upon graduation as a standard service.

Dr. Wellford "Buzz" Wilms of the Center for Research and Development in Higher Education at the University of California, Berkeley, is directing the largest study of private and public vocational training to date. He received cooperation from fifty schools (twenty-nine proprietary and twenty-one public schools, mostly community colleges) in four cities, teaching six occupational fields. He was able to study about 4,800 students and graduates.

At a November 1974 briefing on his study in Washington, Dr. Wilms commented on the old question of "shadiness" in the proprietary sector: "It's an interesting sidelight that if you read the Boston *Globe* series [see Bibliography] and some of the other exposés, you get the feeling that every other proprietary school is a rip-off. This was not at all borne out in our data. Of 29 proprietary schools that we asked to join the study, only two turned us down. That's a pretty small percentage. No evidence was found that proprietary schools, which attract applicants with fewer educational skills, either exploited their students or used deceptive advertising. The concept of 'shadiness' is not borne out at all."

Wilms's study reports that out of twenty-nine private schools, *only one* went out of business in the two years covered by the study and only two were sold in that period. Wilms concluded that it was a stable industry.

As yet, Wilms has produced no data on attrition or dropout rates. However, he has said: ". . . our survey in Chicago in September 1972 showed that although the proprietary and public postsecondary schools started with about the same number of secretarial and data processing enrollees, the proprietary schools graduated 4 to 6 times as many as the public community colleges. This same pattern seems to hold in the other locations we are studying" [see Appendix E].

One of the great misconceptions about private schools is that complaints are not dealt with by the schools, that proprietary schools leave great numbers of dissatisfied students behind. At the Federal Trade Commission, several lawyers told us that vocational schools led all categories in consumer complaints to the Better Business Bureau. This was a serious charge, and we checked it out in two reputable places. The first was the Better Business Bureau itself. In a letter to the FTC, the Council of Better Business Bureaus brought the FTC up short:

> . . . a review of statistics maintained by our Research Department revealed that on the basis of complaints received by local BBBs, the classification for trade and vocational schools ranks approximately 35*th* out of 85 categories. This ranking has remained quite stable for several years.

Just to be sure, we brought up the subject with Henry Cabell, an attorney in the Legal Division of the FTC, who has had more experience with the school industry than anyone else at the FTC. According to Cabell:

> Complaints have been steady; there are thousands of schools out there. . . . But we don't get complaints on the schools that really teach you to do something. Seventy to eighty percent of the complaints are generated by a few schools. The rest of the schools take care of themselves. . . . I think [the industry] does a pretty good job.

Similar satisfaction was voiced by Joseph Clark, Commissioner of the Indiana Private School Accrediting Commission, which oversees private schools in that state. In testimony before the House Special Committee on Governmental Investigations, Clark said:

> [Proprietary schools] have proven to the colleges and universities of the country that people want, expect and need education that prepares them for job immediacy. . . . It is time that we call to the attention of the American consumer that there are good schools out there and that they do good, creditable training. . . . In 1973 we had problems ranging from inconvenience to fraud, with 8% of the schools doing business in Indiana. I do not see 8% as constituting a clear and present danger to the American people. For of that, only .02% were hard core fraud cases.

We leave the last word to Phil Chosky, the owner of an electronics school in Pittsburgh. At an FTC hearing on proposed new industry regulations, Phil told his government audience:

> As you go about the business of the Commission, I am sure that you frequently have occasion to travel on the commercial airlines of this country. I would just like to call to your attention that most of the aircraft mechanics and most electronic technicians who maintain aircraft navigational systems are graduates of proprietary schools. Every time you set foot on a commercial airliner you literally bet your life on the qualifications of these institutions and their graduates. This may give you something to think about on those long trips between hearings!

WHAT IS ACCREDITATION?

Accreditation is a long, drawn-out process that a school voluntarily undertakes in order to establish itself as

a worthwhile school to attend,

a school eligible to participate in various government student loan programs.

Accreditation means that after operating successfully for at least two years, a school has been evaluated and found to meet the minimum standards of an accrediting commission recognized by the U.S. Office of Education. For the schools in this book, that means the National Association of Trade and Technical Schools. Although any school can apply for accreditation after operating for at least two years, most schools have been around at least four or five years before they feel ready for a visit from a NATTS evaluation team.

An accredited school:

Truthfully advertises its services.

Clearly sets forth its terms of enrollment.

Charges reasonable tuition fees.

Admits only qualified students.

Offers up-to-date courses.

Employs instructors experienced in their fields.

Maintains adequate equipment for the courses offered.

Keeps classes to a reasonable size.

Provides guidance and placement services.

Is answerable to the NATTS Accrediting Commission for all of the above.

The schools undergo full reaccreditation (application and evaluation) every five years.

Accrediting organizations cannot close a school; they can only exclude from membership. Expulsion, however, means a school is denied participation in federal programs like the Guaranteed Student Loan program. But the real hammer is the loss of face that would accompany expulsion. School owners are hungry for peer recognition. NATTS is the only fraternity they have.

All accrediting associations operate in a similar fashion. First they establish standards for membership. Then schools measure themselves against those standards, changing and improving various aspects of their operation to meet them. A long "Self-Evaluation Study" is made by the school itself wherein it explains its operation in relation to the published standards of the accrediting agency. After payment of a fee (about $500, generally, for the schools in this book) the school is visited by a team of "knowledgeable persons."

Team members go into the classrooms and listen to the instructors, then wander around looking at equipment and student work. Each member stops to talk to students privately to get their evaluation of the training and listen to any complaints they might have. Meanwhile, a NATTS staff person contacts the Better Business Bureau and local consumer offices to check on the school's reliability. The financial situation of the school has already been investigated, and now student records are checked to see that they are well maintained, and that refunds and complaints have been promptly handled.

Graduates are also contacted to get their unvarnished evaluation of their training. One of the team members is a businessman who is acquainted with the reputation of the school and may even have had occasion to hire one of the graduates himself. The team is trying to evaluate the overall effectiveness of the school in meeting the goals it has set for itself. But the question each member asks himself is simple: "Would I want my son or daughter to attend this school?"

An informal side of accreditation is the "snitching" that goes on between members of NATTS. For example, if one school tries a bit of hard-sell advertising, within days NATTS has been sent a copy of the ad and the offending school is questioned about the incident. This is "peer pressure," industry self-policing. It is effective.

The schools listed in the NATTS Directory are accredited, and accreditation often reassures students, parents, and high school counselors. However, do not limit yourself to only accredited schools. Accreditation of trade and technical schools is a new process, begun in 1966; hundreds and hundreds of good schools are not yet accredited.

HOW MUCH DO THEY COST?

They're not cheap. They don't give these courses away. Here are average *Spring 1975* tuitions for thirteen popular courses in NATTS-accredited schools. These courses account for 85 percent of total NATTS enrollments.

Please remember that these are *average* tuition figures, suggesting the middle ground of tuitions. Schools will charge more in some cases, less in others. Prices vary from area to area. Courses cost what they are worth.

We arrived at these figures by averaging tuitions from three schools in each field, one from the East, one from the Midwest, and another from the West Coast.

SKILL	AVERAGE LENGTH WEEKS	AVERAGE TUITION
Electronics (electronic technician)	72	$3,123
Automotive (automotive mechanic)	45	$1,680
Art (interior design)	100	$4,403
Paramedical (medical assisting)	27	$1,481
Computer (computer programming)	26	$2,139
Air Conditioning	24	$1,769
Fashion (fashion merchandising)	76	$4,410
Drafting (electro-mechanical)	52	$1,883
Aviation (a&p mechanic)	67	$3,146
Welding (general or combination)	16	$1,264
Broadcasting	25	$1,663
Truck Driving (diesel)	3–8	$1,291
Travel (air travel career)	28	$2,095

Accredited NATTS schools are required to charge *reasonable* tuition fees. Private vocational schools figure their tuitions by adding a reasonable profit to the *total* cost of instruction. Generally, the higher the tuition the better the training. Shorter, intensive courses also tend to be higher priced. School owners know students will pay for quality courses and are distrustful of "bargains" in such matters.

Some schools charge by the hour, others by the day, week, month, or quarter. Some charge as little as $1.50 per instructional hour. More common is a $3–5 per hour figure, but in any case, it is unimportant arithmetic. Cheap courses tend to be long, leisurely, and not as up to date. Since you are paying tuition only *once*, go *first class*.

Getting a skill is expensive. To your tuition you must add the cost of "foregone earnings," money you might have earned while you were attending school. It can add up to thousands of dollars, but it is a worthwhile investment in the long term. In a study of vocational schools for the U.S. Office of Education, the American Institutes for Research in Palo Alto determined the *rate of return* on the investment in skill training:

The 29% rate of return calculated for all alumni indicated that the vocational training programs surveyed are clearly effective from a cost-benefit standpoint, the rate of return being almost six times the return which would have been obtained from having invested similar money in a bank over a similar number of years. . . . It is apparent that it is possible to recover the costs of training within three years.

WHO SHOULD GO?

A machine shop teacher once told us that he could spot the best students the minute they walked into his shop:

> I can tell how a kid will do when he sees the shop, the other students, and the equipment. If his eyes light up, it means he has found what he's been looking for and he's set to go.

This teacher was talking about the Specialty Oriented Student. The concept may be credited to Dr. Ken Hoyt, who, as we write, is an Assistant Commissioner of Education and head of Career Education programs in the U.S. Office of Education. Hoyt defines the Specialty Oriented Student (SOS):

> The Specialty Oriented Student is one whose motivations toward educational achievement are built largely around a desire to acquire a specific occupational skill or set of skills. Courses designed to broaden his potential for avocational living have little or no appeal to this student. He may be described as expressing relatively more interest in being "trained" than in being "educated."

Since 1961 Hoyt has been devising a vocational counseling system based upon his SOS research program. Over the past dozen years he has studied about twenty-five thousand such students. These are his findings:

> Most SOS students are under twenty-one years of age.
> They come from lower-middle-class backgrounds.

They receive only a portion of their school expenses from their parents.

They rate their training programs as good.

They complete their training.

They enter into training-related occupations.

The term Specialty Oriented Student straightens out much slack and disparaging thinking about those students who do not want to truck off to college. It has little to do with the terms "occupationally oriented student" or "vocationally oriented student." It says that some students are distinguished from the average academic students in that they want to specialize right away. The beauty of the term SOS is that it lends needed dignity to a student who has made an early choice about what he or she wants to do in life. Those are the high school students who are generally looked down upon. Seeing them as "specialty oriented" rather than "work oriented" helps us understand who and what they are. The term suggests a maturity which in fact they possess.

This is the student we have met up with in proprietary trade and technical schools. These schools exist for, and are predicated upon, the Specialty Oriented Student. This book is *for* the Specialty Oriented Student.

It is also for unemployed college graduates who need skills to get jobs. Unemployment statistics for college graduates are higher than the national average.

Arch Booth, President of the Chamber of Commerce of the United States, wrote in *JOBS for Veterans,* September 1974:

> College graduates would be making a big mistake not to consider work outside of the fields regarded as the traditional preserves of the degree holder. The skilled trades pay very well today; so do many technical fields.
>
> In the 1980's the number of college graduates will far outstrip the supply of jobs for them.
>
> According to the American Movers Conference, there is a shortage of truck drivers in the interstate moving industry. . . . There are undoubtedly other jobs like that going begging, just waiting for

someone adventurous enough to take off the blinders and find work that suits him, regardless of his official educational status or the preferences of his mother-in-law.

For those who cannot escape their mothers-in-law, successful schools also exist for training legal assistants, midwives, childcare specialists, and for teaching various medical and veterinary skills. College graduates seem to like the intensive training, usually lasting only four to six months, and if they choose, they can find employment in professional offices that want to lower costs by reorganizing their workloads. We see new "career ladders" being established that will allow more of this kind of thing.

Proprietary schools should also be considered by unemployed older workers who do not expect to find work in their previous occupations. Older people are reluctant schoolgoers. But a sprinkling of older people is now attending these schools, and school officials describe them as generally excellent students, not hard to place in jobs. The schools themselves are improved when older, experienced people are attending.

One day we were sitting in an advanced electronics class in a small proprietary school. We had interviewed a number of students and been impressed by their maturity and sense of direction. As we are dumb when it comes to numbers, the lecture was passing over our heads. Afterward we asked a student what it was all about. "Well, to simplify it: Electronics has to do with *control*; electricity has to do with *power*. The lecture was discussing the design of gadgets that bring the two together."

We blinked, looked at the array of pens, pencils, and slide rule in his shirt pocket, and were reminded of a line in a Barber College catalog: "One of the benefits of training is that you learn it the *right way*."

CAN I GET IN?

Yes. Private vocational schools have "open admissions" providing you have

a desire to take the course,
a basic aptitude for the skills involved,
a high school diploma, G.E.D., or demonstrated ability,
some way of paying for the course, and
a probability for successful job placement.

Each school has determined job requirements for the skills it teaches. The schools know fairly precisely what sorts of people employers are looking for. Dental assisting schools won't enroll obese women; they're hard to place. For the bench trades, an applicant must show mechanical ability. Commercial art schools want to see a portfolio of work demonstrating the student's talent. Drafting and architectural technology courses demand strong spacial perception, patience, and neatness. Electronics depends on a basic mathematical ability; sometimes applicants must know trigonometry. If you are going to take a travel agent course, do you like to travel?

During the first interview the schools will give an aptitude test or question the applicant closely to determine the suitability of the course. The schools are looking for desire. Students with some remedial deficiencies can always be brought up to speed.

"We found out that the students couldn't use simple hand tools. We had to teach that first."

—A DEEP-SEA DIVING SCHOOL

DO PROPRIETARY SCHOOLS AWARD ANY KIND OF DEGREES?

Yes. Several states now allow accredited proprietary schools to award specialized *associate degrees* for selected two-year programs meeting established standards. These degrees have equal standing with those given at community colleges. They may have unfamiliar titles, such as Associate of Applied Arts, Associate in

Specialized Technology, and Associate in Occupational Studies.

The courses that are given degree status are the longer—eighteen months to twenty-four months—that have college equivalency, such as architectural engineering technology, data processing, electronics, commercial art, fashion merchandising, interior design, and the like. The degree offerings differ from community college courses in that they have a decreased emphasis on general education and much more emphasis on applied skills and job preparation.

It is debatable whether or not this is a healthy trend. Private schools have gotten along without degrees for years. Employers and students have always valued the diplomas and certificates awarded by reputable schools. Although associate degrees may, in the short run, give private schools a competitive edge, we feel that they will eventually water down the basic advantage of the private school—that training lasts just long enough to qualify the student to get the job he wants. When a school sets up an "academic calendar," strings out its courses to unnecessary length, and hires a "registrar," watch out. Trade schools don't need such "couth."

CAN I TRANSFER COURSE CREDITS FROM A PRIVATE TRADE SCHOOL TO A COLLEGE?

There is an old saw around the school industry: when college enrollments are down, suddenly proprietary school graduates find it possible to gain advanced standing in some colleges and universities. This is true today.

If you match the right private school with the right college, you can use your proprietary training as the basis for a college degree. When the colleges take a look at the schools' courses they often realize they are superior to their own.

If you are interested in credit transferability, be in early contact with both schools. Many business schools and some trade and technical schools have already worked out transfer arrangements which they can explain to you.

WILL I FINISH?

Yes, the figures are with you. Course completion is the strong suit of private vocational schools.

Courses 1–6 months long: 70–90 percent finish

Courses 6–12 months long: 65–75 percent finish

Courses 12–24 months long: 50–70 percent finish

Typically, 2 to 5 percent are asked to leave for academic reasons with the rest moving on to something else in the classic manner of dropouts.

Some courses have two streams, one shorter and less demanding with a certificate at completion; the other geared for the upper technical end of the skill involved, with a diploma at graduation. It is possible to move from one to the other if it will help you persist in school.

Naturally, the shorter the course the better your chances of finishing.

If you finish, you'll have gotten a skill.

WILL I GET A JOB?

These schools depend upon successful graduates to stay in business and it is a stable industry. They work for your success. Each school has a placement office that maintains contact with employers that have hired the school's graduates in the past. Toward the end of the course, placement officers begin to match students and jobs. They keep at it until most students are placed and most are placed within a month of graduation.

"It's good when you know."

—A SEWING SCHOOL STUDENT

FALLING INTO THE UNDERGROUND

Originally this book was to be about fulfilling work and meaningful jobs. We had figured out that there must be some way other than experimental colleges, on-the-job training, and counseling for young people to gain competence and autonomy, and to learn how to *do* something. The students we had known were desperate for skills.

Someone, someplace, we figured, must have discovered how to teach skills without hurting. Someone must be providing a nourishing environment where people could learn a job skill and get out on their own, in an independent fashion.

We went to the West Coast, looking. It began by accident, our discovery of the world of private trade and technical schools. Driving down a street in Seattle, we saw this big sign: "Seattle School of Mixology." A bartending school.

Nobody knows for sure, but there are probably three thousand resident private trade and technical schools in the United States today, enrolling one and a half million students, and teaching just about everything. Schools like the little Seattle School of Mixology don't show up on anyone's list. We recently dialed Seattle Information to see if the school still had a phone. If Seattle wasn't hiring any more bartenders, or if the owners wanted to retire, there wouldn't be any more little school. In November 1975, it was still listed in the phone book and in the Yellow Pages under "Schools."

Let's read its two-page catalog, which we were given when we walked in the door:

THE SEATTLE SCHOOL OF MIXOLOGY

This brochure for our school answers your questions about the Northwest's finest bartending and bar management school. We have a complete course in Mixology, including cost control and financial management. There is a course in Dinner Wines, and you will also become thoroughly qualified in the art of handling, dispensing and serving draft beer at the Rainier Brewing Company.

The course is designed and presented so that new students and experienced bartenders can work and learn at the same time, using the newest electronic liquor dispensers and mechanical mixing equipment. Each student in the school has the opportunity to learn and practice on this speed equipment with individual instruction.

AFFILIATIONS

The Seattle School of Mixology is a member of the Seattle Chamber of Commerce, the Better Business Bureau, and the State of Washington Restaurant Association.

INSTRUCTORS

A professional, college trained staff provides your instruction. Our staff has had years of experience in the food and beverage management field.

GRADUATION REQUIREMENTS

By learning and practicing five drinks a day you will acquire the ability to mix 110 drinks before graduation. A practical exam is given at the completion of the course and each qualifying student receives a diploma in Mixology and Wine Service. If for any reason the student does not pass the exam, he is given the opportunity to study further and take the exam over at a time arranged by the instructor.

With day and evening classes offered, there is no need to leave your present position while you learn. The morning class is from 10:00 A.M. to 1:00 P.M.; the evening class is from 6:30 P.M. to 9:30 P.M., Monday through Friday.

Classes form on a continual basis through the month, and tuition is $325.00 for the four week course, terms are available at a slightly higher rate. You are welcome to drop in at any time. Thank you for your interest in our Seattle School of Mixology.

The school is located just outside the downtown area in a small two-story office building. It shares the ground floor with an insurance office and a hairdresser's. The entire school is about fifteen feet wide and fifty feet long, with a partition dividing the office from the classroom—all in all, about the size of a large bus.

The classroom contains some student desks, a table covered with various bottles of syrup and colored water, a blackboard, and a long bar, completely stocked with everything but liquor. Colored water is used so as to keep the school sober. Tom is the only teacher for the day class; another instructor teaches evenings. Out front are the president and his secretary. Tom teaches bartending while the president and his secretary enroll students and place graduates in bartending jobs all over the Pacific Northwest. Ten students are in the day class at any given time; a new student can enroll as soon as someone graduates: in college they call this setup "personalized instruction."

The school trains all students to be lounge managers or owners. It is called a school of "mixology" because, Tom says, anyone can tend a bar, but it takes education to blend liquors into drinks. Furthermore, "mixing" is distinct from "tending" in that it demands accuracy in making drinks. This is the secret to operating a bar profitably. "Overpouring" each drink by a fraction of an ounce becomes a loss of thousands of dollars in inventory in a year. Bars go out of business because the barkeeps do not pour the exact, costed amount each time. The school teaches you how to do this.

Doug Wagoner, the owner, says that many large cocktail lounges and restaurants in Seattle send their managers to the school to learn how to run a profitable bar. Each day the students work on four or five cocktails they have memorized at home the night before. At the end of the course Tom can assign any one of 110 drinks to his students and each one should be able to mix it accurately. At first everyone is shy, a bit afraid. The first thing people do at the school is mix a drink for someone. The theory comes the next day; first a little "hands on" to break the ice. The class plays the part of a bar crowd and puts on the pressure. This type of training helps create confidence in the student that he'll be able to handle anything when the real thing comes along on the job. The school tries to match graduates with jobs that most appeal to them. Then they often send an experienced bartender along on the student's first day of work to ease him or her into the new job, because they know it may be the worst day of his or her life.

We liked the atmosphere of the school. There was a retired truck driver, looking to open up a tavern, being tutored in rum collinses by a third-week student. There was also an art student, dropping into this school to learn a skill to help her earn her tuition, and a longshoreman with a bad back. We noticed a long-haired person sitting in the corner reading a sociology textbook. He turned out to be a recent graduate of the school. Keeps coming back, he says, because the place "works." He now acts as an informal "teaching assistant," helping newcomers start out. He likes the "active participation" in the school and dislikes his college classes because they are all study, lecture, and tests. He told us there is more learning and good human relationships in one day at the School of Mixology than in a year at the university. He turned back to his sociology text, while Tom was saying: "As a general rule, women do not like the taste of hard liquor, therefore mix less of it in the typical lady's drink. This also saves money for the bar. Use your judgment with customers."

The curriculum is built around the 110 drinks that must be

learned by heart. Then there are a number of lectures on such things as how to keep the bar area clean. For example, point six:

> Keep Looking Up: Watch for chipping, peeling or scaling of paint on walls or ceilings. Be sure light fixtures, cords, ducts and hoods are free of dust and grease. Climb up where the tops of refrigerators and equipment are visible to be sure they are clean.

Or from the lecture on Bar Control:

> Cash Registers: The simpler the better and the closer to the bartender the better. Best is to have the keyboard by the bartender and the cash drawer two steps away and away from the bar counter to avoid stealing by customers.

That sort of thing three hours a day five days a week for a month. We kept overhearing students say to one another as they were deciding a disputed point, "Well, Tom says—" Tom told us there would continue to be a strong job market for bartenders, for by the year 2003, distilled spirits consumption should approach one billion gallons a year. As if aware of their bright future in this bleary business, the students were enjoying one of the highspots of Pacific Coast education.

As we hit the sidewalk, we knew we had a book. At the first phone booth we stopped to look under "Schools" in the Yellow Pages. Sure enough, there they were, the educational underground: local schools that taught piano tuning, deep-sea diving, welding, dog grooming, motel managing, short-order cooking, bookkeeping, electronics, building maintenance, bank tellering, body and fender repair, real estate, oil burner maintenance and repair, industrial instrumentation, and printing. Are we *surrounded* by these invisible schools?

THE DISCOVERY OF PROPRIETARY SCHOOLS

Slim, gray, and all figured out, Bill Goddard has been waiting for years. "It's wonderful to be discovered," he says. Goddard and the private school industry are ready. But as he looks back down the road to World War II, when returning vets caused a trade school boom, Goddard is both amused by and wary of the train of visitors who tell him that "proprietary" is now all right and his schools are "in."

Bill Goddard is the no-rust, no-tarnish, stainless-steel Executive Director of the National Association of Trade and Technical Schools and Secretary of its independent Accrediting Commission. Goddard's style and that of the association are built on an assiduous avoidance of flash and pomp. Goddard understands that you sell the sacred things of life—in this case, education—very, very carefully, or they get you. The offices of NATTS, located on L Street in downtown Washington, have the physical appeal of a ward room on a newly commissioned destroyer: they are functional, clean, a bit awkward, and no one can get the wrong idea. Goddard has a way with the bland. He is also an interesting man and, concerning his industry, has heard it all before.

"I guess we're discovered once a week. Educationalists, researchers, corporations, educational associations, and writers like yourself. Yes, we're *hot* right now. Folks are finding out that we do what we say we do: train people in the shortest amount of time for the best possible job. Why, I even think that we're getting to be considered part of the educational establishment! Dangerous waters."

"What have you learned from all this exposure to the rarefied air of Higher Education?" we asked.

"Simple. I see the same people at all the meetings. If one were conspiracy-minded, which I am not, one would say that there was a Higher Education conspiracy. Most decisions seem to be made by a very few people. They're always getting together in some commission or council.

"I look around those meetings sometimes and wonder. They never talk about students. Now at *our* meetings, we *have* to talk about students; they're our bread and butter."

Goddard feels that the major misconception about the private school industry—that their salespersons lure students in with deceptive promises and then fail to deliver—is finally being laid to rest. "We don't go out and oversell," says Goddard. "The

schools that do generally get severely criticized. But as enrollments wane, colleges and universities will have to get out and recruit, too. As they go in for that type of salesmanship they're going
to get the same type of criticism. Schools that do a good job of
training and placement don't get the criticism. They aggressively
recruit, but they don't do it in such an obvious way. I don't think
there is anything wrong with aggressive promotion. I think we
have an obligation to let the people that need help know about
our schools; you have to reach and find them to let them know
what's available. You *have* to advertise, promote, print up literature, mail it out in a broad distribution. The private schools are
merely trying to reach those people who feel that what we offer
is a very valuable thing for their lives."

"Do you see a conflict between education and profit?" we
asked.

"I see a *connection* between education and profit," replied
Goddard, "not in conflict. I think the profit motive in education
is very beneficial. It brings in ambitious, intelligent folks who
want to do something better and to better themselves. In a free
market, private schools have to deliver the services they promised
or go under. And we do deliver. We:

figure out in which fields there are jobs,

find an experienced worker who is able to teach well,

recruit students likely to do well in the field,

train them intensively, in short segments that give a sense of
achievement to people who often have not felt successful
before,

demand proper work habits, and

work hard to place graduates in jobs they want.

That's what we do successfully. Years of criticism, competition
from everything the public schools can throw at us—Area Vocational Schools, Comprehensive High Schools, Community Colleges, and now two-year state university career programs—all

these have tried to do what we do and they haven't touched us yet."

WHY NOT COMMUNITY COLLEGES?

Goddard's claim that private trade and technical schools are superior to public offerings in the field is backed up by outside assessments. Many government studies are critical of public school occupational training. It appears that in high schools the poorer students end up in shop training and most of them eventually drop out. Nationally, only about one-third of those originally enrolled complete high school vocational programs. Hopes were high when community colleges began offering trade and technical courses, but the results could not have been much more disappointing.

If you want to go to college, try the local community college. If you want to get skilled, forget it. Community colleges are not set up for skill training. Only about 30 percent of community college students are enrolled in occupational programs; the rest are in college-oriented transfer programs, which are the real business of community colleges. This naturally affects the vocational programs they do offer.

Teachers in community colleges tend to have academic credentials rather than impressive work experience. They spend a lot of time doing committee work and research necessary to hold on to their jobs, whereas proprietary school teachers are hired—and fired—on the basis of their work experience and teaching ability. There is no such thing as tenure in proprietary schools.

Very few CCs do a responsible job of placement. Unlike the private schools, whose income depends on successful placement, the community colleges get their money from taxes, so their stake in training and placement is much smaller. They do not need to be selective in their admission policies, choosing only those applicants who seem likely to persevere. Nor do they provide the kind of disciplined, work-oriented learning environment that private schools strive for. Very few community colleges take the initiative in contacting potential employers and, because they produce so few employable graduates, it is not worth local employers' time to keep in touch with *them*.

The biggest danger in these schools is that students will drop out of courses, which generally are two years long. Nationally, only *one-quarter* of the students enrolled finish community college vocational programs. In his study for the Center for Research and Development in Higher Education at the University of California, Buzz Wilms reports that he had a difficult time finding community college vocational programs with sufficient numbers of graduates to compare or test with proprietary school graduates. One community college secretarial course started with one thousand students and graduated one. Remember, in most of these programs you also have to take *required* courses in General Studies. Consequently, the skill training is not intensive. Where in private schools you would have thirty hours of class a week, all in skill training, in most CCs you have classes only fifteen hours a week, and perhaps only half of those hours are spent in skill training.

Community colleges are new and are only now being evaluated.

"Community college—it's like thirteenth grade," said a young man in conversation on the beach at Nag's Head.

"It's high school with ashtrays," said Mrs. Porro's son on Vashon Island.

Illinois is the only state to date to carefully evaluate its community colleges. The system in Illinois is similar to that existing in most states. The following remarks are the conclusions of a survey of the Illinois Public Junior College System by the Illinois Economic and Fiscal Commission, Springfield, 1973.

—The response to our administrative survey indicated that only about eight campuses (of 48) have specific, formal evaluation procedures to determine occupational course effectiveness. . . . The colleges themselves are unlikely to know what their programs are achieving.

—It appears from the evidence that the occupational instruction in many junior colleges is not oriented toward the actual manpower demands and job opportunities in the state.

—Our survey showed that at least four of the forty-eight had no personnel specifically assigned to placement and that twenty-two had only one part-time professional working in the area.

—Placement personnel are available evenings on only sixteen campuses. The vast majority of schools rely primarily on bulletin boards or circulars to communicate job openings to evening students.

The best available figures nationally:

■ Only about 30 percent of community college students are enrolled in occupational programs; the rest are in college-oriented transfer programs, which are the real business of community colleges.

■ 65 percent of students entering community colleges drop out and never return.

■ Only one third of the students who enter community college transfer programs actually transfer to four-year colleges; the rest drop out.

■ Only 12 percent of students in community colleges complete four years of higher education.

■ Only 25 percent of community college students in occupational programs actually finish their courses; the rest drop out.

From all this we conclude that community colleges are not the best places to invest the time, money, and energy required to complete what should be the essentially uncluttered process of gaining a certain skill and taking it out on the job with confidence.

There is extensive personal and institutional failure revealed in the statistics mentioned earlier. Until the nation's community colleges either accept strict educational and financial accountability or are recycled into comfortable prison farms, it is our urgent suggestion that young people not only look the community college gift horse in the mouth, but stay out of its way; it has a mean kick.

WHY PRIVATE TRADE AND
TECHNICAL SCHOOLS?

Americans see schools as a utility, rather like the power company and the police force. They pay their tax money and they send their kids off to school. They also correctly or incorrectly view public education as a force for Democracy. They assume that Horace Mann was right:

> "Never will wisdom preside in the halls of legislation, and its profound utterances be recorded on the pages of the statute book, until Common Schools . . . create a more farseeing intelligence and a purer morality than has ever existed among communities of men." (1849)

A hundred years later we have learned differently:

> The public schools, which are still the main institutions of education for children aged six through eighteen, cannot carry out many of the missions assigned to them. Most of the schools do not build character, open the mind, implant an appreciation of beauty, or otherwise serve as the great humanizer or the social equalizer as educators would wish them to do. In desperation it is suggested now that the schools concentrate on teaching the three Rs, and it is common knowledge that they have a hard time doing even that.
> —AMITAI ETZIONI, *Saturday Review*, June 3, 1972.

Private trade and technical schools continue to flourish because they understand students, and they try to be different from the public schools. As Bill Goddard of NATTS puts it, "If this is truly a free society, a man or woman should have the opportunity to choose the level at which he or she wants to enter an occupation and to prepare for that level. He should not have to expose himself to training that he does not think relevant. Look at all the people leaving school; they consider what little vocational training they are getting not worth what they have to take to get it."

Private schools offer success on the *students'* terms, not the professors'. As Goddard points out, "Very few people go to our schools because mom and dad want them to. The student makes the decision. What the student feels in attending one of our schools is that he or she will *finish quicker,* get more *specialized* training, and less training *unrelated* to the occupational goal. Plus, he or she will be attending school with *motivated* people with similar goals. They will find the *cost is less* because they will be on a payroll earlier and they will find that the proprietary school is much more interested in the individual student's success because the private school has no alternative. The school and the student are on the same side of the fence: the school's ultimate success depends on the student's ultimate success. Students know from their own experience in the public schools that the teachers and administrators look upon students as problems. They seem to feel they could get along a lot better if it weren't for the damn students. You don't find many of our schools that think about students that way. Students appreciate that. You know, a private school has to get 'em and keep 'em happy in order to get 'em and keep 'em. We give people what they *want* in addition to what they need."

The school is on the students' side. Unlike the community colleges, it is always thinking about ways to deal with morale problems that cause dropouts.

On our bulletin board, a note listing things we saw at Dick Diggs's automotive school in Detroit.

1. Individualized classrooms. Each classroom was done in a different motif, achieved via bright paint, false ceilings, and pictures. The tune-up lab was the "Bavarian Alps," with a shingled interior roof and a little flowerbox. It was nuts, but made the room (part of a former Safeway Store) a fun place to study automotive repair.

2. A letter to all parents, asking them to visit the school regularly. It also included suggestions on how parents can support their children during the intensive course of study at the school.

3. Food as morale builder. A cozy dining area, with good, hot food available at cost.

4. Men's Room mirror with sign painted above it: "Would you hire this man?"

5. A poster announcing a forthcoming raffle for a toolbox, and an award for the student with the best attendance.

6. "Mass meetings." Diggs holds weekly Dale Carnegie-type self-improvement meetings with his students. They talk about everything from moral issues to job interviewing. Students reported they didn't mind the get-togethers.

7. Job placement desk at the *front door* of the school, so that every student has to pass the placement officer daily. The man gets to know them and they are constantly reminded of that job at the end of their training.

8. A sign over the tool room door: "Honesty."

9. A monthly alumni newsletter with a prize for the best letter from a working graduate.

10. Five students working part-time keeping the school clean.

Obviously, this school gives a damn.

Another school director described his strategy for dealing with the potential dropout:

> The "bitter quitter's" excuses are poor school facilities, inferior curricula, inferior instructors, low morale, bad scheduling, and many other negatives. We used to match wits with them and try to out-talk them.
>
> In recent years we have taken the attitude that the best solution to the dropout problem is prevention. We divide our preventative activities into four stages.
>
> In the *pre-sell*, the prospect receives a catalog and is told to be ready with questions for the field man's visit. During the interview with both parents present, the representative tells the prospect how difficult our program is and often asks pointed questions. He makes him promise to work harder and do better than he did in high school. The application requires a $95 deposit.
>
> *Re-sell:* After the application has been accepted, the president writes the enrollee a letter announcing the fact. Two weeks

later we send an information folder answering questions about the student's first trip to our city. We also type a letter for the pastor of his denomination to sign and another for the mayor's signature. Three weeks before the entry date, the principal sends a letter giving the last minute details. In the meantime we have made the financial arrangements necessary to keep the student in school.

On entrance day we plan to eliminate or minimize surprises. The new student is greeted and taken on a personal tour by a student guide and is escorted to his boarding house. An orientation program is provided during the afternoon. He may take placement tests and files an application if he wants part-time work. Finally we prepare a news release for his home town newspaper. The anticipation of publication and clippings on the bulletin board builds his morale and helps keep him in school.

Every day, we encourage a sincere smile on every face. We issue grade reports monthly. We maintain bright, clean, comfortable facilities; all space is air conditioned. We provide recognition through a monthly honor roll, a gold pin for three months on the honor roll, and notices in home town papers for the gold pin. We use student names—not numbers.

We provide effective full- and part-time employment services. We reserve for advanced students those part-time jobs which might turn into full-time jobs. We could easily create a dropout problem by giving such jobs to beginners.

We carefully select our front office staff. We keep after absentees. Within 15 minutes after every class begins, we know who is absent and then we get on the telephone. We keep a record of the conversations on the back of our Key-Sort attendance cards.

We help those students who need it most. We insist that our people search out and give extra attention to the shy students, the slow learners, the unattractive personalities, the loners and loafers. As most potential dropouts are in this group, we can often save them before they turn bitter. We have materially cut down on our "bitter quitters."

That's how it is done in well-organized schools. Everything is controlled. Such organization generally extends into the training and placement of students as well.

PRIVATE OWNERSHIP

Public school vocational programs are run by educators who must concentrate a lot of their energy on "input"—such questions as the political process of funding and the changing views of educational theorists who influence how public schools will teach. Private schools are mostly concerned with the "output"—employable graduates. They try to take the simplest, cheapest, most effective route toward that goal. Every activity is costed-out.

In contrast, public job-training programs cost twice as much as they should, and, consequently, most go bust before they do much good. Twenty billion dollars has been spent on government manpower programs in the War on Poverty. In Washington, D.C., $61 million has been spent in various other programs in recent years. A 1973 General Accounting Office survey summed up the result:

> No one knows how many people are being trained, where they are being trained, for what occupation they are being trained, or the impact of the training on the demand for skilled workers.

So it goes across the country. When industry tries to co-sponsor programs with the government, it does not do any better. Tuition-free programs in skill training are too loose to establish the disciplined atmosphere required for vocational training. When a contract is involved—that is, when money changes hands—the schools put out and so do the students.

The difference between private and public vocational schools is reflected in their respective attitudes toward dropouts. Public schools view the dropout as a defective; he wasn't able to compete effectively and he let the school down. The problem is solved when the kid drops out and stops disrupting his class. In proprietary schools, a dropout means lost revenue, because the student stops paying and usually badmouths the school, affecting future enrollments. A teacher does not like to see a kid drop out; it reflects on his teaching ability. For all these reasons, an effort will therefore be made to deal with an unsatisfied student's complaint.

Bill Hyde, a researcher at the University of Chicago, views the proprietary school as a "supplier of a product—namely, an opportunity to acquire a job skill under *specified conditions.*" These conditions are detailed in a contract signed by both the student and the school. The student himself pays the tuition as specified in the contract. He thus develops an equity in the training and a certain control over the quality of that training. Proprietary education is dependent upon student choice and personal financial investment.

We see four features of proprietary education that distinguish it from public education: its *pedagogy*, its job *placement* function, its *problems,* and the *profit* motive.

PEDAGOGY

Private schools teach differently. As Tyrrell Burgess has written in *Ekistics* magazine, May 1973, "There is, of course, an educational tradition, which, to put it baldly, starts with the student not the subject. Its object is to make the student competent at something, not just to tell him things. It rests on the educational commonplace that people learn best by solving problems." Proprietary schools start with the student who has paid to learn something. That student wants to study intensely.

PLACEMENT

Proprietary school educators know precisely what the employer needs and train motivated students to meet those established requirements. The realistic goal of job placement binds the student and school owner together. Placement assures accountability.

PROBLEMS

Like mammals, private schools either adapt or die out. Currently, community colleges are attempting to teach everything taught in private schools and they're almost giving it away. School owners either come up with programs that are better and shorter than the community colleges' or they go out of business.

Competition with the public sector and with one another keeps private schools lean and hardy.

Proprietary schools don't hang on after their usefulness has passed. When the airlines stopped expanding in 1974, the excess airline schools closed. Problems weed out the weak schools, firm up strong ones, and create new ones. When a· new technology happens along, it is the private schools that are able to move, with courses designed and students enrolled in a matter of weeks. Welding schools are now sending hundreds of welders to the Alaska pipeline and to developing countries.

New ideas in the school business usually come out of the new schools. A person gets a new and good idea, starts a school. When a school has "arrived," it often becomes mild-mannered and content. Its publicity, public relations, and recruiting efforts may lose steam and the far end of the student pipeline begins to dry up, without the owners' realizing it. Content with offering sound training, a school owner lets the business go hang, until suddenly panic sets in. Students are admitted whether they can pay tuition or not; collections fall off, and soon it's all over.

PROFIT

The profit motive is essential to skill training in schools. This is ticklish. Few of us have had any experience with private, independent school operators, except for local ladies who teach piano to unwilling kids. Public-school people believe in the public trough, while liberal school reformers always loudly organize into "nonprofit" schools (which may mean they are short-lived, have trouble functioning, and have transient leadership).

We have developed great affection for the notion of a person starting up a school. Entrepreneur-educators get the job done with long hours, hard work, and consideration for their students (they often refer to them as "young ladies" and "young gentlemen"). Lou Dimasi, a school owner in Pittsburgh, has written, "The incentive of reasonable profit in the proprietary institutions encourages quality education, for profit is the result of meeting the needs and demands of the students, graduates, and their employers."

It is curious that in this country, which publicly applauds free enterprise, we have an arrogant public monopoly in education—so much so that proprietary school owners tiptoe through their communities wondering when the next criticism of them will fall. They live in a rather Stalinist world, carefully tending their little garden plots of skill training, watching the state-owned giants gobble up and misuse the resources—in this case, young people. But large numbers of those young people are showing where, given a free choice, they would turn to prepare for their futures.

In December 1970, the Center for the Study of Public Policy completed a study called *Education Vouchers*. Christopher Jencks, director of the Center, reported in the study:

> It is true that when students begin to make their own decisions about their education, they are more likely to enroll in profit-making institutions. Driver training schools, foreign language schools, computer programming schools, secretarial schools, beauty schools, and a host of others testify to people's willingness to attend institutions which operate for a profit when they want specific skills rather than more general education.

We have been inside the profit motive in education, and the student-centered training that follows from it, and found that it works.

It also works much better than the alternatives. Lewis B. Mayhew, professor of education at Stanford University, writes in *Higher Education for Occupations:*

> . . . careful observers of the apprenticeship system judge it generally inadequate to prepare the large number of skilled workers which the technological society demands. Trade unions limit the number of apprentices accepted, in part to protect the job equities of their members. Employers frequently restrict apprenticeships on the ground that it is more efficient to pay overtime to experienced workers than to pay lower wages to less experienced and less effective apprentices. Another alternative is to expect business and industry to provide extensive educational programs. . . . Other studies, however, do not corroborate these

opinions. They discover that only larger firms operate formally organized education and training programs, and that these are more frequently for managerial and professional employees than for technical or skills-level workers.

SIZE IS DAMN NEAR EVERYTHING

Noel Adams, owner of Tulsa Welding School and member of the NATTS Accrediting Commission:

"You know, I'm working harder today than I ever have; and with *one school* specializing in one thing, with 100 good students, I'm making more money than I ever have."

The most significant, arresting feature of the private vocational schools discussed in this book is their typical sizes: 250 to 300 students and fewer than a dozen teachers and administrators. We believe that this characteristic, together with private ownership, generates successful schools.

Large size is one of our complaints about public community colleges. If they were smaller they would work better and be more respected. In his study "The Effectiveness of Public and Proprietary Occupational Training," Dr. Buzz Wilms describes the twenty-one community colleges randomly selected for comparison with twenty-nine proprietary schools.

Our average proprietary school offered *two* occupational programs, compared with an average of *eleven* programs for the public schools. First-time visitors at public schools often need a map to avoid getting lost in new and sprawling complexes. Proprietary schools sometimes set up shop in equally fancy headquarters over the local dime store, in refurbished factories, or in storefronts. The twenty-nine proprietary schools in this sample had full-time enrollment ranging from fourteen to 2,300 students, but the average proprietary school enrolled 291 students. Public school enrollments ranged from 120 to a whopping 14,000-plus, with a large average school enrollment of 7,867—some 27 times larger than the average proprietary school.

Students particularly can appreciate what such large size does to institutions and the people in them. Dr. Roger Barker of the University of Kansas and the Midwest Psychological Field Station listed the results of studies comparing the behavior of people in small, undermanned schools and work settings with behavior of people in large settings or institutions.

1. People in small settings are absent less often.
2. They quit jobs and positions less often.
3. They are more punctual.
4. They participate voluntarily more frequently.
5. They function in positions of responsibility and importance more frequently, and in a wider range of activities.
6. They are more productive.
7. They demonstrate more leadership behavior.
8. They have broader role conceptions.
9. They are more frequently involved in roles directly relevant to setting tasks.
10. They are more interested in the affairs of the institution or setting.
11. They engage in more greetings and social transactions per person.
12. They find it easier to communicate with each other.
13. They receive more "satisfaction."
14. They speak more often of participation as having been valuable and useful.
15. They find their work more meaningful.

We think it is important to understand that the country's thousands of small private schools are an important resource to students; we also think it is important to understand how they become threatened by large organizations or by growing too large themselves. This problem of size relates to Americans in many ways. Harmful largeness is all around. Even big farms do not work. In an article in the Washington *Post*, July 11, 1971, Peter Barnes raised the question of agribusiness and land reform.

Beyond a certain point, there is nothing gained by having one vast farm in place of several smaller ones. In fact, small farms are often more productive per acre because their owners work harder and take better care of the soil.

In mid-1973 we interviewed Karl Hess, a Fellow of the Institute for Policy Studies in Washington, D.C. Hess is working on the development of community-controlled businesses and service organizations. He believes that if neighborhoods learn to feed, house, and clothe themselves they can do better than City Hall. We explained to him about private, independent, profit-making vocational schools. He responded, "That's the thing I'm trying to get at. We need institutions that are:

concerned with people,
small scale,
locally managed,
decentralized,
operating in a free market,
permanent, belonging to the community,
entrepreneurial (innovative and resourceful)."

Hess's ideal is, in effect, embodied by our proprietary schools. But instead of existing as a valued alternative to the big institutions around us, the small, independent private schools have been hard put to withstand the pressures to abandon their supposedly outdated nonconformity and enter the conglomerated present—the world of Big Business and Big Universities. As David Riesman commented in *The Lonely Crowd:*

> . . . big monopolies, taken as a single group, are in devastating competition with the not yet grouped. . . . These little scattered followers find what protection they can in the interstices around the group-minded.

Luckily for students desiring to get skilled, the private vocational schools have not yet been "grouped." But they have been able to find precious little protection from the group-minded—in the media and private industry, especially—who have worked hard at either discrediting or co-opting the successful private schools. Here is what they have tried to do. Students will note how the schools have adapted and have, so far, come out on top.

THE MEDIA

Monday, February 25, 1974, Ten O'Clock News, Metromedia Television, Channel 5, in Washington, D.C. We were sitting with cassette recorders at the ready. We waited through Watergate, an energy crisis report, the Local Scene, buffered antacids, and then, at 10:24, it began—the "first in a series of Special Reports on Career Schools."

Audio: a drum roll, leading into a jolly tune for ten seconds. Video: cartoon of diplomas, fluttering about on bird's wings. Audio: an announcer with the voice of a hustler: "Earn 200 to 300 dollars a week in your spare time! That's right, 200 to 300 dollars a week—thousands of jobs go begging—our school training guarantees your placement—glamour, excitement, and big, big money!"

Video: cut to face suggesting wily school owner (we know that face—it is taken from an FTC brochure warning against proprietary trade schools). Audio: a few seconds of the one-time hit song "Promises, Promises." Video: cut to reporter at cluttered studio newsdesk. Audio: "At the outset, let us say, this is meant to be neither a broad, all-inclusive report on, nor a blanket indictment of the multi-billion-dollar, multi-million-student Vocational or Career School industry. . . . We will be employing the negative. In the context of this series, we are in the consumer protection business. We will point out the Good, but our principal role will be to point out the Bad and the Ugly . . ." Video: cut to one-shot of sad-looking young black woman. Audio over: "Elaine Brown completed a $2,000 computer course, says she applied for dozens of jobs, says she still works for the library. . . ."

Video: cut to an angry-looking young black man. Audio: "What did you think about the promises they were making you?" "I think they were quite false." Announcer: "The Jerome Clairs are lured by promises, outright or implied, sometimes in advertising, more often tumbling from the lips of so-called Guidance Counselors, Enrollment personnel, School Reps."

Video: cut to a downcast student. Audio: "I thought this was a new beginning for me and I was let down." Announcer: "Some of those who think they come out on the losing end of empty promises perhaps wonder why the government or the FTC is not doing more to protect us, *crack down* on the schools."

And it went on for five more minutes, each night for five nights at 10:24.

Perhaps because of America's expensive commitment to public education, the media finds an occasional "exposure" of alleged corrupt schools an easy and obvious story. Most cities are treated to one every four or five years. They give lurid details of a school's nefarious practices, quote some angry students and parents, then find an "expert" to sum it all up in favor of the public sector. In 1970 the Washington *Post* ran a famous series which did quite a bit of damage. Later on, Bill Goddard, Executive Director of NATTS and Secretary of its Accrediting Commission, investigated the *Post* report. He found out who the students interviewed were and what the facts were in each case. He discovered that some of the students interviewed had, in fact, been offered good jobs; others had had poor records at the schools they attended; one student who had complained of being left high and dry when his school suddenly closed had been placed in another school with little inconvenience to him. Goddard wrote up a report on his findings, but instead of calling a press conference, he simply placed the report in his drawer. "Our industry," Goddard says with a smile, "has finally learned that criticism is good. When our schools got important, they started getting criticism. As long as those stories don't attack the students, most of whom have been hurt by the public school system, we just let them go by."

THE CORPORATE STYLE

Much of this recent criticism has sprung from the involvement of major corporations in the private school business. As the American involvement in Vietnam began to peak in 1965, the Bank of America did some market surveys for American industry, suggesting postwar investment possibilities. One such report pointed out that the returning GIs would be in the market for job training, and stated that there were high profits to be made in technical schools.

So it happened. At least thirty major U.S. corporations turned on the private vocational school industry and began buying up small technical schools. Almost overnight, these corporations found themselves in the school business: Lockheed Aircraft, LTV Aerospace, Philco-Ford, Lear Siegler, Ryder Truck, ITT, IBM, Litton Industries, Macmillan Publishing, Bell and Howell, American Express, Honeywell, CBS, and many others.

The problem was that the Bank of America surveys were wrong. Schools do not make big money. Like a restaurateur, a school owner can expect a tidy personal income, at best. Disappointed with their first-year profits, the corporations began cutting operating expenses at the same time that they pushed to increase enrollments. The inevitable happened. The schools slumped and slowed as former presidents became mere employees. The dropout rate increased sharply; many tuitions became uncollectable. Schools that had overexpanded to handle increased enrollment were in trouble. Most corporations took about four years to learn their lessons and sell out. But behind them they left educational carnage. Many schools that had enjoyed fine local reputations were now burdened with falling enrollments and rising complaints. In the uproar over this small percentage of mismanaged schools, the whole industry got tarred.

A CASE STUDY

A veteran schoolman wrote for us this case study of a corporate acquisition:

A classic case of a corporation purchasing and then losing a successful school operation happened in the vicinity of my school. This school was founded in the early 1900s and developed into a very large and successful business school which had multiple locations within the same metropolitan area. The school enrolled some 10,000 students during 1967, primarily in short-term type-writing, shorthand, and other business courses. The courses were relatively inexpensive. The main school location grossed a million dollars or so that year and showed a healthy 20 percent profit. Along came the big corporation which literally begged the family that owned and operated the school to sell out to them. The family did sell out and did stick around for a short period. The school immediately inherited a 15 percent corporate overhead factor which would cut the profit line to 5 percent, assuming the school continued to operate at the same business level. However, most disastrous was the immediate change of the marketing end of the business. The family had believed in spending a considerable amount of revenue for advertising. Further, they could manipulate the owners of advertising space and secure substantial discounts. In essence they could secure $500,000 worth of advertising coverage for $200,000, more or less. Along comes corporate, which doesn't believe in bargaining for discounts and which believes in using an advertising agency as an intermediary. The result is that the corporation spends the same $200,000, for which it receives $170,000 worth of advertising with the other $30,000 being spent for the agency's fees. All of a sudden the school has one-third the effective advertising coverage it previously enjoyed. The school also suddenly has one-third the number of enrollments but with the same basic overhead costs which can't be reduced quite so suddenly. In short order the school has gone from a 20 percent profit venture to a staggering loss venture. The corporation, which originally had great visions of expansion under its proven business management acumen, then began closing branch locations, employed a great succession of quasi-experts to solve its problems, continued to lose vast amounts of money in addition to losing its original capital investment, and finally, in mid-1974, the corporation closed the doors of this school. The students were trained out before the closing so they were not damaged by the closing.

It is interesting to note that during this same six years one member of the family that sold the school to the corporation did strike out on his own. He purchased a small school out of his share of the proceeds received from the corporation. He observed the noncompetition constraints placed on him by the corporation for the period he was so encumbered. At the time the corporation closed the doors on its school this young man had developed his new school business to a high level of revenue and profit.

Corporate America assumes that "larger" means "more profitable," yet their large schools have gone out of business. The best people in the school business say that the key to success is keeping the schools simple, smallish, and cheap to operate.

Mo Gaebe has been in the school business in Providence, Rhode Island for twenty-seven years. Most years he has turned a profit with this simple education philosophy:

1. A school must offer *courses* that people want to study.
2. Courses must be offered at a *time* when people are available to take them.
3. The courses must utilize teaching *methods* for the average student that result in satisfied customers.

If the result of corporate involvement in private vocational education wasn't so sad, it would be comical. The corporations had less savvy than most students.

•

THREE

PRIVATE TRADE SCHOOLS—PROFILES

Guidebooks can be deadly affairs. We like to think that ours have flesh and blood. Also, guidebooks are published for one audience and invariably get read by another. We wrote this for students, but we know that parents, teachers, counselors, and government people need such a guide, too.

In the following four profiles we tour representative private trade and technical schools. It is a personal tour, introducing school people and students. We try to show what the schools are like and how they teach.

These particular schools were selected because each holds down a corner of the universe of private occupational schools.

■ The first school is an electronics school. Electronics schools are currently the most numerous of all schools in the NATTS

Directory. We will meet a successful schoolman there who will describe his operating philosophy.

■ The second, a gunsmithing school, is a family-run "mom and pop" operation. It is a specialty school, the kind it's the most fun to visit: right before your eyes you can see fine guns being created by hand.

■ The third school is a combination home study and resident training school. It is accredited by the National Home Study Council rather than the National Association of Trade and Technical Schools, NATTS. But it could just as easily be a resident school. The combination of prior home study and short resident training is very workable and the mechanics of a truck driving school are interesting. We include the course outline to suggest how it is all done.

■ The last school is oriented to women. It is a fine school whose students pay a great deal of money to attend. The owners are among the country's most successful. The school demonstrates how creative people can honestly make a sizable profit in education.

AN ELECTRONICS SCHOOL

Few taxpaying, school-bond-supporting Americans can appreciate the idea that an individual can *own* a school. Phil Chosky *owns* a school in Pittsburgh, Pennsylvania. There is more to be said about Phil Chosky and his excellent electronics school, but the dimension of ownership, that Phil Chosky *owns* a school, must be understood first. He can make a small universe of his own decisions, and anyone studying the independent private school industry of America must deal with that. Chosky and his electronics school will continue to recruit students, train them, and place them in electronics jobs around the country without regard to what people think about a person owning a school and making a profit from that school. We don't think his school will close down, go out of business, or be much threatened by any crusading reporter carrying out the periodic scourge of the private trade school business. In the years to come, hundreds of Pennsylvania young people are going to be "trained out" at Electronics Institutes. Phil Chosky *owns* this school in Pittsburgh, Pennsylvania. Once again.

Chosky looks like a cartoonist's likable gnome, and Pittsburgh in the winter is a mammoth cavern. Streets tunnel through the fog, walls run wet, bridges disappear into other caves, and your rope's untied and you wonder why you are there. And Chosky is not looking like an "educator," but like a merry troll who knows all the secrets of the cave. He said he would pick us up, and in about fifteen minutes a black Lincoln Continental crept up to the curb. Deep inside was a small round man who motioned us to get in the back seat. King Toad?

Down Penn Avenue we went, away from city center, sliding between buildings, hills, and railroad tracks. Then suddenly at a warehouse—just a warehouse—we stopped. He turned gnomishly in his seat. "This is it." We were nowhere. And here was where Phil Chosky *owns* a school.

The Electronics Institutes occupies the second floor of the Pitt-Penn Terminal Building. The building is a postal warehouse running for blocks alongside the Pennsylvania Railroad tracks. Loading docks flank the doorway to the school. We went up, crowding past students who were eating sandwiches on the stairs. Emerging at the top we looked down the longest hallway in the world. Chosky led the way, wading through more students. After a few steps, his head swiveled. "This may not be the best school in the world, but it's the longest."

A private school is not like high school; it is not like college. A private school owner is different in mentality from a public school official or administrator. Put them in a classroom together and you could tell one from the other, because the school owner would have a gang of door keys in his pocket and would turn out the lights as he left the room. Phil took us on a tour of his school. Going through a ring of thirty keys like it was a well-fingered rosary, he showed us stockrooms, computer maintenance classrooms, closets, bathrooms. Classes in session had about thirty students at long tables, each with an open black briefcase that created a private study carrel. And a teacher was "on platform" in front, explaining a circuit or drafting principle.

We started asking questions and Chosky had answers.

We get our students, some from Pittsburgh, but most of our kids come from surrounding towns and cities. Lots of them commute in. . . . Most university and community college programs stink. That's why kids come here. Our objective is vocational.

We teach what a kid wants to know to get a job. Eighteen-year-olds have needs, and we have need for discipline, because this is learning-under-pressure. We try to get a balance between the student's needs and the need to get the work done. . . . The courses take 24 months, 2,772 clock hours. Half of that is lab; cost is $3,700.

No romance. Kid has to work to get through. Sixty-five percent of them graduate. Community colleges? Take a look at their figures: kids don't graduate from their programs. Programs are too small; not enough students to afford a large staff. We have *sixteen* full-time teachers here, plus others that come in for special subjects. Kids study one subject for five hours a day, five days a week, year round.

A proprietary school has to deliver a product; an employable graduate. To do that we have to keep the kids in school. We don't let good students drop out. We get on the phone if a kid is not in school for a couple of days. They have to have an 85 percent attendance to stay. We take attendance at the beginning of every class. We don't have "excused absences"; employers want good attendance records.

We have 300 students, 250 in electronics and 50 in drafting. And most of them are in class right now, I'll guarantee. High school graduates. And they all had algebra. That's our admission requirement. Algebra. Here is the course outline:

ELECTRONIC AND COMPUTER TECHNOLOGY

		CLOCK HOURS
1st Term	Elements of Electricity and Electronics	231.00
	Lab	115.50
	Mathematics	115.50
2nd Term	Basic Electronic Circuits	231.00
	Lab	231.00
3rd Term	Solid State Devices and Circuits	231.00
	Lab	231.00
4th Term	Communications Technology	231.00
	Lab	231.00
5th Term	Computer Technology	115.50
	Lab	115.50
	Computer Mathematics	115.50
	Fundamentals of Programming	115.50
6th Term	Technical Writing and Oral Expression	115.50
	Industrial Organization and Management	115.50
	Drafting for Electronic Technicians	231.00
	TOTAL CLOCK HOURS	2,772.00

This is typed on no-nonsense mimeograph and there is no Western Civ to distract anyone. The business is to produce electronic technicians; this unrelenting schedule does it.

Like tired milers, we followed Chosky to his office. A desk loaded with forms, government regulations, capacitors, and catalogs was occupying the middle ground of the office, which was decorated with industrial tile. The buck obviously stopped before it got here. We sat down in two unmatched chairs.

Chosky peered at us. We looked at each other. Chosky is not a conversational leader. Finally we said, "Phil, how much money do proprietary schools make?"—and held our breath. There, we had asked it. "About like any other business . . . ten, twelve percent profit in good years, often lucky to break even. Want to know how much a school makes?" We nodded. "Multiply the tuition by the number of students. Then, take ten percent of that!" He chuckled. "To make it, you have to recruit. Most kids come here because of friends. But you can't make a profit that way. Recruit. It's all overhead in this business. Can't cut back on your costs or kids will leave."

Later, as we walked back toward the longest hall, he gave us a list of last year's graduates and their addresses at work. "Give them a call." He went back to work.

Across town, Lou Dimasi, owner of the Penn Technical Institute, was saying, "So you met Phil. Good. Phil and I have been competitors for at least twenty-five years. We have lunch once a month. He runs a damn good school. Different from mine, same subjects generally, but different. That hallway would drive me crazy. His school is a one-man show. He can't delegate at all. I bet he answered your call when you phoned the school, right? I thought so. That school is his life. I like having Phil Chosky in town. Keeps me on my toes."

Pittsburgh has the largest number of private schools per capita of any city in the country. We visited eight more of the thirty-eight: a gunsmithing school, a medical-dental school, two art schools, a dressmaking school, a barber college, a carpet installation school, a drafting school. Each one was a different world. Some characteristics they shared. They all advertised. They were small, ranging from forty to three hundred students, and they rented space, usually downtown. The courses were concentrated, lasting most of the day, and there was a certain strictness about them—one school used to terminate students for stopping in a tavern on the way home. Most of the day is spent in practical learning situations. What came through in all our conversations with Pittsburgh school owners was a sense of belief or investment in the students. The schools depend on the students' doing well. As Phil Chosky said, "If a student isn't happy or doing as well as he can, we've probably made a mistake somewhere and I hear about it and move on it."

Phil Chosky, we're pleased to report, *owns* a school in Pittsburgh, Pennsylvania.

A GUNSMITHING SCHOOL

The Thatchers told us to drive west out of Pittsburgh along the Ohio River. At Avalon we were to go slow and look for a red-shaked building on the left overlooking the river. We drove past it, stopped, and turned around. The school is easily missed. It's only a hundred feet long and twenty-five feet wide. It's one of two gunsmithing schools in the country and is probably our favorite private vocational school: the Pennsylvania Gunsmithing School.

The Thatchers have owned and operated the school since 1947. It is one of that species of "mom and pop" schools that taught bench trades to a vanishing America.

George Thatcher figures you learn here in seventeen months what it would take you four years to learn apprenticed to a gunsmith. There are twenty-six students in the day course and twenty in the evening course. Students must register first in the night course; then, as people graduate, they rotate into the day schedule. There are only twenty-six benches and George Thatcher is determined not to expand. "We feel we have the finest program anywhere."

The course costs $170 a month for a total of $2,870—that covers exactly 2,496 hours of instruction and practice. A professional tool chest with necessary hand tools and materials is also required, at an estimated extra cost of $1,350. The day begins at 8 A.M. and goes strong until 3:30 P.M. We got there at lunch—a Big Mac and a shake, eaten around a 10" Clausing lathe, 36" between centers. Gunsmithing is precise. So are the Thatchers.

The students work on each other's guns. Then, as the course progresses, they make their own rifles.

George Thatcher doesn't care if a student hasn't had previous mechanical experience. Most students have never taken a gun apart before. But generally they do like to hunt. "These fellows," according to Thatcher, "rebel at a theory situation. You can tell about kids when you are working with them. They like this business because they can see what is accomplished. We

THE COURSE

	HOURS
Introduction	60
Blueing	480
Stockmaking	660
Machine Tool	330
Heat Treatment	30
Welding and Soldering	60
Barrel Fitting and Chambering	60
Chambering	60
Sight Mounting	36
Repairing and Custom Alteration	600
Reloading and Simple Ballistics	60
Business Practice	30
Total hours for the Master Gunsmithing course:	2,496

work along at the student's pace, what they call individualized instruction, but we keep telling them, 'Lay down your screwdriver and you are not producing.'"

Students come from all over. They have seen occasional ads in the *National Rifleman*. Most are in their early twenties; many are Vietnam veterans. They all work part-time to support themselves while studying. And they like the school. They must—attending the evening course for six months or more before they can enter the day classes is rough.

The school is an actual machine shop with lathes, mills, drill presses, bandsaws, sanders, an anvil, a forge, and blueing room. Like all vocational schools, the school simulates the workplace. The catalog states: "No machine the student uses in school will be beyond his own facilities to own after graduation. Precise gunsmithing is done by coordination of the hand and mind. It does not require large production machinery. On the contrary, the finest available custom work is found coming out of small shops."

The course assumes that most of the graduates will go into business for themselves. The school itself is a small business; Mrs.

Thatcher is able to give the students a good introduction into small business management.

When we asked about the four instructors, one fellow answered, "Gosh, if I only knew what those guys have forgot. . . ."

It's not easy to get into the Pennsylvania Gunsmithing School. The Thatchers want students to visit the school first, with a parent if possible. A high school diploma is desired, and good references are needed. George Thatcher says he can tell if a person is going to succeed in his school immediately after a walk-through of the shop. Thatcher can sense a fellow's motivation to work with guns.

They have never had a woman student; they say it's impossible, what with the benches being so close together and all. The school is a bit straitlaced, but if some women really want to be gunsmiths, they could probably talk the Thatchers into it.

A TRUCK DRIVING SCHOOL

Ryder Technical Institute is a different breed of school from the others in this book. Before one can attend the actual resident truck driving school—there are four regional centers—one must complete a forty-lesson home study course that covers everything from steering a semi to public relations for the truck driver. We like this combination of home study and three weeks of short, intensive, resident training. Because they've studied at home, students arrive at the Center psyched up, confident that they will do well.

Ryder Technical Institute is accredited by the National Home Study Council, the recognized accrediting agency for correspondence schools. The Home Study Council has accredited sixteen other combination resident and home study schools. Subjects that are taught by this method include motel-hotel operation, data processing, electronics, dental assisting, camera repair, diesel mechanics, and motorcycle mechanics.

In the spring of 1975 the truck driving course costs $1,295. And this is what it is like.

The Home Study End of It

The lessons are bound ten to a looseleaf binder. There is an introduction explaining what the lesson will cover, the lesson itself with drawings and an occasional photograph, ending with a self-study quiz and an objective quiz that is mailed into the headquarters in Atlanta for grading. After one book of ten lessons is finished, another set is mailed out. You pay as you go. Eighty percent of those who sign up don't finish, which is the way of all home study courses. They require discipline and a desire to complete things. Ryder's first home study lesson opens with a cartoon of someone named "Ryder Gyder." Ryder Gyder, with twenty-four-inch biceps and a Gibraltar jaw, is wheeling his rig round a curve, saying, "Hello and Welcome to Our Ryder Family!" Sort of a Paul Bunyan Teamster. The first lessons are filled with this kind of hype about truck driving. It is supposed to get the student "in gear." The course doesn't really begin to give out much information until lesson five, but after that it picks up speed and begins to work. Each lesson is sixteen to twenty-four pages long. The average completion time for the whole home study course is said to be eighty hours.

LESSON NO.	SUBJECT
1	Your Future as a Professional Driver
2	Let's Get Aboard
3	Back of the Cab
4	A Truck Is Born
5	The Drive Train
6	Let's Put Her in Gear
7	Steering
8	Putting on the Brakes
9	Natural Laws and Moving Vehicles
10	Coupling and Uncoupling
11	Pre-Trip Inspection
12	The Power Plant (Engines)
13	The Electrical System
14	The Engine Fuel
15	The Engine Air System

16	The Engine Lubricating System
17	The Engine Cooling System
18	Tires
19	"Gentlemen, Start Your Engines"
20	Mid Program Review
21	Engine Troubleshooting
22	Trailer Troubleshooting
23	The Privilege of Driving
24	Safe Driving—Elements and Precautions
25	Preventing and Fighting Fires
26	Accidents
27	Instrumentation
28	Accidents and Driver Assistance
29	Defensive Driving, Part I
30	Defensive Driving, Part II
31	Reporting the Accident
32	Load Distribution
33	Freight Handling, Part I
34	Freight Handling, Part II
35	D.O.T. Regulations, Part I
36	D.O.T. Regulations, Part II
37	D.O.T. Regulations, Part III
38	D.O.T. Regulations, Part IV
39	Public Relations
40	Let's Wrap It Up

That seems to be a reasonable flow of information. Much work, money, and modern teaching theory have gone into the development of the course. The students we asked at the training site agreed that it did the job for them. But they, of course, were of that slim 20 percent who were going to finish what they had begun.

The Atlanta Training Center

Harold King, training director at the Resident Training Center, calls himself "the fat man." He is not. He is a block of a man —Mr. Ryder Gyder, a stern, bandy-legged captain for every boy who dreamed of travel that first motel night away from home as he listened to the rigs outside down-shifting, horning their way into the wee hours. How's your rig pullin', Harold?

Harold had been chief instructor at Atlanta until a month before we arrived. His office squats in an asphalt field of fifteen acres, with an old warehouse and loading docks at one end, the driving range at the other. The course contains a hundred-foot alley, a thirty-foot alley, a serpentine, a jack-knife parking hazard, and a perimeter road with turns, bumps, stops. There is a maintenance shed for the dozen or so diesel and gas trucks the students learn on. Harold's main administration building is a former house trailer sans wheels.

Every three weeks 120 students—divided into two shifts—pass through the Center. They go at it, forty hours a week, under the guidance of eighteen instructors, all experienced drivers. This is the course:

TRAINING CENTER SCHEDULE

FIRST WEEK

Monday	Orientation—Classroom—1 hour
	Coupling/Uncoupling & Pre-Trip Insp. on the truck—6 hours
	Simulator—1 hour
Tuesday	Driving on Concourse—8 hours
Wednesday	Backing Exercises—6 hours
	Simulator—½ hour
	Classroom Logs—1½ hours
Thursday	Driving on Concourse—6 hours
	Driving over-the-road—2 hours
Friday	Backing Exercises—8 hours

SECOND WEEK

Monday	Driving over-the-road—8 hours
Tuesday	Backing Exercises—8 hours
Wednesday	Driving over-the-road—8 hours
Thursday	Backing Exercises—6 hours
	Classroom (DOT Reg.)—2 hours
Friday	Driving over-the-road—8 hours

THIRD WEEK

Monday	Backing Exercises—5½ hours
	Classroom (DOT & Logs)—2 hours
	Simulator—½ hour
Tuesday	Driving over-the-road—8 hours
Wednesday	Backing Exercises—5 hours
	Classroom (Driving Pra.)—2 hours
	Simulator—1 hour
Thursday	Backing Exercises—5 hours
	Final Written Exam & Road Test —3 hours
Friday	Backing Exams—4 hours
	Graduation & Placement—4 hours

Harold sure didn't know what we were about. He didn't know, but he began to talk because he was proud of his trade, himself, and his Center.

"These men here (now we got some women) are jus' tryin' to upgrade theirself. They read an ad for Ryder or saw that big van saying 'Learn-To-Drive This Rig' passing them on the Interstate or saw a commercial on TV. Anyhow, they took the correspondence course, passed it, and signed up for the Resident Training. Here they'll learn safety, how to couple-up and how to trip. Most of 'em are truck driver material, some are the college types. (They gotta get their heads turned around, that's the only problem there.) But you look out that window there—see those trucks doin' that course? Trucks all over the damn place, backin' and fillin', jack-knifin', moving out onto the Interstate there. With all that, we've only had one road accident here.

"We run this place like a Marine boot camp. We go at it for three weeks. It takes about a year on the road to make a professional driver, but believe it, you should wish that every driver coming at you has been to school like this. After that three weeks—which includes five hundred road miles of four-lane, two-lane, and mountain driving—we know that if a student passes, he is equipped and safe to be on that highway. Now we don't get a 'natural driver' very often, but we make truck drivers out of 95 percent of the men that come here. If they have finished that correspondence course they're with it and ready to learn to drive.

"I'll tell you why some guy wants to drive truck. One, you don't have a boss except at either end. Two, you are alone. Three, working for a higher goal, like your own truck or a house. Four, don't have to stay in one place. Five, you got freedom and some money. You get a whole release on life, gettin' in that rig."

King sent us out to the course and told us to talk to anyone we saw. Crossing the field was like running out of gas in a spaghetti-bowl interchange. But we made it to where some students and an instructor were backing into a "loading dock," simulated by painted stripes and a barricade. Groups of students were riding around the perimeter road on three trucks; two trucks were in the serpentine; one was doing alleys; and we assumed that some were off on the Interstate highways that menace what remains of Atlanta. From the air it must look like a Parchesi board or a county fair. We talked to some students.

Mr. Jackson: "I wanted to better myself. I was working for $3.50 an hour in a real sweatshop in Columbus. . . . This course is not as easy as a man would think."

Joe Sommersle, black, thirty-three, New York City: "I work at Hunter College, a Custodian, if you dig. When you come from the ghetto, you learn to wait, wait and sacrifice . . . it's slow. But I saved $100 a month for this course."

Mr. and Mrs. Willie Talent, Sanford, Florida: "My wife knows more about trucking than I do. She worked for a trucking outfit and gave me the idea we could do this together and get ourselves a truck. We used to have a tavern. Damn hours about killed us. This is going to work out. Look at my wife backing over there. Damn good, isn't she?"

Mr. Carter: "Me, I was working third shift in a tampon factory. Shhhh. Don't say anything. Kimberly-Clark doesn't know I'm here. This is better than I thought it would be. I started the Home Study a little over a year ago."

The chief instructor came over and asked if we would like to get into a rig and ride with some students. Stowing our notepads as best we could, we got instructions in how to navigate the eight feet from ground to cab. We got into the little bedroom behind the front seat, a place we'd always wanted to see. Two other students were there already, waiting their turn to drive. Meanwhile, they observed and listened to the instructor talk to the driver. This run was going to be the student driver's first sortie out onto the Interstate. The first! The kid was nervous and apologized in advance that it was going to be a rough trip. Instructor: "No, it ain't. You been doin' good all week. No problems. Just watch your RPMs and your side mirrors. OK, you've made your pre-trip inspection, check the coupling again. Checked your mirrors and gauges. Hit your air brake a few times. Good. Let's roll it. Put in the clutch. Good. Hit it!" And so it went.

The Ryder Truck Simulator, Jim Ryder's brainchild, costs $30,000 and each of the four training centers has two or three. It simulates the driving and control of an International Harvest 4070 tractor equipped with a Cummins NDC 250 engine and a 13-speed RTO 9513 Roadranger transmission. It uses three synchronous slide projectors and provides all the sounds and responses of a real truck. You sit there and drive, looking at screens, one big one in front, and one each for your rear-view mirrors.

King got into the simulator and showed how it works, how the instructor can throw mechanical problems into it to see if the students are watching the gauges, etc. King came to life behind the wheel. We could actually see him heading out of Atlanta, the wife and kids behind.

Ryder Technical Institute is now being sold. Though more successful at it than most corporations, Ryder is getting out of the school business. Back to trucks, where they belong.

A FASHION MERCHANDISING SCHOOL

> en-tre-pre-neur: A person who organizes and manages any enterprise, esp. a business, usually with considerable initiative and risk.
>
> en-tre-pre-neuse: A female entrepreneur.
>
> —*The Random House Dictionary*

Most of us have been entertained on long bus or subway rides by the advertising card above the window opposite us: "k u re th? if so u k ri 120 wpm & gt mo pa." Thousands and thousands of young people have been challenged to decipher that message, enroll for the Speedwriting course, and move up in the world. Edward Porter created that ad and it helped his first school—Massey Business College, Atlanta, Georgia—become the largest and most successful private business school in the South.

Atlanta shouldered itself to the top with battalions of office workers trained and placed by the schools Sir Edward and Lady Anna Lee Porter founded in Atlanta. Rural young people would read in their hometown newspapers that they could learn a skill and get a job in Atlanta, and they poured into the city from all over the South. For those who couldn't make it in, the Porters provided temporary term schools—units that could be set up in the smallest town within two weeks, with a class to be graduated in sixteen weeks. The Porters sold the business schools in 1965, after fifteen years in Atlanta, and moved to Miami to establish the International Fine Arts College, one of the most successful proprietary schools in the country.

We went and looked over their school, and then the Porters—Sir Edward and Anna Lee—had us to dinner at their fabulous and slightly loony house out on the Miami Beach Gold Coast.

Lady Porter, Anna Lee, a handsome woman in her middle years, is Southern, sharp, and tough. "Edward taught me everything I know about selling. When we first started out, I enrolled as a student in the Speedwriting course, but since I couldn't pay the $107 tuition fee, Edward hired me to work in the office. After the first few weeks on the job, I wanted to learn how to enroll students, so I listened through the partition to Edward selling away. 'You'll *love* it, you can learn Speedwriting in six weeks,' and all that stuff. Anyway that's all I knew, so when the phone rang one time, I said, 'Oh yes, Speedwriting, you'll *love* it, learn it in six weeks!' Edward came tearing around his partition calling me a thief for stealing *his* material. Here I was working for him and he was angry! Well, he got over it.

"Let me tell you how Edward sold. A girl would walk into

his office and he started closing the sale before she even sat down. He would smile and say, 'Hello, how are you? Day school or night school? Will you be paying by cash or check?' "

Edward hurried into the conversation.

"If that effort at 'closing' didn't work, I went on with a bit more of the sales talk. I find that many people sell, but not many *close*, get that signature. I was so busy running that school that I didn't have time to waste on selling that didn't pay off. I had to close the sales and I had to be innovative to do it. When a prospective student would hit that top step, I'd say, 'Day school or night school?' and you'd be surprised how many times they would suddenly make up their minds to enroll, and then I'd say, 'Write your name exactly as you want it on your diploma' . . . wouldn't you say this is a *buying signal*, when they write their name?"

Just then the phone rang. The housekeeper answered it and announced, "Sir Edward, it's for you." At that moment we knew we had left ordinary proprietary schools and entered the world of theater. This was no mere school we were visiting, this was musical comedy. As Lady Porter had said earlier, "We're not like anyone else in the world." The International Fine Arts College in Miami and the Porters who built it are special to the school business. Their school is a Longest Running Show, full of pizzazz, expensive seats, comic characters, an old-fashioned "bevy of beauties," and the remorseless click of sound business decisions. It's what you'd have if Ethel Merman and producer David Merrick left Broadway to start a school.

The International College is right there on Biscayne Bay, downtown Miami, near everything. The school's quarters are in a five-story fifty-year-old building, a Spanish palace on the water, surrounded by a park. It horseshoes around a lovely patio, complete with hanging plants, palm trees, and girls studying, chatting, waiting to be photographed. There are about 170 young women enrolled in the school. They were born into middle-class and wealthy families and have come (or been sent) to learn the graces while studying fashion merchandising or interior design in an "academically-oriented vocational school."

The school is expensive. Tuition and fees are $5,317 a year. This includes books, tuition, all fees (field trips and social activities), and rather elegant living accommodations in a waterfront apartment complex owned by the Porters. The school keeps college hours: three classes in the morning, starting at 8:30, and two in the afternoon, starting at 1:45. Most courses meet three or four times a week, with students carrying seventeen to twenty-two hours per quarter. All students take the same freshman core courses and then branch out in the second (and final) year to either Fashion Merchandising or Interior Design. International was accredited by NATTS in 1969.

CURRICULUM

FRESHMAN YEAR

Fall Quarter
History of Fashion I
Marketing Principles
History of Art
Speech
Fashion Trends

Winter Quarter
History of Fashion II
Economics
Dynamics of Art
Great Books
Fashion Show Production
Psychology of Drama

Spring Quarter
Retailing I
Survey of Fabrics and Textiles
Fashion Illustration
Literary Craftsmanship
Fashion Coordination
Interior Design Principles

FASHION MERCHANDISING MAJOR: SENIOR YEAR

Fall Quarter
Management and Organization
Consumer Psychology
Display
Merchandising Math
Fashion Design I

Spring Quarter
Marketing Management
Fashion Buying
Advertising
Business Law
Business Policy

Winter Quarter
Sales Management
Retailing II
Bridal Consulting
Survey of Business Components
Fashion Design II
Placement Seminar
Interior Design Concepts

INTERIOR DESIGN MAJOR: SENIOR YEAR

Fall Quarter
History of Furniture and
    Architecture
Consumer Psychology
Interior Design I
Architectural Communications
Layout and Space Planning
Management and Organization

Winter Quarter
Interior Design II
Architectural Communications II
Color Psychology
Survey of Interiors
Commercial Interiors
Placement Seminar

Spring Quarter
Interior Design III
Commercial Interiors II
Lecture Series
Business Law
Administrative Procedures &
    Budgeting
Professional Presentation
    Techniques

We spent three days at the school, wandering from class to class, interviewing students, faculty, and staff. Our first class was referred to by the students as "Lipstick 101"; the Bulletin calls it "Fashion Trends." The instructor is Charlene Parsons, a leading model and fashion consultant in Miami. She has taught at the school for five years. Fashion Trends has a little bit of modeling in it, basic makeup, papers to write on current and future fashions, field trips to clothing factories, working at fashion shows, and, we suspect, a good bit of personal development advice from Mrs. Parsons. This is the first course the girls take.

The class is held in the Mirror Room. A makeup table with lights runs around the mirrored walls with a small stage in the center. On Mrs. Parsons's desk are piles of *Women's Wear Daily,* attendance sheets, eye shadow, and pancake makeup. Mrs. Parsons is talking about a recent visit to New York.

"In the collections this time, faces were mostly pale, not a lot of color. They're applying the color to the face the same way we've been doing but they don't blend it in. You leave a pretty big red spot on the cheek. The foreheads were shiny. The hair was curlier, some straight and under. You can see it in *Women's Wear.* You have to look at the pictures carefully. Speaking of *Women's Wear,* use it for your Thanksgiving assignment, 'Trends for Spring and Summer.' Remember, if you are a buyer you've got to make those decisions six months ahead, so you can get your orders in. Don't be swayed too much by your own personal taste."

As class ended, Mrs. Parsons came over to us, wondering how it had gone. We said that the girls had been bending our ears with various complaints.

"I see changes the girls don't see. I'm with them day and night for both years. We involve them, expose them fully to the fashion world. There are Internships for a few senior girls where they get to work with fashion executives. A lot of the senior girls are working in stores. At least once a week, we organize some sort of activity for the freshmen, like a merchandising presentation at Burdine's, a fashion show at Saks, another at the Doral Country Club, a visit with the president of Burdine's. I always take a girl with me on modeling assignments. After this first quarter, the girls have more confidence, it seems to me. By graduation, they will tackle any job."

After lunch we went to the first-year marketing class. The school's academic dean is Sandra Broaddus, a woman of about twenty-eight. She is good.

"What do we mean by holding costs? . . . Yes, warehousing is part of it. Also insurance, taxes, obsolescence, what else? . . . What is involved in a shortage cost? . . . Replenishing costs? OK, you have this central area with warehouses in the middle, now they have a fleet of trucks to distribute out to their stores.

OK, stimulation techniques: Johnson and Johnson, with falling birthrates, has to take its products to the adult market; now adults are using their baby oil and shampoo. If you were Gerber's Babyfoods, what would you do . . . ?"

The class went on like that for an hour and fifteen minutes. We looked at the text: *Fundamentals of Modern Marketing*, Prentice-Hall, 1973. A standard college text.

After class, we asked her what she thought of her students.

"I teach a course at Florida International University. We have better, more motivated students here. Being small, it's more fun."

In a senior interior design class, we talked to the pros, the girls who had stayed at the school and knew it well. Susan West talked with us while struggling with the project for the week: a bachelor apartment, with bar, bay window, and three seating areas. Susan is twenty, tall, brown hair to her waist; a striking young woman.

"What does your father do?"

"He's a wholesale grocer and also owns two discount stores in Bristol, Tennessee. He wanted me to come here. He didn't want me to meet a 'Bristol Pistol' and get married right away. He wanted me to come to a 'nice' place and meet 'nice people.'

"A lot of the freshmen you talked to complained about the school, right? Every freshman goes through that—they don't like the school, they want to go home. They're not used to seeing so many girls just like themselves. You find out you're not as unusual as you thought. The ego goes bump. It's all part of growing up. I love the school now. I came here because I wanted fashion merchandising—you can't get it in many colleges and, besides, well, let's say I was deficient in math . . . I wanted to avoid math. I think that's true for a lot of the girls here; I wasn't the only one."

Later in the week we talked to the two men who help keep the girls involved, feeling special, and the school oiled and running. While the Porters create ambiance, set strategy, and move the school around the upper reaches of Miami society, Dr. Nimrod Thompson, vice-president of International, ramrods the whole show, day-to-day. His sergeant major is Charles Wright, the school's custodian. We talked with Dr. Thompson (Dr. T.) first. He is fifty, with an elegantly bald head and an imposing Southern accent.

"What do you do here, Dr. Thompson?"

"I'm Director of Admissions, do much of the placement work, and handle 'accounts receivable.' When you bill people, you get to know them very well. There is nothing wrong with billing and collecting money. Most of our girls pay in advance. When there is a problem, we try to make other arrangements. If there are still more problems, I'm the one to phone the parents. I know the parents as well as I know the girls. Fifteen to twenty percent are what we call 'sacrificing parents.'

"For the girls, I'm a father figure. They come to me with their personal problems, even after they graduate. I keep track of them."

Just then a girl walked by his door. He called after her, "Hey, you're gorgeous; what are you doing, being so pretty today? I *love* that dress!"

The school's fourth leg is Charles Wright. Wright, a black Bahamian, has been with the Porters from the beginnings of the school. He was the first person hired; he'll be the last person let go. He is the custodian, builder of partitions, driver, solver of problems for the girls, everyone's confidant. A man of immense dignity, he has the most interesting background of any staff person.

Wright is a graduate of Jack Johnson's Training Center for Domestic Workers in Nassau, a proprietary school that trains butlers, doormen, waiters, and valets for high society in the Bahamas. Before he came to this country he was considered one of the two best chief butlers in the islands.

We asked Mr. Wright about the school.

"With Lady Porter and Sir Edward, I built this school. We worked long, long hours. We had only forty-one students at the beginning. . . . This is my life. When the school expands, I profit. When the school grows, I grow. A business must pay for itself and I try to help."

FOUR

HOW DO I FIND THE RIGHT SCHOOL?

Any young person locked into high school has a time of it, trying to figure out the world and how he or she might fit into it.

Unless you are in an unusual high school, your introduction to proprietary schools will not come from your school's guidance counselor. In most schools, counseling's essential purpose is to maneuver the majority. into college. An article about school guidance counseling in the October 3, 1974, *New York Times* stated:

> A majority of students said "changing a class schedule" was the only service they received from counselors.

> Only one in 10 parents surveyed felt that counselors were helpful in getting a student a job, and only 18 per cent felt counselors had aided in getting their children accepted by a college.

■ 73

Whatever counselors may wish to do, their days are filled with clerical business and the never-ending tide of students with schedules to be changed. With paperwork and college counseling taking up the hours, only one high school student in five—20 percent, nationwide—receives *any* vocational counseling.

Dr. Ken Hoyt, Director of Career Education at the U.S. Office of Education, tells of a study of Des Moines, Iowa, high school counseling he made a few years ago. First he asked that the counselors send him tapes of what they considered their best counseling sessions. He listened to two hundred and found that *all* the sessions chosen were with college-bound students with an average IQ of 136. Apparently no one had had an exemplary session with a vocational student. He wrote all the counselors again and asked them to send him tapes of vocational counseling sessions. In summary, this is how the counseling went:

1. Tell me about your problems.
2. Beware of gyp schools.
3. Try the Army training programs.
4. Good luck.

Counselors expressed concern that they could not relate to the work-oriented student; they did not know what to ask. They did not have answers to the basic questions:

1. What will happen to me if I choose to become this?
2. What are my chances of getting into this type of training and getting a job?

Listening to the tapes, Hoyt realized the vocational students had no confidence in what they were hearing from counselors. In any high school, word soon gets around. Students that aren't going to college stay away from the counselors' offices.

There are about 70,000 school counselors in the United States. They should be helping students get job skills. Yet 750,000 bored, ignored, and embittered students drop out of high school each year. Another 850,000 students drop out of college. The National Advisory Council on Vocational Education, in its Sixth

Report, "Counseling and Guidance: A Call for Change," 1972, reported the following:

—Counselors are much more competent in guiding persons toward college attendance than toward vocational education.

—Job placement and follow-up services are not now being routinely provided as an important part of counseling and guidance programs.

—Most counselors know very little about the world of work outside education.

—Counseling and guidance services are being rejected by the hard core disadvantaged as irrelevant and ineffective.

Walk into any high school guidance office and there is a tidy table and racks filled with brochures about "Careers." For years they dealt with "Your Future as a Nuclear Scientist," "Why I Chose to Become a Successful Lawyer," "Is Teaching for You?," or "The Health Professions." When the only business of high school was college, you could find out only about jobs that demanded college. There are changes in the literature racks now. We have seen some flat-footed pamphlets like "Technical Education May Be for You!" and "What Is Drafting?" Counselors tell us they still go pretty much unread. So what can a person do?

We say, go to a private trade school to learn a special skill; that is what this book is about. Our premise is that people move ahead on their dreams. And dreams are very specific, detailed workings of the mind. Daydreams have been called the "back burner of the mind."

Most people know what they can do, like to do, and what, in fact, they will be doing. For years psychologists attempted to identify predictors of future job-holding and success. Eventually, it was discovered that the best way to find out what young people would be doing some years from now is to *ask* them. No one had thought to ask them their dreams.

Professor John Holland of Johns Hopkins University has used this finding to develop a very useful counseling tool, the *Self-Directed Search for Educational and Vocational Planning*

(SDS). The SDS is a *self*-administered, *self*-scored, and *self*-interpreted device. The student is asked to list his occupational daydreams, favorite activities, and special competencies. With the aid of an enclosed Occupation Finder, the student comes up with a list of occupations that fit his or her talents and dreams.

Counselors wishing to obtain copies of the *Self-Directed Search* can write:

Consulting Psychologist Press
577 College Avenue
Palo Alto, California 94306

To us it is clear that intensive specialty training, geared to the workplace, is the stuff of dreams for many. And now a word from the same people who gave us large, impersonal public school systems in the first place.

> Our schools are, in a sense, factories in which the raw products (children) are to be shaped and fashioned into products to meet the various demands of life. The specifications for manufacturing come from the demands of twentieth century civilization, and it is the business of the school to build its pupils according to the specifications laid down.
>
> —ELLWOOD P. CUBBERLY, *Dean of the School of Education, Stanford, 1916*

To dream, perchance to weep.

COUNSELORS AND PRIVATE TRADE SCHOOLS

We were out beyond the Beltway in suburban Maryland and it was a wet, hungry, mongrel night. We were scouting a high school Career Day Fair. An automotive school director had told us about it. He said he was going with his school banner, his slide show, some brochures, a cut-away painted car transmission, and little hope.

"No one goes to these things. They hold them at night, supposedly so parents can go, but really they don't want to interrupt their class schedules. It's in the gym and folks will walk around like at a country fair. The Army recruiters will be there, naturally.

"Last year, we had to laugh—the *Encyclopaedia Britannica* salesman got in and got a booth. Everything but the recliner-massage chairs. It's not the way to buy or sell education but I promised the counselor we'd be there. He wants to get at least eighty schools there and he has sent us some students on the Q.T. the last couple of years."

For everybody but us the evening was not much. Desultory perambulating from booth to booth, students and parents warily reaching for brochures while the school recruiters from M.I.T., the University of Maryland, Notre Dame, and the local business and trade schools tried to engage them in talk. Ten percent of the school's students showed. Someone told us that schools hold these Career Days to get all the college recruiters out of their hair at one time.

As we walked in we were given a floorplan of the exhibitors and a leaflet which said in large black type: "Thinking of Job Training? A Correspondence Course? WATCH OUT for the SALESMAN WHO . . ." Then it went on with a scary litany of sales techniques that schools can use to steal your money. The last line read, "Before You Sign Anything, Stop! . . . Go to a school or career counselor." We could not tell you who printed this leaflet—probably the Federal Trade Commission. It seemed unkind to invite the trade schools to participate and then frighten off their prospects with scare propaganda.

Private trade and technical schools have to operate in this hostile counseling environment. Now that there are so many community colleges, few public school counselors are going to take the risks of sending students to the college's competitors. Rarely do they visit the private schools and since they rarely deal with the sort of young people who go to these schools, they don't get any feedback on how well or badly they are trained. So they don't know about proprietary schools and are not going to find out. From the other end, in rather typical fashion, the school owners rarely invite counselors to their schools. Which is a mistake, because good schools always sell themselves.

By and large, this is how school counselors perceive private schools:

1. Private schools are trying to sell. We do not trust the information they give us.
2. Many private schools are no good. Therefore, all are suspect.
3. Private schools are dedicated to keeping the truth from students and parents.

Students have to deal with those biases if they take the government's advice and go to a school counselor for guidance.

On the other hand, there are a handful of counselors who do recommend private schools to students. Often the principal does not know that the recruiter gets into the high school or that the counselor provides the school with names and addresses of possible sales.

We have sensed that high schools are loosening up to private school representatives. One study showed that about half of the private schools found high school representation and liaison work effective. If the school rep does not come on too strong, clearly has the student's interest in mind, and the trade school has a good track record with recent graduates of that high school, then a quiet session in an outer office can probably be arranged between a recruiter and some students who obviously are not going to college. And there is the rub. One school owner wrote:

> We are in the process of making a basic change in our recruiting philosophy. For many years the doctrine of most high school counselors has been that any high school graduate who could possibly do so should go to college. While we have certainly disagreed with this attitude, we have passively condoned it through our approach to high school counselors. In their conversations with counselors, our representatives normally ask permission to talk to those seniors who will not be able to go to college. This has been a rather apologetic, negative approach and has no doubt resulted in our getting lower quality, less motivated students.

He hopes that one day he will get parity with the colleges in the counseling process. "Hell, my grads are going to make more money as electronic technicians than most of the kids that go on to college and I swear to God, they will be just as happy."

Some high schools, particularly in the East where there is a longer tradition of private trade schools, set up assemblies for the school reps. One East Coast airplane maintenance school has three recruiters who go to five hundred schools and talk to nine thousand students a year. A large computer school has what it calls a "high school stroker." She is young and has an M.A. degree. She does not try to talk to students. She makes appointments to talk with counselors. She is welcome in about four hundred high schools. She does not try to "sell" the school. She explains the training and talks about what graduates of the high school she's visiting are doing right at the moment as a result of the computer training they received. In these high schools contact with the trade school is solving some guidance problems. But it is on a limited basis, because the goodwill that is extended to one proprietary school is rarely extended to the industry. If the counselor is certain that a particular school is OK and does right by the referrals it gets from the high school, then the counselor feels confident in dealing with that school. But if a student walks in and asks about other fields or other schools, the counselor is apt to say, "Why don't you try the course down at the community college?"

High school counselors should make a study of all the private trade schools in the region so that intelligent, informed, and candid opinions are possible. It is important that concerned teachers and counselors get out and into the private schools to see what they are doing and how well they are doing it. If they do see the schools, they will have less reason to railroad unmotivated students into college or junior college. They will have an alternative.

DOING IT ON YOUR OWN

Most of the thousands of trade school graduates made their choices on their own, without school counseling. You can too.

The first private trade school student we ever talked to was a young woman at the Seattle bartending school. She had thoroughly investigated the school before she enrolled. She had called the Better Business Bureau, the State Employment Service, and the Chamber of Commerce, then visited the school and talked to students. That's not the usual routine. A student in a Baltimore electronics school is more typical: "Well, I tell you—I got the idea of coming here because I drove past this building for years on the way to work and always saw that big sign there. So I came in one day and signed up."

That's how most of us get through life. We check out blind dates more thoroughly than we do a school where we'll invest thousands of dollars in our future. On the other hand, that electronics student did not make a mistake; things had probably been working quietly in his mind for some time. When the time was right, he made his move. Most people dislike checklists. When a dream starts to work, decisions get made on many levels, both rational and emotional. One school owner told us that when a kid makes his mind up, nothing can stop him—counseling, advice, nothing. But a checklist is a place to start. So start with this one:

■ *Write* to the schools that appeal to you, that teach the skills you desire; ask for their catalogs. Write to a number of schools. Write nationwide.

■ *Visit* the schools that fit your needs; talk to everyone in sight. When you speak to the school owner, tell him you are visiting a number of schools before making up your mind.

■ *Evaluate* them in terms of your needs. If the school is accredited, this process is simplified; if it's not accredited, check it out as you would an automobile.

WRITING AWAY

Good trade and technical schools are everywhere. The directory of NATTS-accredited schools in the back of this book is a fine starting point.

Further sources of school names and addresses:

The Yellow Pages under "Schools."

Appendix D, Consumer Advice Offices. Each state approval and licensing agency listed there publishes a "Directory of Approved Private Trade and Technical Schools." Write the state office and request that directory. These are schools that have been approved for veterans. The state directories include both nationally accredited and state-approved schools.

The back pages of magazines. *Popular Mechanics, True, Argosy, Glamour, Seventeen,* male- and female-oriented magazines, and special-interest magazines carry school advertisements.

Here is a sample letter to a private vocational school:

Date _____

Admissions Office
Name of School
Street
City and State and Zip Code

Dear Sir or Madam:

You school was listed in the NATTS Directory, as published in *Getting Skilled* by Tom Hebert and John Coyne. I am interested in learning _____. Could you send me material about the school and those courses? Can you send me a complete catalog including tuition costs?

Thank you very much,
(*sign*)
Your address:
(*carefully print your
name and address so the
material will reach you*)

SCHOOL CATALOGS AND THE WRITTEN WORD

You have to know how to read a school catalog. If you do, few things in life will tell you the truth as fast and as sure. Anything a school knows about itself ends up in its catalogs. Good or bad, it all comes out in its printed material. If the school has something worthwhile to offer, one way or another it communicates that. If it is a shuck, the absence of detail, and the presence of distortion, promises, overstatement, and a too-good-to-be-true quality rushes you: you better poke at it with a stick.

These catalogs are expensive to print; some run one dollar each. The schools do not throw them away; they would rather send a simple brochure first to see how interested a person is. So write a letter to each school that you want to research.

Most schools will respond within a couple of days. You can also use the phone numbers we have included. With rare exceptions, the accredited NATTS schools listed here will be in business when you contact them. The unaccredited schools suffer a certain fallout: 10 or 15 percent of them change hands or go out of business each year when their usefulness is past or their management has become less efficient.

Except for those published by chain schools, all catalogs are as different as dogs in the pound. Large and small, fat and thin, rich and poor. Here is the simplest catalog we have ever seen. One sheet of typing paper, folded and stapled; a rough mimeograph job. We believe what this lady says about her school. If we are ever in Eagle Creek, Oregon, we will look her up to find out how her graduates have done.

SCHOOL OF MASSAGE

CLASS BEGINS   First Monday in October and will continue through April
9:00 AM to noon 12:30 PM to 4:30 PM
Monday through Friday
1000 hours in class required to earn a diploma. Special hours may be arranged in some cases.

TUITION $525.00—payable either in advance or on a budget plan of $75.00 down and $75.00 the first of each month until paid in full.

ENTRANCE   High school or equivalent. Students who do not have
REQUIREMENTS   a high school diploma should enquire how to qualify.

SUBJECTS

Anatomy	250 hrs.	Electrotherapy	25 hrs.
Physiology	100	Exercise	50
Hygiene	50	Massage Theory	150
Hydrotherapy	50	Massage Practice	325

This is a vocational school for the purpose of teaching the art and science of massage, with an introduction to related phases of Physical Therapy.

The school is licensed by the State Department of Education and is bonded in accord with state law.

Here is the contents page of another catalog, from an old-line automotive school. Anything you could want to know about this school and about automotive training is in the catalog:

CONTENTS

A medical technician school we know makes sure that its large catalog looks about twenty-five years behind the times, giving the school a settled and secure image. More important, it supplies pages and pages of detailed information. For example:

URINALYSIS
Physical, Chemical and Microscopic

Preliminary Examination of Urine: description of tests, and explanation of terminology used. Description of types of specimens; preservatives to be used to prevent bacterial and chemical decomposition. Specific Gravity, transparency, volume, reaction, color and the determination of total solids are reported under this classification. Procedures for concentration and dilution tests for Renal Function and the Phenosulfonphthalein (P.S.P.) test. Normal values in the determination of these tests on urines and the significance of abnormal results.

The principal requirement of a catalog is that it make sense. A good school emphasizes the *training offered.* It doesn't wander off into discussions about space travel. A certain New York school's catalog offers only one specific detail—that the course is 415 hours long. It does not discuss fees, rules, or history of the school—just empty talk like this:

ELIGIBILITY
High school graduates, adults, and veterans may be admitted for training.

Average or above average general intelligence.

Top 15 percentile in mechanical reasoning aptitude as determined by a standardized test. Request testing at your school or at M.B.V.S.

Average or above average reading ability.

Good citizenship—Dependable, honest, energetic.

TECHNICAL SERVICE CAREERS ARE REWARDING
Thanks to our system of private enterprise, you can really go as far as your effort and capabilities will merit. The more technical training and practical experience you can get, the better are your opportunities for advancement.

Things to look for in a catalog:

■ Does the school claim lots of things are "free," like placement, housing assistance, or parking? Nothing in a proprietary school is "free." Student tuition pays for it all. Placement should not be described as "free"; it is *always* provided without additional charge.

■ Look out for words like "oldest" and "largest."

■ Endorsements and testimonials—are they current, relevant, in context, meaningful?

■ Are photos and illustrations appropriate? Might they create false impressions? Does that airplane belong to the school or United Airlines?

■ Does the catalog bear a date? It should—a recent one.

■ Check the back-page approvals. Is the school listed for membership in a lot of organizations that an individual can simply join? Or does membership in the organization really say something about the quality of the school?

■ Accreditation and Approvals: About the only accreditation the schools in this book will have will be that of the National Association of Trade and Technical Schools (NATTS). A few are also accredited for some courses by the National Home Study Council or the Association of Independent Colleges and Schools. A NATTS document points out:

> Reference in advertising to accreditation is limited to official accreditation achieved and currently held by the school through nationally-recognized accrediting agencies and associations as defined and listed by the U.S. Office of Education.

Incidentally, "accreditation" does not mean that course credits are automatically transferable to other schools or colleges. Transferability of credit is based on an agreement between two institutions and usually requires the approval of the receiving school.

■ On veterans' benefit approvals, be careful. Almost any school can get an approval, allowing it to accept students on veterans' benefits. This is OK, in that it gives veterans many alternatives for study and training. But do not rely too much on a school's being "Approved for Veterans' Training"; the record of the state approving agencies has been very patchy, although it is fast improving.

■ The phrase "Guaranteed Placement or Your Money Back" is in disfavor now and is rarely used. No school can "guarantee" a job. We must admit, though, that two of the best schools we came across guarantee placement. They select their students very carefully and have, in fact, returned money to graduates who were not able to get jobs. Of course, schools that make a placement guarantee can never be accredited or approved, but since these particular schools are in fields with many job opportunities, they have no problems and do not need accreditation.

■ Give high marks to schools that print the curriculum in the catalog. First there should be work in basics. Then see if the course moves on to apply *basics in realistic settings*—the more practical, the better.

■ See that conditions of enrollment and refund are clearly stated. Remember, catalogs can be only "imitations of reality" at best. The good schools try to tell you about themselves in factual terms. But there should also be some *glamour* in their catalogs. Sometimes a school, like the gunsmithing school described earlier, can go easy on the glamour, because there is a built-in glamour for many people in fine guns, blue-steel barrels, and exotic woods. But every student wants to think he or she is going into a life's work that is useful, in demand, and respected by other people. A catalog that shows a graduate solving a complex problem for an employer or customer is a good one. Our favorite is the school catalog that led off with the slogan "Morticians enjoy life!"

TALKING TO A SALESPERSON

Once you have written to a school, it will probably follow up on your interest by having one of its salesmen or saleswomen contact you. Most schools prefer that you visit the school and have this talk on the premises. But if you cannot make it during the day, or if you want your parents to be present, a salesperson can visit you at home. This is where the process of *recruitment* begins.

We should first lay out some of the essential vocabulary used in the trade:

■ *lead:* The name and address of someone who has expressed an interest in the school or who is looking for training. Leads come from returned advertising coupons, counselors, state employment agencies, friends, and relatives. When you write for a catalog, you become a lead.

■ *aggressive selling:* The key to a school's health. Seeking out every possible enrollee, telling the school's story straight and true, and getting a decision.

■ *conversion:* A successful enrollment, from expressed interest to signature on the bottom line. Sometimes called a "close."

■ *in-house conversion:* Sale of a course made on the school premises, as opposed to a home sale.

■ *blue suede shoes:* A term from the boom years of proprietary education, 1946–52. It refers to the hard-sell salesman, the kind who will sell *any* student *any* course. He lives off student deposits and leaves the problems to others. He may represent a bad school; sometimes he will represent a good one. But he tends to move on.

■ *entrance examination:* A sometimes good, sometimes bad, enrolling device used in the home sale or at the school. These have been used extensively in the past but are now frowned upon by accrediting agencies. An honest salesperson can use an exam to find reading problems, an aptitude for mechanics or lack thereof, and so on. A high-pressure salesperson can use one to convince a shaky sale that he has more talent than he actually possesses. Exams are entirely appropriate *after* the sale as a counseling device.

■ *front-money schools:* A crooked operation that exists on prepaid tuitions. Such a school demands a large payment at the "front of training," then delivers a cheap product or, more rarely today, skips town.

■ *high-pressure selling:* Forcing someone to buy something he or she did not intend to buy. Bad.

■ *negative selling:* Telling the student of every possible disadvantage to attending the school. The Marine Corps has used the technique for years. It is suggested to the student that even if he manages to qualify for entrance, the school may prove too difficult for him. Used honestly and not to spur an unqualified or questioning prospect, negative selling creates an "I can do it!" attitude in the student and helps keep the school out of trouble by disclosing everything from the beginning. Also called "affirmative disclosure."

■ *recruitment:* To deliver a qualified enrollment to the school's door.

■ *retention:* In good schools, what recruitment is all about. Finding students who will stay in the school for the length of the course and pay their full tuition. High-pressure selling results in a high dropout rate and low retention of students. This costs the school money because its facilities are budgeted for certain numbers of students. Dropouts also cause trouble around the school. Proper recruiting yields high retention.

■ *sales-force rollover:* How long the sales force stays with a school. Good schools have satisfied, stable salespersons. Fly-by-night schools have a constantly changing sales force, a lot of blue suede shoes.

■ *sit-down student:* A lead that has signed, started paying tuition, and is attending classes. A sit-down student is the end product of the school's recruitment effort.

To talk to a recruiter directly, we answered some ads in magazines and newspapers. One fall night we got a call about eight P.M. from Sam Nelson, who represents an electronics school with both home study and resident training divisions. Sam readily agreed to talk to us about selling education. "I do not do hard *negative selling* like the old-time encyclopedia man, where you tell the guy that he owes it to his kids not to let them grow up stupid like their old man. But you do find out the prospect's problems and remind him that he does not have much in the way of a future without training. At this point you can tell him that he is making the right decision, if you think he is. People like to be told that you have the right school for them. A prospect wants answers. I give them. Then I tell him that our resident schools can give him two things: (1) a theory of electronics and (2) practice on good equipment. A top technician can make $15,000 a year. Hell, I used to make that. . . . If the student is married, I have to talk to the wife. If she does not have any confidence in the husband, if she knows that he never finishes what he starts, she won't let me *close* the sale. After we show the material we have with us, we ask the *closing question:* 'Well, do you think you can do it?' If the student does not change his mind in the next three days, he sends in the down-payment, which is $100."

We asked Sam to talk about some of the abuses of selling. "Well, I would distrust the salesman who made fantastic claims or said the course was too short or too easy. No one should guarantee jobs. Some crooked salesmen won't leave a copy of the contract with the prospect and won't outline the Federal Trade Commission rule on cancellation—that you can get your deposit back if you change your mind within three days. [See the sample contract, pp. 112–113.] By God, a person has the right to back out of a sale if he wants. If you have been honest and the course is the best thing for the person, he will stay with it. But he should know his rights."

What are some mistakes that prospective students make? "Well, we spend one to two hours making a sale. We read all the material to them out loud (I can read upside down), but people don't ask questions when they get a chance. We ask them, 'Any questions?' But people don't want to *look stupid,* so they don't ask questions. They postpone them. Look, if I have one piece of advice, it is to ask every question you can think of and go over the enrollment terms very carefully." Just then Sam apologized, said he was sorry but he had to stop; he had a hot prospect to talk to that night. As he hung up, he said he hoped we would not come down too hard on salesmen.

We don't. We think that good salespersons have a positive role to play. Pump them for what they know about the school.

THE OLD WALK-THROUGH ROUTINE

If after a thorough study of the school's advertising and catalog, and perhaps a conversation with a salesperson in your home or over the telephone, the school still looks good, it's time to arrange a personal visit. Most schools will *want* you to visit them at some point in the enrolling process. If you have a number of interesting schools to visit, put together a bus tour, and take off cross-country to see what's what.

We emphasize that you should try to go *away to school.* Your chances of completing training are better if you get at least two hundred miles away from home with all its associations and distractions. After you find a school with a *good training program* and a *positive learning environment,* worries about leaving home will be left behind. Schools appreciate your traveling a distance to attend them and do their best to help you get settled. You are not limited geographically.

You have to leave behind your biases about "schools" and what they are supposed to be like. We have been in dozens of private schools and no two were alike. A deep-sea diving school in Seattle is an old scow with an office and classroom built on deck. The students spend a good part of their day mucking about on the bay bottom; watch you don't trip on that coil of rope. A classy computer school outside Washington, D.C., has carpeted classrooms with potted plants, and the students live in elegant apartment towers across from a shopping plaza. Airplane maintenance schools are at airports, and heavy equipment schools need a hundred acres, so they're likely to be in out-of-the-way locations. Some schools have relocated in the suburbs, following the students. But most depend on bus service and low rents, so they take over second-floor office space in the downtown area, within a ten-block radius of the center of town. After getting off the bus, you walk around the corner and up a couple of flights.

School owners have to understand square-feet and short-

and long-term leases. They like to have flexible space so that they can expand cheaply for a new course and added enrollments, or drop the lease on a couple of classrooms if recruiting is down. What we are saying is that these schools are practical places, designed to get the job done. They are *adult schools*. Students realize that they pay for everything they see. This works to keep the schools simple. You won't see ivy walls, lovely auditoriums, and large grounds. In the case of the computer school mentioned above, the nice surroundings are meant to suggest the type of setting a graduate will work in. Don't look for a romantic environment in a converted warehouse in Pittsburgh. In any case, the lack of glamour does not matter. Most students don't make the school home—come 3:15, they are gone.

Phone or write ahead that you are going to be in town such and such a date and that you would like to visit the school. When you arrive, you will probably be taken around by one of the salespersons; in small schools your guide will be the owner or a student. In large schools you may have a two-step interview. First a salesperson will explain the course (how long it takes, what it costs, what kind of people the school is looking for) and take you on a tour of the facility. Afterward, if it looks like you are interested, you will be taken in to see the owner or director, who will press home the advantages of the school, answer further questions, and ask you when they can enroll you for class.

This visit is a complex event. The school is trying to convert a lead (you) to a sit-down student; you, on the other hand, are attempting to determine if it is the right school to attend. With most schools there is no conflict. The visit helps the school to see if you have the right attitude, the ability, and enough money to complete the course. They want to see if you are employable.

You will be struck by the friendliness of the school. Folks are going to be personable. They are, after all, salespeople and/or small business people. But a good school is a happy school and it sells itself. We liked most of the private school people we met. If the person escorting you comes on too strong at first, tell him or her that you don't need to be sold on the school, you are there to let the school sell itself. Carry paper and pencil; take notes.

You are visiting the school for two reasons: (1) to get the *feel* of the place as a learning and working environment and (2) to determine if the training is adequate and what *you want*.

You may be alone with the salesperson or with a group of students who are going to be given a tour and a talk. Some schools schedule "open house" once a month for prospective students. These can be helpful because the owners and salespeople spend more time talking about the occupation they are training for than they do selling. But if you go to an "open house," try to come back alone another day.

The school is accustomed to visitors, most of whom do not sign up for the course. After an initial flip-chart or slide show in the sales office, you will be walked through the shops, classrooms, labs, or whatever. One of the curious details of the industry is that the lab or classroom doors all have little windows that let you watch a class in session. Or there will be one-way windows in the wall that allow visitors to see the action without distracting the paying students. We think it best, though, to visit *inside* a classroom, to sit there and listen to a typical lecture or demonstration. This is a bit of an imposition, so you may have to plan it in advance. But it is invaluable in getting an idea of the courses and it gives you access after class to the instructor and students.

As you walk around the school, you will notice wall plaques that tell of the school's civic memberships or the accomplishments of graduates, and trophies from the school's winning entry in a local craft show or something. You will see school banners for sale ("Ace Auto Tech") and rings and badges that students can buy to give themselves a sense of belonging.

Almost all schools have *student motivation* displays. The usual kind is a notice board covered with photos and notes from recent graduates telling how they are doing out in the real world. The school works hard to keep track of graduates because their stories reinforce what the instructors are teaching the current class of students. Many of the students will know the graduates mentioned on the board and their success keeps everyone's eye on the ball: the job at the end of training. When students can see that the training *does* work and is worth it, they are motivated to complete their own course. Take a look at these displays.

The dining facilities will be a stand-up area surrounded by coin-operated vending machines for sandwiches, candy, and Coke, about all the students want from lunch. Sometimes the school operates them for profit, sometimes they are contracted out. Prices are what you would pay anywhere. This is a good place to buttonhole students for a private chat about the school.

The premises should be clean. Most of the schools we visited were far tidier than their public counterparts, for reasons we don't fully understand. It probably has to do with the students' efforts to develop proper work habits (a clean bench means a clean job) and the school's efforts to protect its investment in whatever equipment the students work on.

MEASURING THE SCHOOL FOR YOURSELF

Dr. Ken Hoyt, whose work we discussed earlier, has carefully researched what questions students have on their minds when investigating a vocational school. He says that the educational consumer is *not* interested primarily in such variables as the number of square feet in the building, the number of degrees held by instructors, the number of books in the library, the history of the school, how the owners maintain and operate the schools (often students graduate from a proprietary school without ever realizing that it was private). Instead, the generic question asked by the prospective student is, "What is likely to happen to me if I choose to enroll in this institution?" Hoyt has also identified the important subquestions most frequently asked by students:

1. What kinds of people would I find in classes with me?
2. What would be my *total* cost to complete training—expenses in addition to tuition?
3. How do students pay the costs of attending this institution?
4. How does the institution compare with the expectations of those who enroll?

5. How do present students evaluate the institution?
6. What proportion of students complete their training at this institution?
7. What proportion of students find employment upon leaving this institution?
8. What kinds of employment do graduates find?
9. Does the institution effectively help graduates find jobs?
10. How much money do graduates make on their jobs after training?
11. Does this training help graduates find and advance on jobs?

That is an effective list of questions to ask of the school and its students. Those are the questions on your mind. You might carry the list with you as you make your way around each school. As you investigate the equipment, the teaching, placement, drop-out rate, and other areas discussed below, you will find those questions are being answered.

TEACHING EQUIPMENT

The equipment used for teaching should be adequate for that purpose. In an automotive course, there should be a number of engines on test stands. These won't be in good shape, because the purpose of having them is to give the students practice in diagnosing troubles and working out solutions. But there should be enough of them—maybe half a dozen—so that every student gets his chance. In a diesel course there had also better be some *operating* engines. We visited a school once that was attached to a large commercial repair facility. It depended on off-the-road trucks for practice in diagnosing difficulties and making repairs. This is not educational. Engines that the staff has worked with for a long period are real teaching machines.

A school for medical assistants made a big deal out of its basal metabolism machine. But doctors do not use basal metabolism tests much any more, so the training was irrelevant. In a commercial art school, is there enough air-brush equipment, enough photographic material? If you know much about the trade, you can answer these questions yourself. Otherwise, ask the students if there is enough equipment. Naturally, they will say that there are shortages sometimes, or not enough material for every technique. Expect some complaints. But if they are *angry* about supplies and equipment, then there is a problem.

The equipment should be *adapted* to teaching. Good technical schools paint different parts of sample equipment different colors. In an electronic school, the outlines of screwdrivers, solder guns, and common testing equipment assigned each student may be painted on the student's work surface, so that they are laid down in the exact same spot each time. This teaches proper work habits. It is a good sign. A school with a concerned faculty will be filled with imaginative teaching aids, well-stocked shelves, enough materials for everyone, and equipment that works when it is turned on.

TEACHERS

There should be a mix of older and younger teachers. This is generally the case in private schools, and it is one of the keys to the superior teaching found there. Older teachers have greater skills, both technical and teaching, while the younger ones can provide more up-to-date information about the workplace because they have just left it. Ask to see background descriptions of the teaching staff. Expect that some of the teachers will be graduates of the school. That is excellent, if they have had two to four intervening years of work in the field. Graduates who return to teach have that special feeling for what is needed from the school and what it is like to be a student just learning the skills. Look to see if the staff has had responsible positions in the field they are teaching. Be wary if they have been teaching for a long time in the public schools. They may be spoiled; they will not be job-oriented.

Some schools hire only full-time teachers while other schools hire part-time teachers, but hire more of them. One art school we know has over one hundred teachers on the staff, but each comes in only for short segments of the course. Another school across town, same size, has twelve permanent teachers. We thought the first school had more pizzazz, while the second was more stable. Who's to say? Whatever you need. *Talk to the teachers.*

Understaffed schools have problems. The 1974 University of California study, "The Effectiveness of Public and Proprietary Occupational Training," asked this question: "Are Certain Kinds of Schools Better Than Others?" The answer is well said.

> . . . we usually found the most successful graduates had gone to medium-to-large schools* with higher paid teachers who worked fewer hours. This finding did not necessarily mean a school would get better results simply by increasing teachers' salaries. We interpreted this finding to mean that moderately large schools had more resources and could pay their teachers more. These more successful schools provided generally better working conditions than poorer schools, many of which had dwindling enrollments and underpaid teachers. Those marginal schools had to eke every ounce of productivity out of their teachers and worked them more hours each week, which set a tone of bare survival.

CURRICULUM

Each school will be different. The courses, though, should have a roundness. They should begin with the basics, move on to the specifics, and then to the job. A main consideration: When in the course do you get hands-on? It should come right away. Something to ask the students: did they have to wait weeks before they used the screwdriver? Hands-on should start at the "front-end" of the course. Many schools have driven students away because they spent too much time on theory at the beginning, boring everybody to death. Theory is necessary, but a well-designed course scatters it throughout.

Many schools arrange "externships" with local businesses. It is cheaper to have students in the field than in the school and often it is more educational, as well, but it should not be a

---

* In the context of this study, enrollments of 200–400 were considered "medium-to-large." These are still small schools when compared to their public counterparts whose students number in the thousands.

major part of the course. It is up to the school to provide the same environment in school as you will find in the workplace. Do not be overly impressed if the school brags about how many professionals come in and give lectures. Instead, be impressed if the professionals come in looking for graduates to hire. However, a smart school does schedule professional visitors because they help the morale of the school; just having them around is enough.

If the course is one that logically can lead to self-employment, is there a section of the course that deals with setting up your own business? In small schools you often pick up this information by talking with the teachers. Have teachers run their own shops?

Two situations to be aware of:

"Stepchild courses." These are new courses hurriedly established to take advantage of a popular public interest. Example: an auto repair school sets up a motorcycle repair course without sizing up the market for graduates or taking time to fully work out the curriculum and train teaching staff. If the course that interests you is outside the normal offerings of the school, check thoroughly.

Too many courses. If a resident school is offering a veritable cafeteria of courses, the school must be truly well established and prosperous, or some of the courses will be inadequate. If your favorite course is one of many, check thoroughly. We were in a small school once that offered air conditioning, refrigeration, drafting, blueprint reading, electrical installation, advertising art, sign painting, showcard writing, and cartooning. They were doing too much with too little.`

FULL DISCLOSURE

Full Disclosure is upon us. Career Education and Consumerism have come together and had a baby—Full Disclosure. Now students will be able to make easier, more informed decisions in the area of career training. Facts about a school's performance now have to be turned over to the prospective student.

The Veterans Administration, the U.S. Office of Education, and the Federal Trade Commission are readying new rules and regulations that will oblige all schools to provide any interested person with placement figures, average starting salaries for graduates, and noncompletion—dropout—rates.

Veterans will soon be able to ask for statistics that the schools supply to the VA. Students needing Guaranteed Student Loans will be given figures required from the schools by the U.S. Office of Education, as of the 1975–76 school year.

In any event, all NATTS schools have to provide dropout and placement statistics in their annual reports to the NATTS Accrediting Commission. Ask the school for those figures.

PLACEMENT

Get a full description of the placement process. Forget about "Lifetime Placement" because you'll never use it. What steps does the school take to get *first* jobs for graduates? Does the school have regular contact with employers? Ask for a list of employers who have recently hired graduates. Does the school actively deal with employers, or just hand graduates the Yellow Pages and the want ads? Most schools have an end-of-course orientation that deals with interviews, job hunting, and placement. Some schools will devote weeks to preparing graduates for specific interviews they have set up. Other schools find that their graduates do not need as much grooming and orientation. (If you are from out of state, placement in your home state may be more difficult. The school will explain what it can do in that case. It may have friends in your home state or it may be able to act only as a strong reference.) Some schools write your résumé for you, others set up appointments and tell you to take your tool kit because the job may begin that afternoon if the employer thinks you can handle it. The Seattle bartending school sends out an instructor to assist the new graduate on the first night on the job, to help her or him over those few panicky first hours. Again, ask current students about the placement process. Students invariably know how recent graduates, their friends, got their first jobs;

if the school did the right thing or not. Ask to have the placement record explained. *Federal regulations now require that
schools do this.*

On February 20, 1975, the U.S. Office of Education published new regulations for vocational schools, *both* public and
private, that desire to participate in the Guaranteed Student Loan
program. This is what such schools must now provide to prospective students:

> Each participating institution shall make a good faith effort to
> present each prospective student, prior to the time the prospective
> student obligates himself to pay tuition or fees to the institution,
> with a complete and accurate statement about the institution (in-
> cluding printed materials) . . . , such statement shall include
> information regarding the employment of students enrolled in such
> courses, in such vocation, trade or career field. Such information
> shall include data regarding *average starting salary* for previously
> enrolled students entering positions of employment for which the
> courses of study offered by the institution are intended as prepara-
> tion and the *percentage of such students who obtained employ-
> ment* in such positions. This information shall be based on the
> most recently available data.

DROPOUTS

Get the dropout figures. NATTS-accredited schools have an
average dropout rate of about 35 percent. According to information on file with the FTC, however, this figure includes "those
who were dismissed for disciplinary or academic reasons, those
who accepted employment before their course was completed,
and those who terminated their studies due to personal reasons
such as illness, homesickness, marriage, pregnancy, financial problems, and so forth."

The FTC misunderstands the issue of dropouts. It believes
that dropouts are the result of high-pressure sales. The fact is,
people drop out for many reasons, including all of those listed
above. Examine the figures carefully. If a course is short but the
dropout rate is high, there is probably a problem at the school

and you had better stay away until it is solved. Worry if there is much dropping out in the middle of a course, but be less concerned with dropouts at the beginning of school and just before graduation when jobs develop. A school with a rather high dropout figure may simply have higher standards than the current group of students can handle. We have known of bad schools whose courses were so easy that hardly anyone ever dropped out.

THE BOTTOM LINE

"Are you getting what you paid for?" That is the key question to ask current students. When talking with students, try to get past their first superficial remarks. People are always somewhat critical of things they are paying for. But if you ask straight out, "Are you getting what you paid for?" and "Should I come here?" you'll get straight answers. Make a point of talking to at least six students. If it is difficult inside the school for you to corner that many students or if they aren't free to talk, stand outside the school at closing time as the students rush out. Tell them you are a prospective student and could use some information. Take some to coffee. When one starts to talk with you, others will chime in and give you the lowdown.

As you talk to students, as you walk through the school, as you sit in on the classes, note how *serious* and *purposeful* the atmosphere of the school is. Where students are learning, there won't be much noise or horseplay, late arrivals, and wasting of time.

TALKING IT OVER

After you've toured the school and met some teachers and students, you will talk to the school's director. You may already have talked to a salesperson in your home. Probably you haven't signed a contract yet, because you wanted to visit the school first. Or you may have signed and made a deposit conditional on a successful visit to the school. Now you are ready to interview at the school.

One school owner told us that he uses the interview to discover the student's attitude to the trade—does he *like* design and layout? He has two questions he wants answered in the interview. (1) Is this course what the student wants? (2) Can he or she *cope*? Another owner told us that he uses the interview not to sell the school but to size up the student. He said that after thirty-five years in the business he can tell within minutes whether they'll make it or not: "Kids look the part or they don't."

In some schools you will be formally rated by the interviewer. Here are the criteria one school uses for admissions:

Appearance	_____
Personality	_____
Apparent Intelligence	_____
Dress	_____
Neatness	_____
Enthusiasm	_____
Poise	_____

Others give you a long, detailed questionnaire to fill out. The answers you write down are not important in themselves, but the director can tell by your tidiness or lack thereof, your ability to follow the instructions, and your reading ability, whether or not the training is appropriate to you. We have noted that "entrance examinations" are no longer in favor, because of past abuse in selling. However, most schools do something to see if you can follow the trade. Truck driving and heavy equipment schools obtain your driving and arrest record from your home state. If they have received it in time for the interview, they will quiz you about it. They can't place drivers with poor records. Computer schools often use the IBM Aptitude Test for programmers. It tells very accurately how the student will do.

The director will also want to find out if you meet his school's specific admission requirements. Dr. Harvey Belitsky's study showed that NATTS schools generally have the following admission policies: 55 percent require a high school diploma; 40 percent have an age requirement, usually over 17 or 18; 47 percent of NATTS schools call for a passing grade in an achievement or aptitude test. Half the schools have certain physical requirements for entrance. No school is looking for slackers. The Hanson Mechanical Trade School in Fargo, North Dakota, lays out its expectations right there in the catalog:

> An applicant must be 17 years or older and he must be willing to study, work hard and have the desire to get ahead. He must be *willing* to study at night to get ahead.

A school's director also uses the interview to protect himself against overeager, blue-suede-shoe salesmen. Many directors will not meet with the student alone; they want the parents there. If the student is married, they want to see the spouse. Like the salesperson who made the initial contact, the director knows from experience that if the family isn't behind the decision to go to school, a dropout is likely. "I make all the final decisions on recruiting," the director of an automotive school told us. "When a salesman has signed up a kid who doesn't want the course, or isn't willing to work—you know, just isn't serious—hell, I won't take his money. And that salesman will get a royal chewing."

Another school director likes to correct immediately any misinformation a prospective student may have received.

> I usually start the interview off by asking if they have any questions on points brought up at the interview with the field rep. Invariably, the parents, and/or student, will have a list of questions that they feel were not covered, written down on a piece of paper. If for some reasons our sales rep misrepresents our school in any way, I have the perfect opportunity to make sure that the misunderstanding is understood and that the people will go out of my office feeling that all of their questions have been answered to their satisfaction.

The same director described for us the remainder of his on-the-premises interview.

> Also, at this time, I ask the newly enrolled student to tell me a little bit about himself, which he does, and his likes and dislikes in high school, as far as subjects are concerned, and why he is inter-

ested in going into the field he has chosen. I also explain to them that I do not often get a chance to meet every student in the school and this is the one way that I can assure myself that I know who is attending our school in the different classes. After this I ask the student if he has read the Student Handbook and if he understands everything contained in it. If he has not received the Student Handbook, I see that he gets one and also see that he gets a list of the cost of materials for his particular course. By this time, the family is usually warmed up to the school and to the career their son or daughter has chosen.

I then check with them to see if their son or daughter needs housing or a part-time job, or needs to talk with our loan coordinator about the completion of the loan papers. We try to cover all of these areas in one interview, and the student and his parents are taken around to the different offices. After they have completed all of their interviews with the respective people on the staff, they are brought back to my office for a final two-minute session. At this point, we usually give the enrolled student either a T-shirt or one of the school notebooks to take back to his high school or home town.

If the director likes what he sees during your interview, he'll press for a decision. "Do it now," he'll say, "while you're ready."

Remember, even at this point your decision is not irrevocable. If you have any questions or misgivings when you get back home, call the director. Sitting in a director's office in Boston, we noticed on his desk a bright red phone. "What's that for?" we asked. "I'll tell you what that red phone is for . . . it's a *direct line* to me. At the end of our talk, when I send these families home to think about it, I give them my business card with the direct-line phone number on it. I tell them, 'Now folks, if you have any questions about our school or our training, any questions at all, just give me a call on this direct line and I'd be pleased to answer those questions. Call me anytime.'"

CAVEATS

Finding the right school is more a matter of knowing what kind of training you want than outsmarting a slick salesman. The perils have been enlarged by a press unwilling to do its homework and by public schools that can't understand competition. These days the student-as-consumer is usually able to see through talk of "Guaranteed Jobs with Glamour" with the assistance of various accrediting commissions, the Federal Trade Commission, state associations of private schools, sturdier state laws and regulations, and what we see as the basic integrity of the private school industry.

Yet there *are* abuses in the selling of training. As Bill Goddard of NATTS points out, "Everyone agrees that most abuses occur in marketing—sales and advertising. We hardly ever get complaints about the actual training a school offers. You know what happens—a school's enrollments drop, so it gets panicky and hires fast-talking salesmen. Trouble in River City. But there is less of that than you think. More money in aluminum siding."

To insure that you are not among the rare but unfortunate victims of a less-than-honest school, we are including the following consumer-protection material, compiled from the work of a couple of interested agencies.

THE FEDERAL TRADE COMMISSION

This excerpt is from an FTC brochure dealing with high-pressure salesmen.

Thinking of Job Training? A Correspondence Course? Watch out for the salesman who

- Says he is a school counselor or advisor. (He may be only a salesman. His income may depend on his sale to you.)
- Offers you a special price for a limited time only.
- Says "sign now—this is your last chance." (No good school requires that.)
- Promises a fabulous career or a glamorous job.
- Tells you there are thousands of job openings for someone like you if you take his course.
- Says, "You have received one of the highest grades ever on the aptitude test."

- Offers you a large discount if you pay now.
- Won't let you have time to think it over or won't come back tomorrow.
- Tries to force you to sign before he will leave.

THE BETTER BUSINESS BUREAU

The Better Business Bureau is a semi-useful organization. It has a negative function. The BBB can tell you if a school has received complaints locally or if it has been in hot water; what the Bureau can't tell you is whether a school is good or not. It is not the BBB's role to evaluate anything. The Bureau judges a school by how quickly and cooperatively it responds to a query made by the Bureau. If a school settles claims fast, the Bureau is happy. The BBB is most useful when you have a problem with a school and need an advocate or adjudicator. Shady or high-pressure schools always try to keep a clean file over at the Bureau. However, it is best to give the BBB a call to see how fat a particular school's file might be.

The Council of the Better Business Bureaus doesn't as yet publish a brochure on selecting a private trade or technical school. It has produced one that refers to private electronic data processing schools, *Facts on Computer Careers* (1973). Unfortunately, it was too late with too little. Computer schools, which made the computer revolution possible by cranking out trained operators in the hectic first few years, have now settled down to a fairly stable middle age. Sources in the accrediting agencies tell us that relatively few complaints and problems are now arising out of the computer school field.

The computer school brochure does, however, contain some suggestions that should be constructively applied to the evaluation of any school. We include some excerpts below:

1. Check with employers in your area. Determine their job openings, requirements and if they are hiring graduates from the school in question. Also, check with firms who have hired graduates to determine their satisfaction and how well these graduates are progressing.

2. Contact your local Better Business Bureau or your Chamber of Commerce in areas where no BBB office exists. While the Better Business Bureau will not recommend any school, it will tell you approximately how long a school has been in operation and its record of complaints.

3. Take at least one comprehensive aptitude test covering your area of interest. Preferably, this test should be administered by an independent center or organization. If not, make certain that it is graded in a valid, impartial fashion.

4. Obtain information from a number of schools covering the curricula, resources and facilities, and fees. Check this carefully and compare costs and hours involved, being certain there are no "extras."

5. Determine how long the school has been in existence. While length of existence is only one factor, it does imply a certain amount of financial and operational stability and enables you to seek out information on past graduates and their attainments.

6. Check the various approvals and/or accreditations the school has received. Is it approved by state or local bodies? Do these "approvals" cover its courses or only general physical facilities? Has approval ever been revoked or is the school on probation? Is it accredited by one of the three organizations which accredit private schools? If not, has it submitted a formal application?

7. Read all contracts or other binding agreements carefully before signing. Make sure the school's schedule of payments, tuition refund policy, and clauses covering cancellation are clearly spelled out. Don't be in a hurry to sign. Make certain you understand everything in the contract and that it contains all agreements which may have been presented to you orally. If you are uncertain on any points, request written clarification and, if necessary, obtain outside assistance in reviewing the final contract prior to signing.

STATE AGENCIES

The various state agencies that license and regulate private schools are becoming more reliable each year. In the last six years there has been a major overhaul of these agencies to the point that thirty-six states now have comprehensive authority to oversee school operations. The National Association of State Administrators and Supervisors of Private Schools (NASASPS) was formed in 1972 to coordinate efforts for uniform state legislation and to provide a platform and voice for those involved in regulating private schools.

Charlie Conlon oversees the business and trade schools in the state of Maryland for the State Department of Education. We have been with him on three NATTS accrediting visits. He has been with the state since World War II and knows the field as well as anyone. He has seen it all. He tells what's what. "I tell you, it's the same few schools over and over again. I get 'em cleaned up and some fast-talking salesman comes along and sells the school a tale on how they can make enrollments go sky-high. There are some salesmen, if I hear they're even in the state I get worried. They go to work and if I hear even a breath of hard-sell, I send the school a warning.

"My advice to students? I would listen to the salesman, but I wouldn't sign a thing until I visited the place. Get the names of all the schools and go to all of them before you sign. Also talk it over with your parents; don't try to do it all on your own."

Frank Albanese, whom we met at the 1973 NATTS Convention in Los Angeles, is Executive Secretary of the Ohio Board of School and College Registration. He monitors and supervises private vocational schools in Ohio. He is also a founder of the National Association of State Administrators and Supervisors of Private Schools. Albanese is probably the most respected and knowledgeable state school supervisor in the country.

We asked him about problems with proprietary schools. "My police function is *minute*. We have no problem with the great majority of schools; they do a great service to our state. When we do have a problem, it generally has to do with marketing, false claims."

Appendix D contains the addresses of the state agencies. We have worked with a number of state agencies and have generally found them to be knowledgeable about their schools, enthusiastic about their schools' performance, and able to provide assistance to students if problems develop. Once you've selected a school, make a check of its reputation with your state's proprietary school supervisory office.

ENROLLMENT PROCEDURES

An old story: an applicant wrote to a school, saying, "Please enroll me in your school; if it's any good, I will send you a check."

The school wrote back: "Please send us your check; if it's any good, we will enroll you in our school."

Even after you have found your school and made your decision, there are always things to get ironed out. Before you sign the contract, have all·your questions answered and, if possible and applicable, see that your parents are satisfied. Then go ahead and sign up. These days, with Truth-in-Lending Laws and cooling-off periods, enrolling is not the anxious moment it once was.

About three-quarters of the private schools have quarterly or monthly enrollment periods; the other 25 percent allow you to enroll on shorter notice. There is almost always room for one more student in a class. Most schools operate at about two-thirds capacity.

There are usually three steps in the enrolling process: (1) the application form; (2) the enrollment agreement (contract); and (3) the letter from the school formally accepting the student for training. Sometimes these steps are combined on one long form.

The application asks for basic biographical information about the student. No application money is required at this stage. Some schools want references and your school/work experience.

The enrollment agreement is a binding contract once the three-day cooling-off period is over. It is accompanied by a $20 to $100 registration fee. If an officer of the school later decides *not* to accept the student, this money is returned, unlike college application fees.

Every enrollment is accepted by an officer other than the salesperson. This is to protect the school and the student. School directors keep track of the admissions process by looking over applications to make sure the student and admissions person have understood one another. In the enrollment process, as we mentioned earlier, tests are often given to make sure a student can profit from the training.

Accredited schools have long and detailed contracts. Basically, the school agrees to give the training if the student pays his bills, attends classes, and causes no discipline problem. An important feature of the contract is the refund policy. If the student wants to drop out of school, there is a tuition refund schedule. As we write, the FTC is coming up with new refund policies. At present, however, NATTS Refund Policy sets these minimum provisions for accredited schools:

> *Rejection.* Full refund of all monies paid if applicant rejected by the school.
>
> *3-Day Cancellation.* Full refund if applicant cancels within 3 days after signing contract and making an initial payment.
>
> *Other Cancellation.* Refund all monies, in excess of 15% up to $100, if cancellation occurs after 3 days but before commencement of classes.

First Week. Refund of at least 90%, less $100, but in no event may the school retain more than $300, if termination occurs during the first week.

After First Week. Refund at least 75%, less $100, if termination occurs after the first week but within first 25% of the course (or school year, if more than 9 months).

After 25%. Refund at least 50%, less $100, if termination occurs after the first 25% but within the first 50% of the course (or school year, if more than 9 months).

It allows the school to keep *up to* $100 of the down payment that always precedes the starting of classes. This has always protected the school from frivolous application and the student from last-minute cold feet. That $100 makes both sides serious.

Speaking of refund policies, they can reasonably be challenged by a few good schools. Here is the strict parent-owner of an Oklahoma horseshoeing school:

As for refunds, we have never done this; we have no need for this at the present time. We have never had a person ask for his money back. His enrollment fee is good any time in the future and that is all he pays to enroll in classes. At the beginning of class I tell them they have five days to decide if they want to go back; I do not collect any tuition from them until after that date. Recently I called Long Distance 18 former students and asked them if they could have gotten their money back after the first two or three weeks, would they have done so? Ninety percent of these students said they would have but are certainly glad they stayed. They feel the training they received was excellent. This is hard work and, as in any class, students get discouraged. It is long hours but when a student leaves our school, we are proud of their feelings. I would like you to see just a few of the letters we receive daily from former students; this is our way of knowing we do them right.

Early in the course, the boys are sore and tired and would probably go home if they didn't have money invested. This is why I cannot refund money to the students unless there are reasons other than just wanting to go home; if there is a real cause, I do refund their money.

ENROLLMENT AGREEMENT

PENN TECHNICAL INSTITUTE • 5440 PENN AVENUE • PITTSBURGH, PA. 15206 • 412–441-9000

This agreement made and entered into this _____ day of _____ , 19 _____ at Pittsburgh, Pennsylvania,

between PENN TECHNICAL INSTITUTE, the SCHOOL, and_____ the STUDENT.

Witnesseth: That for and in consideration of the sum of $_____ payable at the signing of this agreement and subsequent payments according to the payment schedule below, the SCHOOL agrees to instruct the STUDENT at its SCHOOL in Pittsburgh, Pa. in ELECTRONICS TECHNOLOGY, leading to the Associate in Specialized Technology Degree.

☐ Morning Classes
☐ Afternoon Classes   2000 hrs. - $2960*   beginning _____ , 19_____ .
☐ Evening Classes

ADVANCED STANDING STUDENT: Present Total Cost*_____ Total Hours _____

*The payments and the total program cost in this contract are based on the tuition presently in effect and are subject to change in case of a tuition increase, with at least six-months prior notice.

PAYMENT SCHEDULE:

Registration Fee – $20 – payable on acceptance of the STUDENT and with this agreement. This fee is not refundable after the third business day following the date of this agreement.

Day Classes: (Quarter System) 21 months

The first quarterly payment, in addition to the $20 Registration Fee, is $420. This payment is due three weeks prior to the class starting date.

Subsequent quarterly payments of $420 are due three weeks before the quarter class starting dates.

Evening Classes: (Term System) 43 months

The first semi-term payment, in addition to the $20 Registration Fee, is $210.00. This payment is due three weeks prior to the class starting date.

The next semi-term payment of $210.00 is due three weeks prior to the mid-term. Subsequent payments are due three weeks before the term dates and three weeks before the mid-term dates.

REFUND POLICY:

If the school is notified in writing by three weeks prior to the class starting date or if the student cannot begin classes because of some unavoidable condition such as serious illness, accident, etc., the quarter or semi-term tuition paid and any other advanced payment made will be refunded.

If the student does not begin the quarter or term classes, he or she will be refunded all but $15 of the quarter or semi-term tuition paid and any other advanced payments made. (The $20 registration fee paid by the beginning student is also not refundable.)

A student who withdraws or is discontinued because of failing grades will be refunded all of the next quarter's or semi-term's tuition paid and any other advanced payments made, even though he or she may have attended the first day of the new quarter or term, a necessity to receive the grades and counseling.

Day Classes:

If the student begins the quarter classes and withdraws or is discontinued therefrom, the quarter payment will be refunded as follows:

If the last day of attendance is the first to the 19th class day $280.00
If the last day of attendance is the 20th to the 38th class day........................ $140.00
If the last day of attendance is the 39th class day to the last day of quarter.............. No refund
Any other advance payment made will also be refunded.

Evening Classes:

If the student begins the term classes and withdraws or is discontinued therefrom, the semi-term payment will be refunded as follows:

If the last evening of attendance is the first to the 12th class evening $140.00
If the last evening of attendance is the 13th to the 24th class evening. . . . . $ 70.00
If the last evening of attendance is the 25th to the 36th class evening. . . . . No refund
If the last evening of attendance is the 37th to the 48th class evening. $140.00
If the last evening of attendance is the 49th to the 60th class evening. . . . . $ 70.00
If the last evening of attendance is the 61st class evening to the end of the term. . . . . No refund
Any other advanced payment made will also be refunded.

The STUDENT understands:

1. That the SCHOOL will be responsible to render only such first aid as the regularly established facilities at the SCHOOL provide, for any accident suffered while in training and which is not occasioned by gross negligence or other acts by the Faculty or employees of the SCHOOL, in which he or she may suffer injuries of any kind.

2. That the SCHOOL reserves the right to change instructors, calendar, schedules, courses, textbooks, tuition rates, and Rules and Regulations when necessary or desirable in its opinion. (The payments and the total program cost in this contract are based on the tuition presently in effect and are subject to change in case of a tuition increase, with at least six-months prior notice.)

3. That the SCHOOL reserves the right to interrupt his or her training if he or she fails to do satisfactory work, or if he or she is a disciplinary or attendance problem.

4. That all financial obligations to the school must be satisfied before he or she will be eligible for graduation.

5. That on graduation he or she is to receive the cooperation of the SCHOOL's employment help at no extra charge, and that the SCHOOL conforms to the Employment Agency Act and does not in any way or at any time guarantee employment.

This agreement does not include the costs of books and supplies required of the STUDENT during the program. (Since all books and supplies are not purchased at the same time, but periodically throughout the period of enrollment, a list of current prices of such items is always posted on the Student Bulletin Board. The present estimated total cost of books is $150. There are no refunds on the purchases of books and supplies.)

It is understood that this agreement constitutes the entire contract between the SCHOOL and the STUDENT and that there are no credit charges or cash discounts. Once the STUDENT withdraws or is dismissed from training, no future obligations will be accrued by the STUDENT. (The date of termination of training is the last day of actual attendance.)

This agreement may be cancelled within three business days after the effective date, the date by which all parties have signed. (Cancellation must be in writing and received or post-marked within the three-business-day period.) All monies paid will then be refunded. (All monies paid will be refunded should the applicant be rejected.)

Signature below indicates that both sides of the agreement have been read and understood, that a copy has been left with the student, and that the student has received the school catalog, student information bulletin, textbook present-price list, and a description of the school's facilities, equipment and general class size.

_____ Date_____
(Student)

If the STUDENT is under eighteen years of age, a parent or guardian must also sign below:

_____ Date_____

PENN TECHNICAL INSTITUTE

By _____ Date_____

Since that letter was written, the State of Oklahoma has passed a law requiring all schools to have a mandatory refund policy.

Refund policies are a good thing for the industry; they allow students to take a gamble. When the correspondence school industry was obliged to adopt a refund policy, schools feared they would go out of business. Instead, the enrollments trebled.

On pages 112–113 is a 1975 enrollment agreement for a NATTS school. It is typical of—but not identical to—other enrollment agreements. We include it only as an example of what is acceptable, and to provide some practice in reading small print.

Note the required three-day cancellation provision on the second page. This cooling-off period allows you to change your mind.

PAYING THAT TUITION

Norman Mailer once observed (in a different context): "Learning is expensive and I have learned that an education is best paid for in cash." We—and many school owners—agree. John Benanti, an owner of an electronic engineering school called Tampa Tech, probably hasn't lost an enrollment in twelve years. He and his people convert 80 percent of their leads into sit-down students without using any government loan programs whatever. "I believe that every student should work his way through school," says Benanti, "and I demand that my students do so. If you came to my school with $2,400 to train your son, I'd give you $2,200 back in change. I'd take a registration fee and tuition for one month, and that's *all* I'd take. He works his own way through school. If he wants it, let him pay for it. You can help him, slide him money under the table, but he has to work!" Old-line school owners like Benanti prefer the student-financed method of payment for a reason—they believe they get a more serious, motivated student when he or she alone is responsible for the tuition.

Most schools have either a *deferred-payment plan* or *pay-as-you-go*. With the deferred-payment plan, you can pay part of the tuition after you graduate and are working. Pay-as-you-go means that you have your tuition paid up for the quarterly term, or, in some schools, paid every Monday morning before class.

Older trade schools tend to have weekly or monthly payment schedules. Finance charges on unpaid tuition are up to the discretion of the school. If they are in effect they must, of course, be lawful. Half the schools make finance charges and half do not. In any case, students are not allowed to become seriously delinquent in their payments. At some schools, the rule is no tuition, no class; other schools may let two or three weeks go by after payment-is-due action is taken.

THE GI BILL, LOANS, AND GRANTS

THE GI BILL

The schools listed in this book are approved for veterans' benefits. Indeed, many of them were established after World War II as "veterans' schools." In 1975, an unmarried veteran receives $270.00 a month, up to thirty-six months, with married men getting more. This is enough to cover—if only barely—a school's tuition and modest living expenses. The school or the VA can give you details and handle the abundance of paperwork involved.

We feel that GIs, particularly from the Vietnam era, should ask for academic and vocational counseling and testing before making any decisions. The veteran does stand a better chance of *completing* his education in a vocational school than he does in an institution of higher education. In one of the quiet scandals of the Vietnam war, veterans have been tracked into college, where they are often "cooled-out," discouraged. They have dropped out in great numbers and remain untrained.

Vets have always had a home in proprietary schools. The director of a rough-and-tumble heavy equipment school told us approvingly, "Vets can take a chewing out." Vets add experience and stability to a school. Today, the State Education Departments that handle VA payments and school approvals are doing a better job than they have in the past. We are getting to the point where the term "Approved for Veterans" means something.

LOANS

About a third of the students in proprietary schools are in some loan program or other. There is the Guaranteed Student Loan Program (formerly known as Federally Insured Student Loan Program, or FISL), the National Direct Student Loan Program, and various state loan programs. Bank loans are expensive and hard to come by. Most students use the above programs.

Here is a U.S. Office of Education fact sheet on the Guaranteed Student Loan Program. All the schools in the NATTS Directory are eligible to participate in this program.

FACT SHEET

GUARANTEED STUDENT LOAN PROGRAM

The Guaranteed Student Loan Program is designed to make it possible for students to borrow from private lenders to help pay for the cost of education and training at universities, colleges, and vocational schools with the Federal Government paying part of the interest for qualified students. Loans are either guaranteed by State or private nonprofit agencies or insured by the Federal Government.

Terms and Conditions of Guaranteed Loans
A maximum of $2,500 per academic year may be applied for in most states if the educational costs require borrowing to this extent. Total loans outstanding may not exceed $7,500 for undergraduate or vocational students. This aggregate maximum may be extended to $10,000 for students who borrow for graduate study.

The repayment period will usually begin from nine to twelve months after the student graduates or withdraws from school. Repayment will normally be made in equal installments over a period of five to ten years. The student will be required to pay a minimum of $360 per year on all the guaranteed loans he has received during his school years. Loans may be prepaid at any time without penalty.

Any student, whose adjusted family income is less than $15,000 will automatically qualify for Federal interest benefits on loans totalling up to $2,000 in any academic year. However, the maximum loan may never exceed the cost of education less other financial aid received. Students with adjusted family incomes of less than $15,000, who wish to apply for subsidized loans in excess of $2,000 or students, having adjusted family incomes of $15,000 or greater and applying for a subsidized loan of any amount, must submit to the lender the school's recommendation for a subsidized loan based upon the school's assessment of the family's ability to pay for the cost of education. For students eligible for interest benefits, the Federal Government will pay to the lender the total interest due prior to the beginning of the repayment period. Students not eligible for Federal interest benefits, or not wishing to disclose necessary financial data required for determining eligibility, may still apply for a loan but will have to pay their own interest prior to the beginning of the repayment period. During the repayment period, all students will be responsible for paying total interest charges.

An insurance premium of up to one half of one percent each year of the total loan amount outstanding may be collected in advance under state or private guarantee agency programs. On federally insured loans, by law the premium is limited to one quarter of one percent. The lender may collect the premium from the borrower or deduct it from the proceeds of the loan.

Repayment may be deferred for up to 3 years while the borrower is a member of the Armed Forces, a full-time volunteer in the Peace Corps or VISTA, or for any period during which he returns to a full-time course of study at an eligible school. The borrower is encouraged to make at least partial payments during such periods of deferment in order to reduce the principal amount of the loan. Payment of Federal interest benefits will resume at this time for eligible students.

Eligible Student Borrowers
Any student may apply who has been accepted for enrollment in an eligible school or who is already in attendance and in good

standing, and who is a citizen or national of the United States or is in the United States for other than a temporary purpose. In many States, half-time students are eligible but some require full-time attendance. Residency requirements also vary in some states.

Eligible Lenders

Banks, savings and loan associations, credit unions, pension funds, insurance companies and similar institutions subject to examination and supervision by the State or Federal Government are eligible to become lenders under this program. Eligible schools and State agencies may also qualify as lenders. Students desiring loan assistance should contact their own local lending institutions first. It is important to remember that loans are made or denied at the discretion of the lender.

Eligible Institutions

Most colleges, universities and schools of nursing and many vocational and technical schools are eligible. Institutions located abroad may also be eligible. However, a student should check with the institution he plans to attend to determine whether or not a school is eligible. The Accreditation and Institutional Eligibility Staff of the Office of Education, Washington, D.C. 20202 or the agency administering the program in a particular State will also provide information on whether or not a particular school is eligible.

In Operation

Applications for guaranteed student loans may be obtained from lenders, schools, State or private nonprofit guarantee agencies or regional offices of the Office of Education. The school must complete a portion of this application certifying the student's enrollment, his costs of education, and academic standing. For students who do not automatically qualify for Federal interest benefits, additional financial information may be required by the school. The student completes the application form and presents it to a participating eligible lender.

If the lender agrees to make the loan, he first secures the approval of the guarantee agency. A state or private nonprofit agency "guarantees" the loans to the lender in many States. In other

States, the Federal Government insures the loans. If the student defaults in repaying to the lender, either the guarantee agency or the Federal Government will pursue the borrower for recovery of the loan. If the borrower dies or becomes permanently disabled, the obligation will be discharged by the Federal Government.

In all cases, the borrower will have to execute an affidavit that the proceeds of the loan will be used solely for payment of his educational expenses. This affidavit will also have to be signed by a notary public or other person legally authorized to administer an oath or affirmation (other than a person who recruits students).

The key to Guaranteed Student Loans is that they have a low interest rate, currently 7 percent. There is also a nine-month "grace" period after graduation before repayment must begin.

We talked with David Bayer of the Office of Guaranteed Student Loans in the U.S. Office of Education. We asked his advice for students about to take out a loan.

"Remember, it is a loan; it has to be repaid. Know your rights and responsibilities under the provisions of the loan."

"Are most students able to get loans?"

"Yes, by and large. Problems are regional in nature. Sometimes there is trouble getting them in some areas of the South; later that clears up and lenders are tight in, let's say, Michigan. Each lender budgets a certain amount for student loans; when that has dried up, he stops lending money. You see, bankers don't make much money on student loans."

"What prevents some students from getting loans?"

"They don't go about it the right way. It is best to start with some sort of lending organization that knows the family. If you have a savings account or your parents do, that's the place to start; banks like to be 'Full Service.' If you keep looking, though, you'll eventually find a source of support."

"We have heard that private schools have a disproportionate share of Loan Defaults under your program. What are the facts?"

"Well, we are in the process of developing a clearer picture of the default situation than we have had in the past. Vocational loans account for less than 40 percent of the Guaranteed Loans. The trouble is, their default rate has been higher than 40 percent. Large numbers of defaulted loans come from a small cluster of schools. You know, there are Cadillacs, Chevys, and Edsels. Some schools are less selective about their students; they enroll students in loan programs without seriously considering whether they are the kind of people to finish the course and repay the loans.

"Of course, another big reason the private sector has as many loan defaults as it does is that our loan program is about the only one they have available to them. If the colleges were dependent solely on Guaranteed Student Loans, they would have an equally high rate of default; as it is, they have a large assortment of private loan programs and scholarships that spread the problems thinner. And, incidentally, we are now tightening up the management of these loans. The schools will be handling them differently in the future and students will not be allowed to default in the merry fashion of the past few years. A loan has to be paid back."

"Should a student take out a loan?"

"Only if he or she can't finance their education or training any other way. We all know that something is more worthwhile if you have an equity in it. Students that are paying for all or part of their education tend to be more serious about it. Yet, these days it is tough to work your way through college. It was easier in my day. So there you are. Only borrow what you need, as the man says."

GRANTS

Another federal program available is the Basic Educational Opportunity Grant Program (usually known as Basic Grants) which is available to those entering an institution beyond high school for the first time, on a full-time basis. This program, like its sister program, the Supplemental Educational Opportunity Grant (which is for the student who is already in school at least one-half the time but who could not continue his education without financial assistance), is based on the student's need. The schools can explain the details.

PART-TIME WORK

Proprietary trade schools generally let out early, in time for students to go to their part-time jobs. As you'll notice in school catalogs, schools help their students get part-time work, sometimes in the field for which they are being trained. (This varies from school to school, depending on how it might support curriculum.) Perhaps as many as two-thirds of the students at any given school are working part-time somewhere. A number of schools are able to provide jobs to students for a few hours each week on the Federal Work-Study Program.

PROMISSORY NOTES

Finally, if the banks can't help you, the school does not participate in loan programs, and there are no part-time jobs, you can sign a *promissory note* with your family. Go to a stationers or a bank and ask for the form. It is similar to a check. You fill in the amount of the loan, the date, the time of repayment, the name of the lender, interest rate, and sign it.

Making a promissory note is one way to finance skill training with available family resources at the same time that you are avoiding misunderstandings about what will be paid back when.

THE ESSENTIAL POINT

Private trade and technical schools are looking for serious, honest students. They beat the bushes for them. If they like your looks they'll figure out a way to put you through training. It's that simple. A good prospect is hard to turn away. With all the loans available, plus part-time work, plus parental support, training is possible for everyone who needs and wants it.

Every private school has a financial Aid Officer. One such

person, Bob Stanek, told us: "Many people never consider specialized career training because they're convinced—without getting the facts—that they can't afford the tuition. We can and do provide financial assistance for anyone who is sincerely interested in career training."

That's the essential point here. If you have found a school that offers the training you want, talk it over with the Financial Aid Person there. Things will work out.

THE TRAINING ENVIRONMENT

"Each private school is a world of its own," observed Dr. El Shoemaker, pouring us a cup of coffee in his office at the College of Education, Catholic University, in Washington, D.C. He is one of the handful of academics that has paid any attention to proprietary trade schools. We were exchanging experiences of small, way-out, unique, and useful schools we had visited. He continued:

"They are all different, with their own rules, customs, standards, and atmosphere. Colleges and universities, even the new community colleges, frequently model their activities on something which is perceived to be a proper and accepted role for institutions of higher education. Proprietary schools, on the other hand, appear to be organized in order to get a *specific job* done."

The butcher, the baker, the candlestick maker—their schools are all different. Poking through our notes, we find:

▪ Out-of-town students at the Clarissa School of Fashion Design are housed in a nearby college dorm. The school itself shares the second floor of its downtown location with a theatrical agent who won't give up his office to the school because he likes young people around.

▪ It's all business at East Coast Aero Tech. Students cannot make or receive telephone calls except in emergencies.

▪ The Montana Auto College bought an old public grade school building and moved in, hermit-crab fashion.

▪ The Richmond Barber College runs a successful program in the federal penitentiary.

▪ The South Bay Trade School has a graveyard shift of classes running from midnight to 6:30 A.M. Half-time students attend from midnight to 3:45 A.M.

▪ If you are in butcher training at the National School of Meatcutting you wear a full butcher's smock and apron. At the Culinary Institute of America you wear a chef's uniform day in and day out.

Whatever a school's particular specialty, they have all honed down their courses to what the students *want* and *need*. They are, as we like to say, purposeful, and here are some of the common traits you can expect to come across no matter what *your* field of interest is.

The school day begins early. In some schools classes commence at 7:30 A.M.; other schools will start at 8:00 A.M. or 8:30 A.M. The school day is almost always six hours, with only half an hour, usually, for lunch. Schools operate as the job will. If a bulldozer operator is expected on the job at 7:30 A.M., you can bet that the heavy equipment school will take attendance at 7:30 A.M. As a catalog stated: "The facilities, business machines and scientific equipment at this school are of the type in current use in laboratories, industry and business offices. Every effort is made to closely approximate the actual 'work environment' that the student will encounter upon graduation." This verisimilitude is a key characteristic of private schools.

A school makes no assumptions about the talent, past experience, or ability of a new student. It assumes the students are green, and prefers them that way. An instructor at Ryder Technical Institute, which teaches truck driving, told us: "We would like our students to have about a fourth grade education. The less they know, the easier they are to teach; they don't know it all."

The courses start with basics: this is a wheel, it goes round and round; this is the kitchen, where we will eventually make glorious meals—today we will discuss clean hands and utensils. An instructor never starts over someone's head. The first few days are crucial to students, who are often scared and at sea, perhaps new in town. At a good school, you will find that there is a *success factor,* some accomplishment, built into the early part of the course. In the first few days students should be introduced to the actual workings of the trade and they should see that they can actually do something in it. At the Seattle School of Mixology each new student mixes his first drink on the first day of class; theory units are postponed until the second day. In computer schools, students get a program done the first week. It is simple, but everyone finishes a program and runs it. This immediate sense of accomplishment is essential. "Some of these kids are high school two-time losers already; this course may be the first success they have had since they started going to school," said Don Finch, a school director.

As the course moves along, the pace picks up. Once the students have acquired some skills, more pressure is applied by the staff. By the end of the twenty-three-week Perry Institute "Fry Cook" course, the new cooks are running the school lunchroom with short-order elan, under the critical eyes of fellow students and school staff. In the commercial art schools, senior students work on their professional portfolios and organize the school's art gallery into new shows. In the aviation maintenance schools, an inspector will happen through and evaluate the students' work. At some point in every course, students begin to pass muster or they leave. Toward the end of the course graduates are expected to be working at "entry-level" competence—that is, doing the same level of work that will be expected on the job, in the plant, in the office, wherever. The last weeks of school are really the first weeks of work. There shouldn't be any surprises awaiting the student on the job.

Because most private schools are small, with a low student-teacher ratio, students can expect to be close to their instructors. Teachers often give "extra-instructional assistance," that is, counseling and/or tutoring. Mr. Hilbig, a truck driving student at Ryder, told us: "We got some real fine instructors. I had some trouble down-shifting. They took me aside and gave me some special time." A classmate of his, Jim Tinch, agreed: "If you're having trouble, they just tell you to get down from the rig and cool off. They really want you to learn."

In effective schools there is no compulsion or fear. Success is in the air as the students try their wings and take off.

THE WORK ETHIC

It has been said that the Work Ethic is the conditioned ability to take a lot of crap. The first week of vocational school often bears this out. *In loco parentis* is the stance taken by much of the private school industry. The schools have a Sunday School quality about them. The staff is strict and won't tolerate much fooling around. We were struck by this early in our investigation of the proprietary school industry. Coming, as we had, from the off-the-wall world of experimental colleges, we were not accustomed to the follow-the-book, we're-here-to-learn attitude that is maintained in these trade schools. Ironically, these profit-seeking schools are closer to the public's ideal of decorum than are the public schools.

We have come to understand that the rigid atmosphere derives from student needs and desires as well as management efficiency. These are students who have decided to specialize, to get certain training as quickly as possible. They are serious. They have contracted for specific training. Whether or not they become "well-rounded" is not the school's business, in their opinion.

The schools, for their part, are selling proper work habits as well as skills. They and future employers are more interested in performance and reliability than personality. Beyond that, school owners see themselves as cogs in the world-of-work machine, the Puritan Ethic. They tend to believe that with hard work and high moral principles, one gets ahead.

The Rules and Regulations listed in the catalogs or handbooks exist principally for the goof-off or the student who is new to work. We haven't noticed a police atmosphere in the schools. But the private schools run their own show and it is best to be prepared to train under Spartan conditions. Judge for yourself these selections from various handbooks:

DRESS REQUIREMENTS [*A Fashion Merchandising School*]
It is Miss Wade's contention that students of fashion should look the part. They are required to dress for class as they would for work.

RULES AND REGULATIONS OF THE SCHOOL [*A Cosmetology School*]
Standard approved textbooks and equipment may be obtained through the school office. No borrowing of such materials will be tolerated.

Students must attend classes regularly and pursue the instruction and practical work diligently.

A late student must first report to the office before attending classes.

Silence is to be observed in the classroom. Unnecessary conversation or noise will not be allowed.

Students must obey all rules of personal hygiene, sanitation and sterilization while in school.

Students wearing soiled uniforms will not be admitted to a classroom.

Telephone calls, except for emergencies, are not permitted while in school. A service charge will be made for such calls.

GENERAL REGULATIONS [*A Technical School*]
1. It is wise to realize that any immature or shady conduct reflects upon you as a student, and on the school. The safety

and educational atmosphere of the general student body should not be jeopardized by the immaturity of a few.

2. A student attending class under the influence of liquor or drugs will be asked to leave the class. A repetition may result in a leave of absence.

3. Smoking is permitted during break periods in the lounges and lavatories. (City fire regulations prohibit smoking in class-rooms, hallways and stairways.)

4. Please bury cigarette butts in the urns so that they do not keep burning. If not, the rooms become clouded with smoke —certainly not a pleasant nor healthful condition.

5. Please do not loiter, take breaks, or smoke in the downstairs front lobby.

6. Being that the front walk is to be used by the public, be careful not to block it, or the office entrance, when taking a break.

7. On leaving classrooms or laboratories be sure to rearrange the chairs in an orderly fashion, dispose of all waste paper, and we would appreciate returning all equipment or parts to the stockroom or storage place provided.

SELF DISCIPLINE [*An Automotive School*]
Should any writing be found on the walls of the men's room, or in the lounges, the Chief Instructor should be informed. At that time a general meeting of all students will be held immediately. At the meeting Mr. Diggs and Mr. Pribish will emphatically detail how behavior such as this affects the reputation of each of our graduates. Self discipline only comes to those who have learned to accept discipline.

ATTENDANCE

Attendance is the most important single factor in a trade or technical education. Most schools have 90 percent daily attend-ance. "If they'll come to school, I can teach them to fix cars," is the way one instructor put it. Poor attendance also clues a school administration that some poor teaching is going on. "They stop coming when they stop learning," said a school owner.

We have been told over and over again that a student has to

attend school every day or he loses out. We said it earlier: employers want to know your school attendance record; it tells them what kind of employee you'll be. The courses are designed with very little fat in them; miss a day and you fall behind.

Strict attendance policies became law after World War II and the GI Bill. Veterans Administration regulations allow no more than three absences in one month. Classes must meet for twenty-five to thirty hours per week. Every absence has to be documented as to reason. (This is another example of discrimination against work-oriented students: veterans who attend college are not bound by such strict attendance requirements.)

Every school takes attendance at the class bell and it becomes a part of the student's permanent record. Some schools specify that after, say, twenty-five hours of accumulated absences, you are liable to be put on probation. In other schools not even one class cut is allowed.

One cosmetology school we visited charges a dollar each time a teacher has to inquire by telephone about a student's whereabouts. In almost all schools, a call to the student's home will be made at about 10:00 A.M.; the student had better be sick-a-bed. We asked a student about all this. She said, "School is school. You should be here."

GRADES AND STANDARDS

Each school grades and evaluates students according to its own lights and in a form useful to employers. Written work is usually of secondary importance. Attitude counts most. A slow student who comes every day and tries hard is going to be placed in a job. Instructors appreciate earnestness. One school describes the grading process this way:

> Throughout his course of training the student is required to take written and oral examinations. During each phase of training a mid-phase and end-of-phase examination are included in the curriculum. A student's grade is based on the following formula:

Classroom Work ⎤
Shop Work ⎦ 40%

Initiative ⎤
Work Habits ⎦ 60%

In addition to the formal mid-phase and final examinations, daily quizzes are included which serve the purpose of reviewing small segments of the course.

Another school carefully weighs and evaluates each student monthly in the following areas. There are thirty-two gradations possible!

Industry, Energy—Application to Work
Relations with Others—Helpful, Cooperative
Emotional Stability—Self Control
Leadership—Ability to Get Others to Cooperate
Appearance, Cleanliness—Good Taste
Ability to Learn—Situation Adaptability
Dependability—Responsibility
Punctuality

One of the secrets of proprietary education is that students always know how they are doing. They don't have to wait until the end of the course to learn their score. Teachers either formally or informally keep the student abreast of his progress, sometimes with daily comments.

Grades and/or evaluations may be given out at the end of each unit, or at the end of the term. Some schools send the grades to the person who is paying the tuition. If a student is having problems, tutoring is offered or required; sometimes the student is asked to drop school for a month in order to think things over and get it together. School directors have heard it all before. They have a good sense of what it takes to get a student through. They'll sometimes chew out a recalcitrant student, sometimes take him for a beer, or just give the money back and say, "My friend, you made a mistake. This training isn't for you." Whatever is needed. For the more competitive there is always an honor roll and often a new tool kit for the best student, but the schools do try to get *everyone* through the course.

THE SOCIAL ENVIRONMENT

According to our research, art schools have more parties than tool-and-die schools. But parties, fraternities, student councils, and picnics are not part of the general fare, "the definite goals," at trade and technical schools. The schools are the boot camp to the world of work, not preparation for home and marriage. When a school includes or encourages social activity of some sort, it usually has a direct connection to training. One art school locks up its students with beer and food for a twenty-four-hour painting marathon; a computer school keeps its computers running all night Friday night and food is provided. And at the International College of Fashion in Miami, social life is essential to school success. As the school's owner, Sir Edward Porter, told us: "There are formal dances, parties, receptions for important people in the fashion world, fashion shows, just any way we can think of to get the girls out of their apartments and mixing with the fashion world. They pick up social skills and, moreover, they can make important contacts in the business. In a given year, every single fashion executive in Miami will come to one or more of these functions. Dozens and dozens of our girls have been placed in jobs through this sort of social contact."

Schools with local enrollments tend to be 8:00 A.M. to 3:00 P.M. affairs, with no sociable hanging-out afterward. Schools that draw from a wider geographic area often sponsor more activities, because administrators have observed that some students new to the area will have no social life at all if the school doesn't provide it. Sometimes schools get involved in civic projects related to their training. One medical-dental assistant school, for example, always runs a blood pressure booth at local community fairs and picnics.

Trade schools make arrangements for student housing if they are asked. They have hotels, apartment houses, or boarding houses they can direct students to which can enhance the school's learning environment. Naturally, much socializing can grow out of these living arrangements, but this varies school to school.

IF THINGS GO SOUR

A school director sadly and reluctantly told us about the Case of the Mysterious Dropouts. Five years ago, he had taken over a drafting school with a good reputation and a respectable enrollment. Nothing seemed amiss; he looked forward to a good life with his new school. But shortly after he took over, students whose faces and work he was beginning to recognize, particularly those in the Advanced Structural Drafting courses, began to show up absent as he checked the weekly attendance sheets. Then one of the students, a quiet, serious party, left school, without much explanation. Months passed; the director lost a handful of students who didn't seem to be part of the usual dropout group. An experienced chief instructor who had been with the school for years was also baffled. The courses were well designed; graduates had always done well.

Our director went back over the years, checking dropout records. Indeed, in that second half of the course, there had always been an unusual number of departures. Back for more discussions with the chief instructor. They had to nail this thing down. Months passed and more money was lost as the director talked to students and dropouts. Most of those who quit eased out of the school blaming themselves, if anybody. Finally, a particularly promising student well into the second year of the course left school. When the director, who had been away on a trip, heard that this student had quit, he got on the phone to the kid and suggested they get together and talk it out. The student came down to the school that night. The director put his question: Why was the student quitting so late in the course? Silence. Again, why? The student fiddled with some clips on the desk, then he said. "Well, I just lost interest in the structural classes. Got lost."

"Mr. Beaman's classes?"

"Yes, sir, Chief Instructor Beaman. I don't know, sir, but all of us dreaded taking his advanced courses. He is a nice man, nothing against him, but I think he is an awful teacher and I can't afford to stay six hours a day with that man."

The director asked the student to hang in there for a few days; he would do something. After the student left, he went back through the files and, sure enough, when the students got to Beaman's classes, some dropped out. Beaman could talk a good game, but apparently he couldn't teach. He was dull, pushed too hard, and wasn't aware of what went on in his classroom. The next day, our director gave his chief instructor notice, recommending that he go back into industry. He told us that the chief instructor had cost him thousands of dollars.

There are two lessons in this story. Directors should always find the *real* reason for a dropout through a careful exit interview with the student. The lesson for students: if you have a problem with your training, *make noise.* If the training being offered by a school fails to live up to its advertising, recruiting, and contract obligations, do something about it. Go to the person in charge and lay out the conditions that are causing you concern. Problems generally are not schoolwide; skimpy or irrelevant training is most often confined to one department or class. In the case above, the situation was masked for years from the management of the school. The students had not put their heads together and gone to the director. School owners have remarked to us often that it is a delegation of students or the spokesman for such a group that has pointed out—and thus enabled them to solve— training problems in their schools. The proprietary sector is nothing if it is not sensitive to student complaints. Schools do not want "bitter quitters" out on the street, sandbagging referrals and putting down the name and reputation of the school. Therefore, if you have a complaint about the training or anything else you're paying for, document it, organize it, perhaps put it in writing, and take it to the director if it can't or won't be solved by the instructor. Sometimes the school has been getting too thrifty with supplies: the instructor may just be waiting for a student complaint to back up his request for added material. School owners, unlike public school principals, expect complaints to come to their desks. Students have signed contracts and are paying for their training.

Serious problems in an accredited school should come to the attention of NATTS, which also has some informal clout with nonaccredited schools. NATTS gets only two or three student complaints a week. The majority are solved with a prompt phone call from a NATTS staffer to the school. The nature of the complaint is explained to the school, the school gives its version of the same story, and an accommodation is reached. We have gotten the feeling that if you are fair to the school, the school will be fair to you. Of course, good management requires that fairness begin with the school. We think these schools are fair; that's why we're recommending them.

If you have decided after speaking with the management of the school and, if necessary, contacting NATTS, that they aren't going to do right by you, only then do you take the steps listed below. You probably won't have trouble getting money back from a shoddy school. These schools give it back in an instant when they see that you are determined to have redress. They don't want trouble. If that fails, take these steps as outlined in a FTC brochure.

For people you contact in person or by mail, you should have copies of all papers, letters, cancelled checks, advertisements, and a statement of all the facts.

State Licensing Agency
Complain to the agency that issued the license for the school to operate. In most states, it is the State Department of Education. Usually, it will look into each written complaint and try to settle it.

Accrediting Agency
If the school is accredited, complain to the national office of the accrediting agency. If you have already tried NATTS, check to see if the school is accredited by some smaller, specialized agency.

Consumer Protection Agency
There may be such an agency in your local area. If not, check with the State Attorney General's office for the agency normally called the Division of Consumer Protection. With a written complaint, they will often attempt to settle the problem, and may prosecute for fraud.

Better Business Bureau or Chamber of Commerce
Check in the local phone book and then write or visit with your complaint. BBBs may have a special panel that will settle a complaint between a school and a consumer.

Media
Write the TV or radio station, magazine, newspaper or bus that carried the advertisement for the school. They may drop the school's ads.

Newspaper "Action Line"
Call or write the "Action Line" column of the local newspapers, especially if the school is located in the local area. The newspaper may attempt to settle your problem and then later print the results.

Government Representative
Write your U.S. Senator, Congressman, State Senator or Legislator. Write or call your City Councilman or Representative.

Government Agency
Send your written complaint to government agencies that provide support for some vocational schools. Write to the Director for: Accreditation and Institutional Eligibility Staff, U.S. Office of Education, Department of Health, Education, and Welfare, Washington, D.C. 20202; or Education and Rehabilitation Services, Veterans Administration, Washington, D.C. 20420.

Finally, if all else fails, you can sue the school.
You will probably need a lawyer. Find out what the fee will be. If you can't afford one, look for the Neighborhood Legal Services Office near you, or call the courthouse and ask where free legal services are available. You can sue the school in Small Claims Court without a lawyer, though it is sometimes a good idea to have one.

We suggest that the quickest and surest redress comes from:

1. the school
2. the proper accrediting agency (NATTS for the schools in this book; NATTS's address is in Appendix C)
3. the state licensing agency (addresses are in Appendix D).

The other sources listed in the FTC brochure might help, but their performance to date is slow and unsure. The school's director is your best complaint and suggestion box. He doesn't want to lose you.

Dr. Louis Bender wrote in *Community College Review,* Fall 1973:

> The proprietary sector has vigorously worked to correct [misleading and dishonest practices] and to improve the image of honest dedicated institutions. Legitimate proprietary school officials are far more concerned with the identification and elimination of unsavory practices than any other group. They have more to lose.

SURVIVING THE TRAINING

The school is Tampa Technical Institute and it is very early in the morning. TTI's vice-president, chief instructor, and director of quality control, Emilio Begué, is "on the platform." Begué has been with the school since the heady years following World War II, when many of these schools got their start under free and easy veterans' regulations. He is now one of the owners because one day the school, like a fat dirigible settling on a flag pole, collapsed around him. The owner gave it to Begué and then flew-by-night.

As we walk in, Begué is scolding his electronics class: "I want you to be concerned about being late. . . . It affects my mental attitude toward you. . . . The rules have been changed? . . . We have much material to cover and we can't afford latecomers." He casts a baleful look our way and then looks at the clock; we're the latest of the late. "OK, if I have a beta-independent circuit . . ." An hour later, Begué crisply lays down his chalk, hitches his pants, and announces, "Tomorrow's lecture will be on the emitter-follower configuration; read the next chapter."

We're sitting between a couple of students who are spending the break catching up with their notes. We've tried to turn on the desk-mounted oscilloscope in front of us but it's no-go; technicians we're not. We interrupt the fellow on our left.

"How do you survive all this?"

"Stick to it. Figure that it is part of a job."

"How do you do that?"

"Bein' the money I put into it, I better pay attention."

"Why do people drop out?"

"Either they are too young, or they have family problems."

"How about you?"

"My wife's parents think I should be out supporting my wife and family. Listen, I'm twenty-eight. I tried truck driving for four years. For two hundred dollars a week I was killing myself; I couldn't get anywhere. This is my last chance."

We turned to the chap on our right.

"How about you, sir—everyone in the school works part-time, and this course is obviously a rough one. How are you doing?"

"My family didn't think I would make it through. They didn't think I had it in me . . . screw 'em."

As we get up to leave the classroom, we see a sign over the door: "A Technician Is Made in the Lab."

We wander down the crowded hall, looking for the Architectural Drafting class. We have heard that between the recession and the energy crisis, construction is off in Florida and there are few, if any, jobs in the drafting field. We ask the teacher, an architect.

"With the economy as it is, are there jobs for these students?"

"No."

"Do they know that?"

"Sure, we don't lie. When they started, there were plenty of jobs. I understand this course may be closed down after this group."

We asked a student how he felt about all this.

"Well, it's not anybody's fault. I'll be able to use the training some way, and construction will pick up eventually. I'll survive; I like drafting."

If the job market in this field continues to dwindle, this electronics school will probably close down the course in Architectural Drafting. Other changes often take place that students do not understand; many of them are prompted by the exigencies of profit seeking. Schools have to survive the training too.

We walk into the office and President Benanti is haranguing a staff person: "I came in last night, I had *three* teachers in *three* rooms in front of *eleven* students; with the cash-flow like it is, I can't have that kind of waste next quarter! I want to know why we've got all these extra teachers."

Adrian Marcuse, president of the Laboratory Institute of Merchandising in New York City, told us about surviving his tough training:

> I got it down to what students really need. I spent eight years figuring it out. Nothing is wasted. If they can't take the pressure of our school, they can't take the clothing business. . . . Something that is too easy to get isn't worth a damn.

WHILE YOU'RE IN SCHOOL

Your aim in one of these schools is to acquire the skills you want and need, persist to graduation, and then apply the skills in the manner you see fit. Here are some "plants" for your thinking and some "pointers" for your success in school.

■ Concentrate on learning the skills well. This is what these schools are for. They cannot guarantee you a "rosy future"; they can give you job skills and work habits that can lead to success but they shouldn't promise that. There are too many variables outside their control. It is up to the student to use the opportunity for serious apprenticeship; it will be rewarded in some way at some time.

■ Proprietary school students are generally realistic about their future job success. The burden rests on the student. There is inequality and inequity in our society. In some of the occupations taught in these schools, college-trained people will be hired first and paid better to do the same work; in many fields, such as computer programming and electronics, better-trained students from private schools will be discriminated against in the job market. You are taking a "career shortcut"; you will have to chart your own course, perhaps, take risks, and, throughout your training, be planning your attack on the job market. You may even go into business for yourself.

■ Involve yourself in the life of the school. Become known to the administration and the teachers. Do not be "cool" and above it all. You are also paying money for the associations you are building in the school. A young woman discussed this with us.

> This school does an awful lot. As long as you show the interest and get involved, the school can help you. Sure, there are some people who didn't get the job they wanted. How can it be the school's fault, it's the person's fault, if they get the training and then didn't do anything with it. If someone around here really tries, they're going to make it. You got to get involved. Get into this, get into that . . . You go to the teachers and say, "I'm interested in this, I'd like to get into that!" You know, people call the school and they say "I need somebody." The school is going to send the person that has been trying, the one they *know*.

■ Don't skip classes.

■ There is a Morale Curve. Dropouts occur at two places in each course: the "theory stage" and when a major holiday, like Christmas, comes along. The first two weeks are the roughest. Two-thirds of the dropouts occur in one of these periods. Watch your morale during these times. Talk to someone if your grip on the training is beginning to slip.

■ Pay attention in class. You do that by putting yourself as close to the front as possible. We have noticed that the potential dropouts hang back in the second tier of students; they can't see or hear. They also can't be seen. Move up; ask questions.

■ If you find yourself able to move ahead at a faster rate than the majority of the class, talk to your instructor. If he or she agrees, other work may be assigned to you. Push yourself forward.

GETTING A JOB

No school will guarantee job placement anymore, but the odds are definitely with you. Many NATTS schools have a full-time staffer assigned to placement, with additional people assigned part-time. Schools involve instructors in job placement as well. The percentage of total staff time given to placement is considerable—as high as 25 percent just before graduation. In many schools, though, the placement process starts long before graduation rolls around.

It's natural for employers to deal with private schools. Both are businesses and operate in similar fashion, with similar concerns. For example, a bank teller school keeps in weekly touch with local banks; the school owner was once a branch manager. He provides selected and trained people, able to "take hold" the first day of work. His students have even been through a simulated bank holdup.

The job placement process follows three routes:

1. An employer phones the school looking for someone to start on the job. The placement person then matches the employer and type of job with the appropriate graduate or student nearing completion. The placement officer keeps track of what students are looking for what kind of job.

2. The placement officer calls up an employer and asks the employer if he would like to interview some graduates. Sometimes they go to the work site; sometimes the employer comes to the school. Every automotive school we've visited has had a placement officer able to give exact details of the personnel,

wages, and morale situation of every automobile dealer in that town.

3. Upwards of half of any graduating class find jobs on their own. Like the schools, these students are independent.

As we've mentioned, you can get a good idea of a particular school's placement record by checking out its bulletin boards for letters from recent graduates, and talking to students about friends who've attended the school. But you should also be aware of—and encouraged by—the overall picture of proprietary schools' performance in job placement.

In 1972 the Inner City Fund compared proprietary business schools with community colleges for the Department of Health, Education and Welfare. "All of the business schools we visited," said its study, "reported that they had many more calls for students from employers than they had students to place." This general overview is borne out by more statistical studies. Of five thousand former private vocational students who responded to a survey conducted by the University of Maryland in 1971, 81 percent reported that their first job was *directly* related to their training. The 1974 Wilms Study, done for the National Institute of Education at the University of California, Berkeley, reported that 81 percent of graduates from electronics courses received jobs in the electronics field, and 79 percent of the women graduating in dental assisting got related jobs within five weeks of graduation. Finally, a recent survey of a large number of NATTS-accredited schools indicated that out of one hundred typical graduates of NATTS schools:

sixty-four were placed in jobs directly related to the objectives of their course of study;

seven were placed in jobs substantially related to the objectives of their course of study;

thirteen were not available for employment;

eleven were untraceable;

five were traceable and were unsuccessful in obtaining positions.

I have spent the last two years examining the way people cope with routine and monotonous work. I expected to find resentment and I found it. I expected to find boredom and I found it. I expected to find sabotage and I found it in clever forms that I could never have imagined.

But the most dramatic thing I found was quite the opposite of noncooperation. *People passionately* want to work. . . . For most people it is hard and uncomfortable to do a bad job.

> —BARBARA GARSON, *All the Livelong Day: The Meaning and Demeaning of Routine Work,* 1975.

CONCLUSION

Enough of advice, caveats, and consumer protection. This is not a Sargasso Sea threatening young travelers, sucking the unwary down into broken dreams and ruin. And, despite the growing problems of the public schools, proprietary vocational schools do not constitute a guerrilla force about to overrun our nation's school systems.

This is an independent world of student- and skill-oriented schools that has been lost—right on Main Street—for a long time. We have tried to map its features, for we have traveled there. We have seen wondrous things. Princes and students, some cabbages and kings in these proprietary schools. And so we have sought to write a personal guide to this unfamiliar industry; we have attempted a close-up, behind-the-scenes look at these schools, hoping to convey something of their dimension and their life.

For a long time we agreed with the school owners that their schools were forts surrounded by bands of cutthroat reporters, thieving public school officials, and government types, all conniving together to cut off the little schools. There is some truth in that, but it is an on-again, off-again thing. More important, we now feel, are the internal factors that the schools themselves control.

We speak of a "school industry," but more appropriately it could be called a "mosquito fleet" of entrepreneur-educators. For years they have been ferrying kids from high school and the military over to the jobs, and deadheading it empty back to the schools without much acclaim, appreciation, or knowledge of how they fit into the Big Picture. It is clear to us that private, profit-seeking, consumer-financed occupational education should be a much larger force in American life. But certain conditions, existing chiefly in the minds of schoolpeople, have kept it on the periphery.

Schoolpeople suffer from a morale problem; they are often apologetic about being in the school business. The school industry must take a more positive view of itself, change its self-concept. On November 15, 1974 we attended a public relations seminar for NATTS schools. A public relations firm that has had numerous private school accounts made the initial presentation:

> . . . It's important for you all to recognize that the natural tendency for career school operators is to insulate yourselves from the community. Far too often, you are the only ones who actually understand the service you are providing. Naturally, you'd rather just provide that service than to have to continually explain it and even defend it.
>
> Today, however, it's more important than ever before that you take the initiative to explain to people what career education—and your school in particular—is all about. You have to communicate to people the facts that stack up overwhelmingly in your favor. The best way to avoid enemies is to make friends.

In a sense, recent newspaper articles critical of the schools have been helpful; they got the industry off its duff and out into the public arena, talking about itself. Unfortunately, NATTS hasn't had time to function as a real trade association. It has been busy since 1966 getting over 400 schools through a rigorous accreditation process. It has created a more positive image for the schools with state and federal lawmakers and the U.S. Office of Education. It has worked effectively to bring the schools to the big table and the better cuts. And it has actively defended the industry from unwarranted attacks like that mounted by the FTC. Now it is time for NATTS to *promote* trade and technical schools. For starters, NATTS should (1) establish an active, formal outreach to unaccredited schools, bringing them into the mainstream of proprietary vocational education, and, (2) it should publish a booklet, "How and Why to Start a Private Trade or Technical School."

The school industry must truly accept the fact that it is doing a fine job. Proprietary schoolpeople define themselves more by their employment orientation (skills they teach) than by their status as independent educators. This should change. Building on their record of substantial achievement, they should find new opportunities for schools and give us all some new alternatives for learning skills. Some possibilities:

■ Teaching "depression skills." In a tight economy, durable goods are repaired, not thrown away. More schools for training repair persons and do-it-yourselfers should be created.

■ Devising more new "para-courses" for the twenty-four- to forty-five-year-olds—courses for women, unemployed college graduates, men who want career changes.

■ Participating in government rehabilitation programs. Private schools now enroll only 17 percent of persons in these rehabilitation training programs. They should be doing more of this.

■ Teaching occupational skills in prisons. Private schools should contract with states to provide voluntary skill training for prisoners soon to be released. They can also provide job placement assistance.

■ Contracting with public high schools and community colleges to do their vocational training. This is being done now in certain areas with great success.

■ Contracting with the armed services to provide their technical training. The Navy has tried this method and found it (1) cheaper than running its own schools and (2) productive of more capable technicians.

■ Exploring the overseas market. Many developing countries would welcome American school entrepreneurs to start up trade and technical schools and then leave behind that tradition.

These are possibilities that exist within the established structure of education and training in America. Once our thinking cuts loose from the limitations that structure imposes, the potential contribution of small, independent, profit-making schools is enormous.

A DREAM

If we were to see signs: "Learn how to Read and Write, Better HERE, Fast & Cheap!" flashing in strobe and neon arrows, hooking down to narrow stairs that lead from the street up to low-rent classrooms and labs above the stores in every American downtown, our taxes would be lower and our young people a lot better off. We think that the large number of students who simply want to learn how to read "fast and cheap" would damn well make sure they got what they were paying for, which they are not now. If they did not have to learn history and English at the same time, they could learn to read within one or two months, Berlitz-fashion. The schools that met their promises would survive. The others would be put out of business by falling enrollments and lawsuits.

For a long time, the question has been "Where do you work?" rather than "What is your skill?" Young people always want competence, but now they are often unaware that skills can be formally taught and learned in a short time. Many hanker after a simpler America and would jam the Oregon Trail to pioneer the land, but they lack the essential itinerant skills to build a new life or to rebuild the United States. They know they want to do something but are vague about how to do it.

If you want to learn a skill surely and competently, if you want to be relatively independent, or if you want some economic safety in these unsure times, try these small specialized trade and technical schools. They work.

Skilled people are confident and apt to be working.

APPENDIX A: NATTS DIRECTORY OF ACCREDITED PRIVATE TRADE AND TECHNICAL SCHOOLS

The schools in this directory have been accredited by the Accrediting Commission of the National Association of Trade and Technical Schools (NATTS). The Accrediting Commission is listed by the U.S. Office of Education as a nationally recognized accrediting agency under the provisions of Chapter 33, Title 38, U.S. Code, and subsequent legislation.

This directory is current up until January 1977. Each year there are some additions to and subtractions from the list. In future years, should you want to obtain the latest directory, write:

NATTS
Department GS
2021 L Street, N.W.
Washington, D.C. 20036

USING THE NATTS DIRECTORY

Schools accredited by the NATTS Accrediting Commission are listed in this directory by types of training and by geographic location.

LISTING BY TRAINING OFFERED

Subjects taught by these schools are listed below. Under each subject heading are listed the schools that offer courses in that general area.

Acting
Calif.:	Merrick Studios Academy of Dramatic Arts, Hollywood
Mass.:	Leland Powers School, Boston

Advertising Art
Calif.:	Academy of Art College, San Francisco
Conn.:	Paier School of Art, Hamden
Fla.:	Art Institute of Fort Lauderdale, Fort Lauderdale
Ill.:	American Academy of Art, Chicago
Md.:	Professional Institute of Commercial Art, Baltimore
Mass.:	The Art Institute of Boston, Boston
Mich.:	Kendall School of Design, Grand Rapids
Ohio:	Cooper School of Art, Cleveland
Ohio:	Ohio Visual Art Institute, Cincinnati
Pa.:	Hussian School of Art, Philadelphia
Pa.:	Ivy School of Professional Art, Pittsburgh

Air Conditioning
Ariz.:	The Refrigeration School, Phoenix
Ariz.:	Universal Technical Institute, Phoenix
Calif.:	American Business College—Technical Division, San Diego
Calif.:	California Trade Technical School, Long Beach
Calif.:	Fresno Technical College, Fresno
Calif.:	National Technical Schools, Los Angeles
Calif.:	Practical Schools, Anaheim
Calif.:	South Bay Trade School, San Diego
Colo.:	Denver Institute of Technology, Englewood
Conn.:	Technical Careers Institute, Milford

D.C.:	Lincoln Technical Institute, Washington
Fla.:	International Technical Institute, Tampa
Ill.:	Coyne American Institute, Chicago
Ill.:	Greer Technical Institute, Norridge
Ind.:	ITT Technical Institute, Indianapolis
Ind.:	Lincoln Technical Institute, Indianapolis
Kans.:	Climate Control Institute, Wichita
Mass.:	Associated Technical Institute, Somerville
Mass.:	New England Appliance Service School, Bost
Mich.:	Detroit Engineering Institute, Detroit
Minn.:	Dunwoody Industrial Institute, Minneapolis
Mo.:	Basic Institute of Technology, St. Louis
Mo.:	Ranken Technical Institute, St. Louis
Neb.:	Universal Technical Institute, Omaha
Nev.:	Education Dynamics Institute, Las Vegas
N.J.:	Lincoln Technical Institute, Pennsauken
N.J.:	Lincoln Technical Institute, Union
N.J.:	Lyons Institute, Cherry Hill
N.Y.:	Apex Technical School, New York
N.Y.:	Berk Trade School, Brooklyn
N.Y.:	Technical Career Institutes, New York
Ohio:	A.T.E.S. Technical School, Niles
Ohio:	ITT Technical Institute, Toledo
Ohio:	R.E.T.S. Tech Center, Dayton
Ohio:	Sooner Mechanical Trade School, Oklahoma
Ohio:	West Side Institute of Technology, Cleveland
Pa.:	Technician Training School, McKees Rocks
Pa.:	Triangle Institute of Technology, Pittsburgh
R.I.:	New England Technical Institute, Providence
Texas:	American Trades Institute, Dallas
Wash.:	J. M. Perry Institute, Yakima

Aircraft Instrument Technician (See Instrumentation)

Aircraft Mechanics (See Aviation Maintenance
    Technician)

Airline Personnel Training

Calif.:	Airline Schools Pacific, Hollywood
Calif.:	Airline Schools Pacific, Santa Barbara
Calif.:	Airline Schools Pacific, San Bernardino
Calif.:	American Business College—Technical Division, San Diego
Calif.:	International Career Academy, Van Nuys
Calif.:	Pacific Travel School, Santa Ana
Calif.:	Transportation Training Corporation, Long Beach
Colo.:	Parks School of Business-Technical Division, Denver
D.C.:	Lewis Hotel-Motel School, Washington
Minn.:	Humboldt Institute, Minneapolis
Pa.:	Wilma Boyd Career School, Pittsburgh

Airplane Pilot (See Pilot)

Appliance Repair

Calif.:	American Business College—Technical Division, San Diego
Calif.:	Practical Schools, Anaheim
Conn.:	Technical Careers Institute, Milford
Mass.:	New England Appliance Service School, Boston
N.Y.:	Apex Technical School, New York
Pa.:	Technician Training School, McKees Rocks
R.I.:	New England Technical Institute, Providence
Wash.:	J. M. Perry Institute, Yakima

Architectural Engineering Technology

Conn.:	Chester Institute for Technical Education, Stratford
Conn.:	Porter School of Drafting and Design, Rocky Hill
Ind.:	ITT Technical Institute, Fort Wayne
Ind.:	ITT Technical Institute, Indianapolis
Md.:	Arundel Institute of Technology, Baltimore
Mo.:	Bailey Technical School, St. Louis
Ohio:	ITT Technical Institute, Dayton
Pa.:	Pennsylvania Institute of Technology, Upper Darby

Art

Calif.:	Academy of Art College, San Francisco
Fla.:	Art Institute of Fort Lauderdale, Fort Lauderdale
Conn.:	Paier School of Art, Hamden
Ga.:	Art Institute of Atlanta, Atlanta
Ill.:	American Academy of Art, Chicago
Ill.:	Ray-Vogue School, Chicago
Md.:	Professional Institute of Commercial Art, Baltimore
Mass.:	The Art Institute of Boston, Boston
Mass.:	New England School of Art and Design, Boston
Mass.:	Vesper George School of Art, Boston
Ohio:	Cooper School of Art, Cleveland
Ohio:	Ohio Visual Art Institute, Cincinnati
Pa.:	Art Institute of Philadelphia, Philadelphia
Pa.:	Art Institute of Pittsburgh, Pittsburgh
Pa.:	Ivy School of Professional Art, Pittsburgh
Pa.:	Hussian School of Art, Philadelphia
Pa.:	York Academy of Arts, York

Automotive Mechanics (See also Diesel Mechanics)

Ariz.:	Arizona Automotive Institute, Glendale
Ariz.:	Phoenix Institute of Technology, Phoenix
Ariz.:	Universal Technical Institute, Phoenix
Calif.:	American Business College—Technical Division, San Diego
Calif.:	California Trade Technical School, Long Beach
Calif.:	Fresno Technical College, Fresno

Calif.:	National Technical Schools, Los Angeles
Calif.:	Sequoia Automotive Institute, Mountain View
Calif.:	South Bay Trade School, San Diego
Colo.:	Denver Automotive and Diesel College, Denver
Colo.:	Denver Institute of Technology, Englewood
Conn.:	Technical Careers Institute, Milford
D.C.:	Lincoln Technical Institute, Washington
Fla.:	International Technical Institute, Tampa
Ill.:	Allied Institute of Technology, Chicago
Ill.:	Greer Technical Institute, Norridge
Ind.:	Lincoln Technical Institute, Indianapolis
Iowa:	Lincoln Technical Institute, West Des Moines
Kans.:	Wichita Automotive Institute, Wichita
Md.:	Lincoln Technical Institute, Baltimore
Mass.:	ITT Technical Institute, Chelsea
Mass.:	Northeast Institute of Industrial Technology, Boston
Mass.:	United Technical School, Springfield
Mich.:	Michigan Career Institute, Detroit
Mich.:	MoTech Automotive Education Center, Livonia
Minn.:	Dunwoody Industrial Institute, Minneapolis
Mo.:	Bailey Technical School, St. Louis
Mo.	Ranken Technical Institute, St. Louis
Mont.:	Montana Auto College, Great Falls
Neb.:	Universal Technical Institute, Omaha
N.J.:	Lincoln Technical Institute, Union
Ohio:	Northwestern Business College-Technical Center, Lima
Okla.:	Southwest Automotive School, Oklahoma City
Pa.:	Automotive Training Center, Exton
Pa.:	Lincoln Technical Institute, Philadelphia
Pa.:	New Castle School of Trades, Pulaski
Pa.:	Pennco Tech, Bristol
Pa.:	Rosedale Technical Institute, Pittsburgh
Pa.:	Technician Training School, McKees Rocks
Pa.:	Vale Technical Institute, Blairsville
R.I.:	Rhode Island Trades Shops School, Providence
Tenn.:	Bailey Technical School, Memphis
Tenn.:	Nashville Auto Diesel College, Nashville
Texas:	American Trades Institute, Dallas
Texas:	Lincoln Technical Institute, Dallas
Va.:	Fogg's Technical Institute, Hanover
Wash.:	J. M. Perry Institute, Yakima
Wyo.:	Wyoming Technical Institute, Laramie

Aviation Maintenance Technician

Colo.:	Colorado Aero Tech, Broomfield
Idaho:	Aero Technicians, Rexburg
Mass.:	East Coast Aero Technical School, Lexington
Mich.:	Detroit Institute of Aeronautics, Ypsilanti
Mo.:	Aero Mechanic School, Kansas City
Mo.:	Mid Continent Aviation School of Aeronautics, Kansas City
N.C.:	Piedmont Aerospace Institute, Winston-Salem
Okla.:	Spartan School of Aeronautics, Tulsa
Pa.:	Pittsburgh Institute of Aeronautics, Pittsburgh
Texas:	Aero Technical Institute, Wichita Falls
Texas:	Hallmark Aero-Tech, San Antonio

Aviation Mechanics

N.J.:	Teterboro School of Aeronautics, Teterboro
N.Y.:	Riverside School of Aeronautics, Utica

Baking

Minn.:	Dunwoody Industrial Institute, Minneapolis

Ballet (See Dance Instructor)

Barbering

Calif.:	Rosston School of Men's Hair Design, Long Beach
Ind.:	Indiana Barber College, Indianapolis
Iowa:	Iowa School of Men's Hairstyling, Des Moines

Mich.:	Flint Institute of Barbering, Flint
Pa.:	Erie Barber School, Erie
Pa.:	Pittsburgh Barber School, Pittsburgh
Texas:	West Texas Barber College, Amarillo
W.Va.:	Huntington Barber College, Huntington

Blueprint Reading

Calif.:	Modern Welding Trade School, Anaheim
Calif.:	Modern Welding Trade School, Downey
Calif.:	South Bay Trade School, San Diego
Conn.:	Chester Institute for Technical Education, Stratford
Conn.:	Porter School of Drafting and Design, Rocky Hill
Ga.:	Academy of Professional Drafting, Atlanta
N.J.:	General Technical Institute, Linden
N.Y.:	Island Drafting & Technical Institute, Amityville
Mich.:	Allied Careers Institute, Hazel Park
Ohio:	Airco Technical Institute, Cleveland
Ohio:	Akron Testing Laboratory & Welding School, Barberton
Ohio:	Hobart School of Welding Technology, Troy
Ohio:	Technichron School of Welding, Cincinnati
Pa.:	American Institute of Drafting, Philadelphia
Pa.:	Breeden School of Welding, Whitehall
Pa.:	Triangle Institute of Technology, Pittsburgh

Body and Fender Repair (See Automotive Mechanics)

Brickmasonry

Pa.:	Technician Training School, McKees Rocks
Pa.:	The Williamson Free School of Mechanical Trades, Media

Broadcasting

Ariz.:	Ron Bailie School of Broadcast, Phoenix
Calif.:	Ron Bailie School of Broadcast, San Francisco
Colo.:	Ron Bailie School of Broadcast, Denver
Fla.:	Brown Institute, Fort Lauderdale
Iowa:	Academy of Radio and Television Electronics, Bettendorf
Mass.:	Leland Powers School, Boston
Mass.:	Northeast Broadcasting School, Boston
Minn.:	Brown Institute, Minneapolis
Minn.:	Elkins Institute, Minneapolis
N.Y.:	Advanced Training Center, Tonawanda
Ohio:	International Broadcasting School, Dayton
Ohio:	Ohio School of Broadcast Technique, Cleveland
Tenn.:	Tennessee Institute of Broadcasting, Nashville
Utah:	Ron Bailie Western School of Broadcast, Salt Lake City
Wash.:	Ron Bailie School of Broadcast, Seattle
Wash.:	Ron Bailie School of Broadcast, Spokane
Wis.:	Trans American School of Broadcasting, Wausau

Building Maintenance

Calif.:	Practical Schools, Anaheim
Mo.:	Urban Technical Center, St. Louis
N.Y.:	Apex Technical School, New York
Ohio:	West Side Institute of Technology, Cleveland
Pa.:	New Castle School of Trades, Pulaski

Business Machine Repair (See Office Machine Repair)

Camera Service and Repair

Colo.:	National Camera Technical Training Division, Englewood
N.Y.:	Germain School of Photography, New York

Camp Instructor

W.Va.:	Meredith Manor School of Horsemanship, Waverly

Carpentry

Mo.:	Ranken Technical Institute, St. Louis
Pa.:	Northeastern Training Institute, Fleetville
Pa.:	Technician Training School, McKees Rocks
Pa.:	The Williamson Free School of Mechanical Trades, Media

Catering (See Culinary Arts)

Chef (See Culinary Arts)

Choreography (See Dance Instructor)

Coin Operated Machine Repair

N.Y.:	Careerco School for Paraprofessionals, Syracuse
Nev.:	Nevada Gaming School, Las Vegas

Commercial Art (See Art and Advertising Art)

Communications (See Electronics)

Computer Programming (See Data Processing)

Computer Technology (See Electronics)

Construction Equipment Mechanics (See Diesel Mechanics)

Construction Technology

Pa.:	Greensburg Institute of Technology, Greensburg
Pa.:	Pennsylvania Institute of Technology, Upper Darby
Pa.:	The Williamson Free School of Mechanical Trades, Media

Cooking (See Culinary Arts)

Culinary Arts

N.Y.:	Culinary Institute of America, Hyde Park
N.Y.:	New York Institute of Dietetics, New York
Wash.:	J. M. Perry Institute, Yakima

Custodian (See Building Maintenance)

Dance Instructor

Conn.:	School of the Hartford Ballet, Hartford

Data Processing

Ala.:	Herzing Institute, Birmingham
Calif.:	American Business College—Technical Division, San Diego
Calif.:	Computer Learning Center of Los Angeles, Los Angeles
Calif.:	Control Data Institute, Anaheim
Calif.:	Control Data Institute, Los Angeles
Calif.:	Control Data Institute, San Francisco
Colo.:	Automation & Training Universal, Denver
Fla.:	Garces Commercial College, Miami
Ga.:	Control Data Institute, Atlanta
Ill.:	Control Data Institute, Chicago
Ind.:	ITT Technical Institute, Evansville
Kans.:	Bryan Institute, Wichita
Kans.:	Electronic Computer Programming Institute, Topeka
Kans.:	Electronic Computer Programming Institute, Wichita
La.:	CBM Education Center, Baton Rouge
Mass.:	Control Data Institute, Burlington
Mich.:	Control Data Institute, Southfield
Mich.:	Institute of Computer Technology, Oak Park
Minn.:	Brown Institute, Minneapolis
Minn.:	Control Data Institute, Minneapolis
Mo.:	Control Data Institute, St. Louis
Mo.:	Electronic Computer Programming Institute, Kansas City

Neb.:	Electronic Computer Programming Institute, Omaha
N.J.:	Brick Computer Science Institute, Bricktown
N.J.:	Chubb Institute for Computer Technology, Short Hills
N.J.:	Electronic Computer Programming Institute, Jersey City
N.J.:	Electronic Computer Programming Institute, Paterson
N.J.:	Empire Technical School, East Orange
N.Y.:	Advanced Training Center, Tonawanda
N.Y.:	Albert Merrill School, New York
N.Y.:	Control Data Institute, New York
N.Y.:	Empire Technical School, New York
N.Y.:	New York School of Computer Technology, New York
N.Y.:	PSI Institute, New York
N.Y.:	Syracuse School of Automation, Syracuse
Ohio:	Control Data Institute, Lakewood
Ohio:	Electronic Technology Institute, Cleveland
Ohio:	Para Professional Institute, Columbus
Ore.:	Oregon Career Institute, Portland
Pa.:	Career Educational Institute—Technical Division, Philadelphia
Pa.:	Maxwell Institute, Norristown
Pa.:	Pennco Tech, Bristol
Texas:	CBM Education Center, San Antonio
Texas:	Control Data Institute, Dallas
Texas:	Texas Institute, Dallas
Va.:	Control Data Institute, Arlington
Va.:	Computer Learning Center, Fairfax
Va.:	Electronic Computer Programming Institute, Norfolk

Dental Assisting

Ariz.:	Arizona College of Medical and Dental Careers, Tuscon
Ariz.:	Blair College of Medical and Dental Assistants, Mesa
Ariz.:	The Bryman School, Phoenix
Calif.:	Andon College—Vocational Health Careers, San Jose
Calif.:	Associated Technical College, Los Angeles
Calif.:	Bay City College Dental-Medical Assistants, San Francisco
Calif.:	The Bryman School, Anaheim
Calif.:	The Bryman School, Canoga Park
Calif.:	The Bryman School, Long Beach
Calif.:	The Bryman School, Los Angeles
Calif.:	The Bryman School, West Los Angeles
Calif.:	The Bryman School, Rosemead
Calif.:	The Bryman School, San Francisco
Calif.:	The Bryman School, San Jose
Calif.:	The Bryman School, Torrance
Calif.:	Galen College of Medical and Dental Assistants, Fresno
Calif.:	Lawton School, Santa Ana
Calif.:	Lawton School for Medical and Dental Assistants, Palo Alto
Calif.:	Long Beach College of Medical & Dental Assistants, Long Beach (Bixby Knolls)
Calif.:	North-West College of Medical and Dental Assistants, Pomona
Calif.:	North-West College of Medical and Dental Assistants, West Covina
Calif.:	Oakland College Dental and Medical Assistants, Oakland
Calif.:	Pacific College of Medical & Dental Assistants, San Diego
Calif.:	San Diego College for Medical and Dental Assistants, San Diego
Calif.:	San Jose Institute of Paramedical Careers, San Jose
Calif.:	Southern California College of Medical and Dental Careers, Anaheim

Calif.:	Southland College of Medical-Dental-Legal Careers, Downey
Calif.:	Southland College of Medical and Dental Careers, Gardena
Calif.:	Southland College of Medical, Dental and Legal Careers, Los Angeles
Calif.:	Southland College of Medical-Dental-Legal Careers, Montebello
Calif.:	United Health Careers Institute, San Bernardino
Calif.:	Valley College of Medical-Dental Assistants, North Hollywood
Calif.:	Western College of Allied Health Careers, Sacramento
Calif.:	Western College of Medical and Dental Assistants, Van Nuys
Colo.:	Colorado College of Medical and Dental Assistants, Denver
Fla.:	Charron Williams College-Paramedical Division, Miami
Ga.:	Atlanta College of Medical and Dental Assistants, Atlanta
Ga.:	The Bryman School, Atlanta
Ill.:	The Bryman School, Chicago
Ill.:	Robert Morris School, Carthage
Ind.:	Professional Careers Institute, Indianapolis
Kans.:	Bryman Institute, Wichita
Md.:	The Medix School, Baltimore
Mass.:	The Bryman School, Brookline
Minn.:	Lakeland Medical-Dental Academy, Minneapolis
Minn.:	Minnesota Institute of Medical and Dental Assistants, Minneapolis
Mo.:	Bryan Institute, St. Louis
Mo.:	Kansas City College of Medical and Dental Assistants, Kansas City
Mo.:	Missouri School for Doctors' Assistants & Technicians, St. Louis
Neb.:	Omaha College of Health Careers, Omaha
N.J.:	The Bryman School, East Brunswick
N.J.:	Lyons Institute, Cherry Hill
N.J.:	Lyons Institute, Clark
N.J.:	Lyons Institute, Hackensack
N.J.:	Lyons Institute, Newark
N.Y.:	Advanced Career Training, New York
N.Y.:	Allen School for Physicians' Aides, Jamaica
N.Y.:	Careerco School for Paraprofessionals, Syracuse
N.Y.:	Mandl School for Medical and Dental Assistants, Hempstead
N.Y.:	Mandl School for Medical and Dental Assistants, New York
N.Y.:	New York School for Medical and Dental Assistants, Forest Hills
Ohio:	Toledo Medical Educational Center, Toledo
Okla.:	Bryan Institute, Tulsa
Ore.:	North Pacific Dental College, Training Auxiliary Personnel, Portland
Ore.:	Portland Paramedical Center, Portland
Pa.:	Franklin School of Sciences & Arts, Philadelphia
Pa.:	Median School of Allied Health Careers, Pittsburgh
Pa.:	National School of Health Technology, Philadelphia
Texas:	The Bryman School, Houston
Texas:	San Antonio College of Medical and Dental Assistants, San Antonio
Texas:	Texas College of Medical & Dental Assistants, Dallas
Utah:	The Bryman School, Salt Lake City
Utah:	Salt Lake City College of Medical and Dental Assistants, Salt Lake City

Dental Laboratory Technician

Ariz.:	Blair College of Medical and Dental Assistants, Mesa

Calif.:	Bay City College Dental-Medical Assistants, San Francisco
Calif.:	California College of Dental Training, Los Angeles
Calif.:	Casa Loma Institute of Technology, Pacoima
Calif.:	Dental Technology Institute, Orange
Calif.:	Oakland College Dental and Medical Assistants, Oakland
Calif.:	San Jose Institute of Paramedical Careers, San Jose
Calif.:	Southern California College of Medical and Dental Careers, Anaheim
Calif.:	Southland College of Medical and Dental Careers, Gardena
Calif.:	Southland College of Medical, Dental and Legal Careers, Los Angeles
Calif.:	Southland College of Medical-Dental-Legal Careers, Montebello
Ga.:	Atlanta College of Medical and Dental Assistants, Atlanta
Minn.:	Humboldt Institute, Minneapolis
Mo.:	Missouri School for Doctors' Assistants & Technicians, St. Louis
N.J.:	Lyons Institute, Cherry Hill
N.J.:	Lyons Institute, Clark
N.J.:	Lyons Institute, Hackensack
N.J.:	Lyons Institute, Newark
N.Y.:	Careerco School for Paraprofessionals, Syracuse
N.Y.:	Kerpel School of Dental Technology, New York
Ohio:	Toledo Medical Educational Center, Toledo
Ore.:	North Pacific Dental College, Training Auxiliary Personnel, Portland
Pa.:	Median School of Allied Health Careers, Pittsburgh
Pa.:	National School of Health Technology, Philadelphia

Diamond Cutting (See Jewelry Design)

Diamond Grading and Appraising
Calif.:	Gemological Institute of America, Santa Monica

Die Design (See Tool and Die)

Diesel Mechanics
Calif.:	National Technical Schools, Los Angeles
Colo.:	Denver Automotive and Diesel College, Denver
Fla.:	International Technical Institute, Tampa
Ill.:	Greer Technical Institute, Norridge
Ind.:	Lincoln Technical Institute, Indianapolis
Iowa:	Lincoln Technical Institute, West Des Moines
Mich.:	Michigan Career Institute, Detroit
Mo.:	Bailey Technical School, St. Louis
Mo.:	Ranken Technical Institute, St. Louis
Ohio:	Northwestern Business College-Technical Center, Lima
Ohio:	Ohio Diesel Technical Institute, Cleveland
N.C.:	National School of Heavy Equipment, Charlotte
N.J.:	Lincoln Technical Institute, Union
Pa.:	Automotive Training Center, Exton
Pa.:	Gateway Technical Institute, Pittsburgh
Pa.:	Lincoln Technical Institute, Philadelphia
Pa.:	Northeastern Training Institute, Fleetville
Pa.:	Pennco Tech, Bristol
Pa.:	Rosedale Technical Institute, Pittsburgh
Tenn.:	Bailey Technical School, Memphis
Tenn.:	Nashville Auto Diesel College, Nashville
Texas:	Lincoln Technical Institute, Dallas
Wyo.:	Wyoming Technical Institute, Laramie

Dietetics
Pa.:	National School of Health Technology, Philadelphia
N.Y.:	New York Institute of Dietetics, New York

Diving
Wash.:	Divers Institute of Technology, Seattle

Doctor's Assistant (See Medical Assisting)

Dog Grooming
N.Y.:	International School of Dog Grooming, New York
N.Y.:	The New York School of Dog Grooming, New York

Drafting
Ariz.:	Academy of Drafting, Tempe
Ariz.:	Arizona Automotive Institute, Glendale
Ariz.:	Phoenix Institute of Technology, Phoenix
Calif.:	Bay-Valley Technical Institute, Santa Clara
Calif.:	California Trade Technical School, Long Beach
Calif.:	Fresno Technical College, Fresno
Calif.:	National Career Institute, San Francisco
Calif.:	National Technical Schools, Los Angeles
Calif.:	South Bay Trade School, San Diego
Colo.:	Automation & Training Universal, Denver
Colo.:	Denver Institute of Technology, Englewood
Conn.:	Chester Institute for Technical Education, Stratford
Conn.:	Paier School of Art, Hamden
Conn.:	Porter School of Drafting and Design, Rocky Hill
D.C.:	Lacaze Academy–Technical Division, Washington
Fla.:	Garces Commercial College, Miami
Fla.:	Tampa Technical Institute, Tampa
Ga.:	Academy of Professional Drafting, Atlanta
Ill.:	Coyne American Institute, Chicago
Ill.:	Electronics Technical Institute, Chicago
Ind.:	ITT Technical Institute, Fort Wayne
Ind.:	ITT Technical Institute, Indianapolis
Ind.:	Midwestern College of Industrial Arts & Science, Fort Wayne
Ky.:	Louisville Technical Institute, Louisville
Md.:	Arundel Institute of Technology, Baltimore
Md.:	Maryland Drafting Institute, Langley Park
Mass.:	The Art Institute of Boston, Boston
Mass.:	ITT Technical Institute, Chelsea
Mass.:	Northeast Institute of Industrial Technology, Boston
Mich.:	Allied Careers Institute, Hazel Park
Mich.:	Detroit Engineering Institute, Detroit
Minn.:	Dunwoody Industrial Institute, Minneapolis
Minn.:	Minneapolis Drafting School, Minneapolis
Minn.:	Northwest Technical Institute, Minneapolis
Mo.:	Bailey Technical School, St. Louis
Mo.:	Basic Institute of Technology, St. Louis
Mo.:	Ranken Technical Institute, St. Louis
N.J.:	Lincoln Technical Institute, Pennsauken
N.J.:	Lyons Institute, Newark
N.J.:	The Plaza Technical Institute, Paramus
N.M.:	AAA College-Technical Division, Albuquerque
N.M.:	Coronado Technical Institute, Albuquerque
N.Y.	Island Drafting & Technical Institute, Amityville
Ohio:	A.T.E.S. Technical School, Niles
Ohio:	ITT Technical Institute, Dayton
Ohio:	ITT Technical Institute, Toledo
Ohio:	Youngstown College of Business and Professional Drafting, Youngstown
Pa.:	American Institute of Drafting, Philadelphia
Pa.:	Dean Institute of Technology, Pittsburgh
Pa.:	Electronic Institute, Harrisburg
Pa.:	Electronic Institute, Pittsburgh

Pa.:	Gateway Technical Institute, Pittsburgh
Pa.:	Greensburg Institute of Technology, Greensburg
Pa.:	Lincoln Technical Institute, Allentown
Pa.:	Lyons Technical Institute, Philadelphia
Pa.:	Pennsylvania Institute of Technology, Upper Darby
Pa.:	Pittsburgh Technical Institute, Pittsburgh
Pa.:	Triangle Institute of Technology, Pittsburgh
Pa.:	Washington Institute of Technology, Washington
R.I.:	New England Technical Institute, Providence
Texas:	Durham's Business College—Technical Division, Austin
Wis.:	Acme Institute of Technology, Manitowoc
Wis.:	Acme Institute of Technology, Milwaukee

Dramatic Arts (See Acting)

Dress Making and Design

Calif.:	Louise Salinger Academy of Fashion, San Francisco
Ill.:	Ray-Vogue School, Chicago
N.Y.:	French Fashion Academy, New York
N.Y.:	Mayer School of Fashion Design, New York
N.Y.:	Traphagen School of Fashion, New York
Ohio:	Virginia Marti School of Fashion Design, Cleveland
Pa.:	The Clarissa School of Fashion Design, Pittsburgh
Pa.:	Fashion Academy of Pittsburgh, Pittsburgh
Pa.:	Tracey-Warner School, Philadelphia

Ecology (See Water)

Electricity

Ill.:	Coyne American Institute, Chicago
Mass.:	Coyne Electrical and Technical School, Boston
Mass.:	Northeast Institute of Industrial Technology, Boston
Minn.:	Dunwoody Industrial Institute, Minneapolis
Mo.:	Electronic Institute, Kansas City
Mo.:	Ranken Technical School, St. Louis
N.J.:	Lyons Institute, Clark
N.J.:	Lyons Institute, Hackensack
N.J.:	Lyons Institute, Newark
Okla.:	Sooner Mechanical Trade School, Oklahoma City
Pa.:	Dean Institute of Technology, Pittsburgh
Pa.:	Greensburg Institute of Technology, Greensburg
Pa.:	Lyons Technical Institute, Philadelphia
Pa.:	The Williamson Free School of Mechanical Trades, Media
R.I.:	New England Technical Institute, Providence
Texas:	American Trades Institute, Dallas
Wash.:	J. M. Perry Institute, Yakima

Electronics

Ala.:	United Electronics Institute, Birmingham
Ariz.:	Ron Bailie School of Broadcast, Phoenix
Ariz.:	DeVry Institute of Technology, Phoenix
Ariz.:	Phoenix Institute of Technology, Phoenix
Ark.:	United Electronics Institute, Little Rock
Calif.:	Ron Bailie School of Broadcast, San Francisco
Calif.:	California Trade Technical School, Long Beach
Calif.:	Condie College of Business and Technology, San Jose
Calif.:	Control Data Institute, Anaheim
Calif.:	Control Data Institute, Los Angeles
Calif.:	Control Data Institute, San Francisco
Calif.:	Electronic Technical Institute, San Deigo
Calif.:	Fresno Technical College, Fresno
Calif.:	National Career Institute, San Francisco
Calif.:	National Technical Schools, Los Angeles
Calif.:	Practical Schools, Anaheim
Colo.:	Ron Bailie School of Broadcast, Denver

Colo.:	Denver Institute of Technology, Englewood
Colo.:	Electronic Technical Institute, Denver
Colo.:	Connecticut School of Electronics, New Haven
D.C.:	Lacaze Academy—Technical Division, Washington
Fla.:	Brown Institute, Fort Lauderdale
Fla.:	Tampa Technical Institute, Tampa
Fla.:	United Electronics Institute, Tampa
Ga.:	Control Data Institute, Atlanta
Ga.:	DeVry Institute of Technology, Atlanta
Ill.:	Control Data Institute, Chicago
Ill.:	Coyne American Institute, Chicago
Ill.:	DeVry Institute of Technology, Chicago
Ill.:	Electronics Technical Institute, Chicago
Ind.:	ITT Technical Institute, Evansville
Ind.:	ITT Technical Institute, Fort Wayne
Ind.:	ITT Technical Institute, Indianapolis
Iowa:	Academy of Radio and Television Electronics, Bettendorf
Iowa:	United Electronics Institute, West Des Moines
Kans.:	Wichita Technical Institute, Wichita
Ken.:	Institute of Electronic Technology, Paducah
Ken.:	United Electronics Institute, Louisville
La.:	R.E.T.S. Training Center, New Orleans
Md.:	Arundel Institute of Technology, Baltimore
Md.:	R.E.T.S. Electronic School, Baltimore
Md.:	TESST Electronic School, Hyattsville
Mass.:	Control Data Institute, Burlington
Mass.:	Coyne Electrical and Technical School, Boston
Mass.:	Massachusetts Radio and Electronics School, Boston
Mass.:	Northeast Institute of Industrial Technology, Boston
Mass.:	R.E.T.S. Electronic School, Boston
Mass.:	Sylvania Technical School, Waltham
Mich.:	Control Data Institute, Southfield
Mich.:	R.E.T.S. Electronic School, Detroit
Mich.:	R.E.T.S. Electronic School, Wyoming
Mich.:	United Electronics Institute, Grand Rapids
Minn.:	Brown Institute, Minneapolis
Minn.:	Control Data Institute, Minneapolis
Minn.:	Dunwoody Industrial Institute, Minneapolis
Minn.:	Elkins Institute, Minneapolis
Minn.:	Northwestern Electronics Institute, Minneapolis
Miss.:	Phillips College—Technical Training Division, Jackson
Miss.:	Phillips College—Technical Division, Gulfport
Mo.:	Basic Institute of Technology, St. Louis
Mo.:	Control Data Institute, St. Louis
Mo.:	Electronic Institute, Kansas City
Mo.:	Missouri Institute of Technology, Kansas City
Mo.:	Ranken Technical Institute, St. Louis
Neb.:	Gateway Electronics Institute, Omaha
Neb.:	Radio Engineering Institute, Omaha
N.J.:	DeVry Technical Institute, Woodbridge
N.J.:	Lincoln Technical Institute, Pennsauken
N.J.:	Lyons Institute, Cherry Hill
N.J.:	The Plaza Technical Institute, Paramus
N.J.:	Teterboro School of Aeronautics, Teterboro
N.M.:	North American Technical Institute, Albuquerque
N.Y.:	Advanced Training Center, Tonawanda
N.Y.:	Apex Technical School, New York
N.Y.:	Control Data Institute, New York
N.Y.:	Island Drafting & Technical Institute, Amityville
N.Y.:	PSI Institute, New York
N.Y.:	Suburban Technical School, Hempstead
N.Y.:	Syracuse School of Automation, Syracuse
N.Y.:	Technical Career Institutes, New York
Ohio:	A.T.E.S. Technical School, Niles
Ohio:	Control Data Institute, Lakewood
Ohio:	Electronic Technology Institute, Canton
Ohio:	Electronic Technology Institute, Cleveland
Ohio:	ITT Technical Institute, Dayton

Ohio:	ITT Technical Institute, Toledo
Ohio:	Ohio Institute of Technology, Columbus
Ohio:	Ohio School of Broadcast Technique, Cleveland
Ohio:	R.E.T.S. Tech Center, Dayton
Ohio:	United Electronics Institute, Cuyahoga Falls
Okla.:	Spartan School of Aeronautics, Tulsa
Okla.:	United Electronics Institute, Oklahoma City
Ore.:	United Electronics Institute, Portland
Pa.:	Berean Institute—Technical Division, Philadelphia
Pa.:	Career Educational Institute—Technical Division, Philadelphia
Pa.:	Electronic Institute, Harrisburg
Pa.:	Electronic Institute, Pittsburgh
Pa.:	Gateway Technical Institute, Pittsburgh
Pa.:	Greensburg Institute of Technology, Greensburg
Pa.:	Lincoln Technical Institute, Allentown
Pa.:	Lyons Technical Institute, Philadelphia
Pa.:	Lyons Technical Institute, Upper Darby
Pa.:	New Castle School of Trades, Pulaski
Pa.:	Penn Technical Institute, Pittsburgh
Pa.:	Pennco Tech, Bristol
Pa.:	Pennsylvania Institute of Technology, Upper Darby
Pa.:	R.E.T.S. Electronic School, Upper Darby
Pa.:	Washington Institute of Technology, Washington
R.I.:	New England Technical Institute, Providence
R.I.:	Rhode Island School of Electronics, Providence
S.C.:	Nielsen Electronics Institute, Charleston
Tenn.:	Tennessee Institute of Broadcasting, Nashville
Tenn.:	Tennessee Institute of Electronics, Knoxville
Texas:	Aero Technical Institute, Wichita Falls
Texas:	American Trades Institute, Dallas
Texas:	Control Data Institute, Dallas
Texas:	DeVry Institute of Technology, Dallas
Texas:	Durham's Business College—Technical Division, Austin
Texas:	Industrial Trade School, Dallas
Texas:	United Electronics Institute, Dallas
Utah:	Ron Bailie Western School of Broadcast, Salt Lake City
Va.:	Control Data Institute, Arlington
Va.:	Electronic Computer Programming Institute, Norfolk
Wash.:	Ron Bailie School of Broadcast, Seattle
Wash.:	Ron Bailie School of Broadcast, Spokane
Wash.:	J. M. Perry Institute, Yakima
Wash.:	Spokane Technical Institute, Spokane
Wash.:	Washington Technical Institute, Seattle
W.Va.:	United Electronics Institute, Charleston
Wis.:	Wisconsin School of Electronics, Madison

Emergency Medical Technician

Calif.:	American College of Paramedical Arts and Sciences, Santa Ana
Calif.:	Southern California College of Medical and Dentail Careers, Anaheim
Calif.:	United Health Careers Institute, San Bernardino
La.:	Paramedical Career Academy, Baton Rouge

Engineering Aide (See Specific Field of Technology)

Engineering Drawing (See Drafting)

Engraving

Ill.:	Gem City College—School of Horology, Quincy
Calif.:	United Health Careers Institute, San Bernardino
Calif.:	Associated Technical College, Los Angeles
La.:	Paramedical Career Academy, Baton Route

FCC License (See Electronics)

Fashion Design

Calif.:	Bauder College, Specializing in Fashion Careers, Sacramento
Calif.:	Louise Salinger Academy of Fashion, San Francisco
Fla.:	Art Institute of Fort Lauderdale, Fort Lauderdale
Ga.:	Art Institute of Atlanta, Atlanta
Ill.:	Ray-Vogue School, Chicago
N.Y.:	French Fashion Academy, New York
N.Y.:	Mayer School of Fashion Design, New York
N.Y.:	Traphagen School of Fashion, New York
Ohio:	Virginia Marti School of Fashion Design, Cleveland
Ore.:	Bassist Institute, Portland
Pa.:	The Clarissa School of Fashion Design, Pittsburgh
Pa.:	Fashion Academy of Pittsburgh, Pittsburgh
Pa.:	Tracey-Warner School, Philadelphia
Texas:	Bauder Fashion College, Arlington
Texas:	Miss Wade's Fashion Merchandising College, Dallas

Fashion Illustration

Ga.:	Art Institute of Atlanta, Atlanta
Ill.:	American Academy of Art, Chicago
Ill.:	Ray-Vogue School, Chicago
Md.:	Professional Institute of Commercial Art, Baltimore
Mass.:	New England School of Art and Design, Boston
N.Y.:	Traphagen School of Fashion, New York
Ohio:	Cooper School of Art, Cleveland
Pa.:	Art Institute of Philadelphia, Philadelphia
Pa.:	Art Institute of Pittsburgh, Pittsburgh

Fashion Merchandising

Calif.:	Bauder College, Specializing in Fashion Careers, Sacramento
Fla.:	Art Institute of Fort Lauderdale, Fort Lauderdale
Fla.:	Bauder Fashion College, Miami
Fla.:	International Fine Arts College, Miami
Ga.:	Art Institute of Atlanta, Atlanta
Ga.:	Bauder Fashion College, Atlanta
Ill.:	Ray-Vogue School, Chicago
Nev.:	Fashion Merchandising Institute of Nevada, Las Vegas
N.M.:	AAA College—Technical Division, Alburquerque
N.Y.:	Laboratory Institute of Merchandising, New York
N.Y.:	Tobe-Coburn School for Fashion Careers, New York
Ore.:	Bassist Institute, Portland
Pa.:	Tracey-Warner School, Philadelphia
Texas:	Bauder Fashion College, Arlington
Texas:	Mannequin Manor Fashion Merchandising School, El Paso
Texas:	Miss Wade's Fashion Merchandising College, Dallas

Flight Training (See Pilot)

Food Management

N.Y.:	New York Institute of Dietetics, New York

Gemology

Calif.:	Gemological Institute of America, Santa Monica
Ill.:	Gem City College—School of Horology, Quincy

Gunsmithing

Colo.:	Colorado School of Trades, Lakewood

Hairstyling (See Barbering)

Heating

Ariz.:	Universal Technical Institute, Phoenix
Colo.:	Denver Institute of Technology, Englewood
D.C.:	Lincoln Technical Institute, Washington
Ill.:	Coyne American Institute, Chicago
Ill.:	Greer Technical Institute, Norridge
Ind.:	ITT Technical Institute, Indianapolis
Kans.:	Climate Control Institute, Wichita
Mass.:	Northeast Institute of Industrial Technology, Boston

Mich.:	Detroit Engineering Institute, Detroit
Mo.:	Basic Institute of Technology, St. Louis
Mo.:	Ranken Technical Institute, St. Louis
Neb.:	Universal Technical Institute, Omaha
Nev.:	Education Dynamics Institute, Las Vegas
N.J.:	Lincoln Technical Institute, Union
Ohio:	ITT Technical Institute, Toledo
Ohio:	West Side Institute of Technology, Cleveland
Pa.:	Triangle Institute of Technology, Pittsburgh
R.I.:	New England Technical Institute, Providence
Texas:	American Trades Institute, Dallas
Wash.:	J. M. Perry Institute, Yakima

Heavy Equipment Mechanics (See Diesel Mechanics)

Heavy Equipment Operator

N.C.:	National School of Heavy Equipment, Charlotte
Pa.:	Northeastern Training Institute, Fleetville

Hi-Fi Servicing (See Electronics)

Horsemanship

N.Y.:	5-H Acres School of Riding, Cortland
W.Va.:	Meredith Manor School of Horsemanship, Waverly

Hotel-Motel Training

Calif.:	American Business College—Technical Division, San Diego
Calif.:	International Career Academy, Van Nuys
D C.:	Lewis Hotel-Motel School, Washington

Illustration, Design

Calif.:	Academy of Art College, San Francisco
Conn.:	Paier School of Art, Hamden
Mass.:	The Art Institute of Boston, Boston
Mich.:	Kendall School of Design, Grand Rapids
Ohio:	Cooper School of Art, Cleveland

Illustration, Technical (See Drafting)

Industrial Electronics (See Electronics)

Industrial Management

Mich.:	Allied Careers Institute, Hazel Park
Pa.:	Pittsburgh Technical Institute, Pittsburgh
Pa.:	Triangle Institute of Technology, Pittsburgh

Inhalation Therapy Technician

Ariz.:	Arizona College of Medical/Dental/Legal Careers, Phoenix
Calif.: .	American Vocational School, Garden Grove
Calif.:	American Vocational School, Los Angeles
Calif.:	American College of Paramedical Arts and Sciences, Santa Ana
Calif.:	College of California Medical Affiliates, San Francisco
Calif.:	Medical Training Institute, Mission Hills
Calif.:	North-West College of Medical and Dental Assistants, West Covina
Calif.:	Southland College of Medical and Dental Careers, Gardena
Calif.:	Southland College of Medical, Dental and Legal Careers, Los Angeles
Calif.:	Southland College of Medical-Dental-Legal Careers, Montebello
Calif.:	Valley College of Medical-Dental Assistants, North Hollywood
Pa.:	National School of Health Technology, Philadelphia

Instrumentation

Mass.:	Northeast Institute of Industrial Technology, Boston

N.C.:	Piedmont Aerospace Institute, Winston-Salem
Ohio:	West Side Institute of Technology, Cleveland
Okla.:	Spartan School of Aeronautics, Tulsa
Texas:	Aero Technical Institute, Wichita Falls
Wash.:	J. M. Perry Institute, Yakima

Interior Design

Calif.:	Bauder College, Specializing in Fashion Careers, Sacramento
Conn.:	Paier School of Art, Hamden
Fla.:	Art Institute of Fort Lauderdale, Fort Lauderdale
Fla.:	Bauder Fashion College, Miami
Fla.:	Garces Commercial College, Miami
Fla.:	International Fine Arts College, Miami
Ga.:	Art Institute of Atlanta, Atlanta
Ga.:	Bauder Fashion College, Atlanta
Ill.:	American Academy of Art, Chicago
Ill.:	Ray-Vogue School, Chicago
Mass.:	New England School of Art and Design, Boston
Mass.:	Vesper George School of Art, Boston
Mich.:	Kendall School of Design, Grand Rapids
N.Y.:	Traphagen School of Fashion, New York
Ohio:	Ohio Visual Art Institute, Cincinnati
Ore.:	Bassist Institute, Portland
Pa.:	Art Institute of Philadelphia, Philadelphia
Pa.:	Art Institute of Pittsburgh, Pittsburgh
Pa.:	Hussian School of Art, Philadelphia
Pa.:	Ivy School of Professional Art, Pittsburgh
Pa.:	York Academy of Arts, York
Pa.:	The Williamson Free School of Mechanical Trades, Media
Texas:	Bauder Fashion College, Arlington
Texas:	Mannequin Manor Fashion Merchandising School, El Paso
Texas:	Miss Wade's Fashion Merchandising College, Dallas

Jewelry Design, Diamond Setting

Calif.:	Gemological Institute of America, Santa Monica
Ill.:	Gem City College—School of Horlogy, Quincy
Nev.:	American School of Diamond Cutting, Gardnerville

Keypunch (See Data Processing)

Legal Secretarial/Assistant

Calif.:	American College of Paramedical Arts and Sciences, Santa Ana
Calif.:	Casa Loma Institute of Technology, Pacoima
Calif.:	Southland College of Medical-Dental-Legal Careers, Downey
Calif.:	Southland College of Medical-Dental-Legal Careers, Montebello
N.J.:	Brick Computer Science Institute, Bricktown

Lithography (See Printing)

Loss Prevention Security

N.J.:	Electronic Computer Programming Institute, Jersey City
N.J.:	Empire Technical School, East Orange
N.Y.:	Empire Technical School, Hempstead
N.Y.:	Empire Technical School, New York
Ohio:	Para Professional Institute, Columbus

Machine Design (See Drafting Or Tool and Die)

Machine Shop

Calif.:	National Technical Schools, Los Angeles
Mo.:	Ranken Technical Institute, St. Louis
Okla.:	Southwest Automotive School, Oklahoma City
Pa.:	The Williamson Free School of Mechanical Trades, Media

Texas:	Industrial Trade School, Dallas
Wash.:	J. M. Perry Institute, Yakima

Machinist (See Machine Design)

Materials Handling (See Industrial Management)

Meat Cutting
Ohio:	National School of Meat Cutting, Toledo

Mechanical Drawing (See Drafting)

Mechanical Engineering Technology
Conn.:	Chester Institute for Technical Education, Stratford
Conn.:	Porter School of Drafting and Design, Rocky Hill
Mich.:	Detroit Engineering Institute, Detroit
Pa.:	Pennsylvania Institute of Technology, Upper Darby

Medical Assisting
Ariz.:	Arizona College of Medical/Dental/Legal Careers, Phoenix
Ariz.:	Arizona College of Medical/Dental/Legal Careers Tuscon
Ariz.:	The Bryman School, Phoenix
Calif.:	Andon College—Vocational Health Careers, San Jose
Calif.:	Bay City College Dental-Medical Assistants, San Francisco
Calif.:	The Bryman School, Anaheim
Calif.:	The Bryman School, Canoga Park
Calif.:	The Bryman School, Long Beach
Calif.:	The Bryman School, Los Angeles
Calif.:	The Bryman School, West Los Angeles
Calif.:	The Bryman School, Rosemead
Calif.:	The Bryman School, San Francisco
Calif.:	The Bryman School, San Jose
Calif.:	The Bryman School, Torrance
Calif.:	College of California Medical Affiliates, San Francisco
Calif.:	Galen College of Medical and Dental Assistants, Fresno
Calif.:	Lawton School, Santa Ana
Calif.:	Lawton School for Medical and Dental Assistants, Palo Alto
Calif.:	Long Beach College of Medical & Dental Assistants, Long Beach (Bixby Knolls)
Calif.:	Medical Training Institute, Mission Hills
Calif.:	North-West College of Medical and Dental Assistants, Pomona
Calif.:	North-West College of Medical and Dental Assistants, West Covina
Calif.:	Oakland College Dental and Medical Assistants, Oakland
Calif.:	Pacific College of Medical & Dental Assistants, San Diego
Calif.:	San Diego College for Medical and Dental Assistants, San Diego
Calif.:	San Jose Institute of Paramedical Careers, San Jose
Calif.:	Southern California College of Medical and Dental Careers, Anaheim
Calif.:	Southland College of Medical-Dental-Legal Careers, Downey
Calif.:	Southland College of Medical and Dental Careers, Gardena
Calif.:	Southland College of Medical, Dental and Legal Careers, Los Angeles
Calif.:	Southland College of Medical-Dental-Legal Careers, Montebello
Calif.:	United Health Careers Institute, San Bernardino
Calif.:	Valley College of Medical-Dental Assistants, North Hollywood
Calif.:	Western College of Allied Health Careers, Sacramento
Calif.:	Western College of Medical and Dental Assistants, Van Nuys
Colo.:	Colorado College of Medical and Dental Assistants, Denver
Colo.:	Parks School of Business-Technical Division, Denver
Fla.:	Charron Williams College—Paramedical Division Miami
Ga.:	Atlanta College of Medical and Dental Assistant Atlanta
Ga.:	The Bryman School, Atlanta
Ill.:	The Bryman School, Chicago
Ill.:	Robert Morris School, Carthage
Ind.:	Professional Careers Institute, Indianapolis
Kans.:	Bryan Institute, Wichita
Ken.:	United Electronics Institute, Louisville
La.:	Paramedical Career Academy, Baton Rouge
Md.:	The Medix School, Baltimore
Mass.:	The Bryman School, Brookline
Mich.:	Carnegie Institute of Detroit, Detroit
Minn.:	Lakeland Medical-Dental Academy, Minneapolis
Minn.:	Minnesota Institute of Medical and Dental Assistants, Minneapolis
Mo.:	Bryan Institute, St. Louis
Mo.:	Kansas City College of Medical and Dental Assistants, Kansas City
Mo.:	Missouri School for Doctors' Assistants & Technicians, St. Louis
Neb.:	Omaha College of Health Careers, Omaha
N.J.:	The Bryman School, East Brunswick
N.J.:	Lyons Institute, Cherry Hill
N.J.:	Lyons Institute, Clark
N.J.:	Lyons Institute, Hackensack
N.J.:	Lyons Institute, Newark
N.Y.:	Advanced Career Training, New York
N.Y.:	Allen School for Physicians' Aides, Jamaica
N.Y.:	Careerco School for Paraprofessionals, Syracuse
N.Y.:	Eastern School for Physicians' Aides, New York
N.Y.:	Mandl School for Medical and Dental Assistants, Hempstead
N.Y.:	Mandl School for Medical and Dental Assistants, New York
N.Y.:	New York School for Medical and Dental Assistants, Forest Hills
Ohio:	Toledo Medical Educational Center, Toledo
Okla.:	Bryan Institute, Tulsa
Ore.:	Portland Paramedical Center, Portland
Pa.:	Franklin School of Sciences & Arts, Philadelphia
Pa.:	Median School of Allied Health Careers, Pittsburgh
Pa.:	National School of Health Technology, Philadelphia
Texas:	The Bryman School, Houston
Texas:	San Antonio College of Medical and Dental Assistants, San Antonio
Texas:	Southwest School of Medical Assistants, San Antonio
Texas:	Texas College of Medical & Dental Assistants, Dallas
Utah:	The Bryman School, Salt Lake City
Utah:	Salt Lake City College of Medical and Dental Assistants, Salt Lake City

Medical Secretarial
Ala.:	Herzing Institute, Birmingham
Calif.:	American Vocational School, Garden Grove
Calif.:	American Vocational School, Los Angeles
Calif.:	Andon College—Vocational Health Careers, San Jose
Calif.:	Bay City College Dental-Medical Assistants, San Francisco

Calif.:	The Bryman School, Anaheim
Calif.:	The Bryman School, Canoga Park
Calif.:	The Bryman School, Long Beach
Calif.:	The Bryman School, Los Angeles
Calif.:	The Bryman School, West Los Angeles
Calif.:	The Bryman School, Rosemead
Calif.:	The Bryman School, San Francisco
Calif.:	The Bryman School, San Jose
Calif.:	The Bryman School, Torrance
Calif.:	California Trade Technical School, Long Beach
Calif.:	Galen College of Medical and Dental Assistants, Fresno
Calif.:	Lawton School for Medical and Dental Assistants, Palo Alto
Calif.:	Lawton School, Santa Ana
Calif.:	Medical Training Institute, Mission Hills
Calif.:	North-West College of Medical and Dental Assistants, Pomona
Calif.:	North-West College of Medical and Dental Assistants, West Covina
Calif.:	Oakland College Dental and Medical Assistants, Oakland
Calif.:	Pacific College of Medical & Dental Assistants, San Diego
Calif.:	San Diego College for Medical and Dental Assistants, San Diego
Calif.:	San Jose Institute of Paramedical Careers, San Jose
Calif.:	Southern California College of Medical and Dental Careers, Anaheim
Calif.:	Southland College of Medical and Dental Careers, Gardena
Calif.:	Southland College of Medical, Dental and Legal Careers, Los Angeles
Calif.:	Southland College of Medical-Dental-Legal Careers, Montebello
Calif.:	United Health Careers Institute, San Bernardino
Calif.:	Valley College of Medical-Dental Assistants, North Hollywood
Calif.:	Western College of Allied Health Careers, Sacramento
Fla.:	Charron Williams College—Paramedical Division, Miami
Fla.:	Garces Commercial College, Miami
Ga.:	Atlanta College of Medical and Dental Assistants, Atlanta
Ga.:	The Bryman School, Atlanta
Ill.:	The Bryman School, Chicago
Ind.:	Professional Careers Institute, Indianapolis
La.:	CBM Education Center, Baton Rouge
La.:	Paramedical Career Academy, Baton Rouge
Md.:	Maryland Medical Secretarial School, Hagerstown
Md.:	The Medix School, Baltimore
Mass.:	The Bryman School, Brookline
Mich.:	Carnegie Institute of Detroit, Detroit
Minn.:	Lakeland Medical-Dental Academy, Minneapolis
Minn.:	Minnesota Institute of Medical and Dental Assistants, Minneapolis
Mo.:	Kansas City College of Medical and Dental Assistants, Kansas City
Mo.:	Missouri School for Doctors' Assistants & Technicians, St. Louis
N.J.:	Brick Computer Science Institute, Bricktown
N.J.:	The Bryman School, East Brunswick
N.J.:	Empire Technical School, East Orange
N.M.:	AAA College—Technical Division, Albuquerque
N.Y.:	Eastern School for Physicians' Aides, New York
N.Y.:	Mandl School for Medical and Dental Assistants, Hempstead
N.Y.:	Mandl School for Medical and Dental Assistants, New York
N.Y.:	Advanced Career Training, New York

Ore.:	Portland Paramedical Center, Portland
Pa.:	Median School of Allied Health Careers, Pittsburgh
S.D.:	Nettleton College—Technical Division, Sioux Falls
Texas:	The Bryman School, Houston
Texas:	CBM Education Center, San Antonio
Texas:	San Antonio College of Medical and Dental Assistants, San Antonio
Utah:	The Bryman School, Salt Lake City
Utah:	Salt Lake City College of Medical and Dental Assistants, Salt Lake City
Wis.:	Wisconsin School of Electronics, Madison

Medical Technician

Fla.:	Charron Williams College—Paramedical Division, Miami
Ga.:	Atlanta College of Medical and Dental Assistants, Atlanta
Ken.:	United Electronics Institute, Louisville
Minn.:	Lakeland Medical-Dental Academy, Minneapolis
Mo.:	Gradwohl School of Laboratory Technique, St. Louis
Mo.:	Missouri School for Doctors' Assistants & Technicians, St. Louis
N.J.:	Lyons Institute, Cherry Hill
N.J.:	Lyons Institute, Clark
N.J.:	Lyons Institute, Hackensack
N.J.:	Lyons Institute, Newark
N.Y.:	Advanced Career Training, New York
N.Y.:	Allen School for Physicians' Aides, Jamaica
N.Y.:	Careerco School for Paraprofessionals, Syracuse
N.Y.:	Eastern School for Physicians' Aides, New York
N.Y.:	New York School for Medical and Dental Assistants, Forest Hills
Pa.:	Franklin School of Sciences & Arts, Philadelphia
Pa.:	National School of Health Technology, Philadelphia

Merchandising (See Fashion Merchandising)

Metallurgical Technology
Pa.:	Dean Institute of Technology, Pittsburgh

Millinery
Calif.:	Louise Salinger Academy of Fashion, San Francisco
Pa.:	The Clarissa School of Fashion Design, Pittsburgh

Motel Operation (See Hotel-Motel Training)

Motion Pictures
Calif.:	Merrick Studios Academy of Dramatic Arts, Hollywood
N.Y.:	Germain School of Photography, New York
Pa.:	Ivy School of Professional Art, Pittsburgh

Motorcycle Mechanics
Colo.:	Denver Institute of Technology, Englewood
Mich.:	Michigan Career Institute, Detroit
Ind.:	ITT Technical Institute, Evansville
Pa.:	Technician Training School, McKees Rocks

Nurses Aide
Calif.:	American Vocational School, Los Angeles
Calif.:	College of California Medical Affiliates, San Francisco
Calif.:	Oakland College Dental and Medical Assistants, Oakland
Calif.:	San Diego College for Medical and Dental Assistants, San Diego
Calif.:	San Jose Institute of Paramedical Careers, San Jose

Calif.:	Southland College of Medical, Dental and Legal Careers, Los Angeles
La.:	CBM Education Center, Baton Rouge
La.:	Paramedical Career Academy, Baton Rouge
Mo.:	Urban Technical Center, St. Louis
Pa.:	New Castle School of Trades, Pulaski
Texas:	CBM Education Center, San Antonio
Texas:	Southwest School of Medical Assistants, San Antonio
Va.:	Fogg's Technical Institute, Hanover

Office Machine Repair

Calif.:	American Business College—Technical Division, San Diego
Calif.:	California Trade Technical School, Long Beach
Calif.:	Control Data Institute, Los Angeles
Calif.:	Control Data Institute, San Francisco
Ill.:	Control Data Institute, Chicago
N.J.:	Brick Computer Science Institute, Bricktown
N.M.:	Coronado Technical Institute, Albuquerque
N.Y.:	Control Data Institute, New York
N.Y.:	Empire Technical School, New York

Oil Burner Service (See Heating)

Operating Room Technician

Calif.:	American Vocational School, Garden Grove
Calif.:	American Vocational School, Los Angeles
Calif:	College of California Medical Affiliates, San Francisco
Calif.:	Southland College of Medical, Dental and Legal Careers, Los Angeles
Pa.:	National School of Health Technology, Philadelphia

Optometric Assisting

Calif.:	San Diego College for Medical and Dental Assistants, San Diego
Calif.:	Valley College of Medical-Dental Assistants North Hollywood

Orderly (See Nurses Aide)

Orthopaedic Assistant

Calif.:	College of California Medical Affiliates, San Francisco

Painting and Decorating

Pa.:	The Williamson Free School of Mechanical Trades, Media

PBX Switchboard

Calif.:	American Business College—Technical Division, San Diego

Photography

Calif.:	Academy of Art College, San Francisco
Calif.:	Merrick Studios Academy of Dramatic Arts, Hollywood
Conn.:	Paier School of Art, Hamden
Fla.:	Art Institute of Fort Lauderdale, Fort Lauderdale
Ga.:	Art Institute of Atlanta, Atlanta
Ill.:	American Academy of Art, Chicago
Mass.:	The Art Institute of Boston, Boston
Minn.:	Elkins Institute, Minneapolis
Ohio:	Cooper School of Art, Cleveland
Ohio:	Ohio Institute of Photography, Dayton
Ohio:	Ohio Visual Art Institute, Cincinnati
Pa.:	Ivy School of Professional Art, Pittsburgh
Pa.:	Antonelli School of Photography, Philadelphia
Pa.:	Art Institute of Pittsburgh, Pittsburgh

Pilot, Commercial

Calif.:	B & J Aviation, Santee
Calif.:	Sierra Academy of Aeronautics, Oakland
Fla.:	FlightSafety International, Vero Beach
Idaho:	Aero Technicians, Rexburg
Okla.:	American Flyers, Ardmore
Okla.:	Spartan School of Aeronautics, Tulsa

Plumbing

N.Y.:	Berk Trade School, Brooklyn
Okla.:	Sooner Mechanical Trade School, Oklahoma City
Pa.:	Technician Training School, McKees Rocks
Texas:	American Trades Institute, Dallas

Pollution (See Water)

Practical Nursing (See Vocational Nursing)

Printing

Minn.:	Dunwoody Industrial Institute, Minneapolis
N.Y.:	Printing Trades School, New York
Pa.:	Philadelphia Offset Printing School, Philadelphia
Texas:	American Trades Institute, Dallas
Wash.:	Washington Technical Institute, Seattle

Radio Broadcasting (See Broadcasting)

Radio-Television (See Electronics)

Real Estate

Nev.:	Education Dynamics Institute, Las Vegas

Refrigeration (See Air Conditioning)

Retailing (See Fashion Merchandising)

Sanitation

Mo.:	Water & Wastewater Technical School, Neosho
Wash.:	Spokane Technical Institute, Spokane
Wash.:	Washington Technical Institute, Seattle

Security (See Loss Prevention Security)

Sewage (See Water)

Sewing (See Dressmaking or Tailoring)

Stationary Engineer (See Building Maintenance)

Surveying

Mo.:	Dunwoody Industrial Institute, Minneapolis

Tailoring

N.Y.:	Traphagen School of Fashion, New York
Pa.:	The Clarissa School of Fashion Design, Pittsburgh
Pa.:	Fashion Academy of Pittsburgh, Pittsburgh
Pa.:	Tracey-Warner School, Philadelphia

Television (See Electronics)

Television Broadcasting (See Broadcasting)

Time Study (See Industrial Management)

Tool and Die

Calif.:	National Technical Schools, Los Angeles
Calif.:	South Bay Trade School, San Diego
Ind.:	Midwestern College of Industrial Arts & Sciences, Fort Wayne
Mich.:	Allied Careers Institute, Hazel Park
Minn.:	Dunwoody Industrial Institute, Minneapolis

Ohio:	ITT Technical Institute, Dayton
Pa.:	Dean Institute of Technology, Pittsburgh
Pa.:	Pennsylvania Institute of Technology, Upper Darby
Wis.:	Acme Institute of Technology, Manitowoc
Wis.:	Acme Institute of Technology, Milwaukee

Tool Engineering Technology (See Tool and Die)

Traffic (See Travel)

Transportation Management (See Travel)

Travel

Calif.:	Airline Schools Pacific, Hollywood
Calif.:	Airline Schools Pacific, San Bernardino
Calif.:	Airline Schools Pacific, Santa Barbara
Calif.:	International Career Academy, Van Nuys
Calif.:	Transportation Training Corporation, Long Beach
Colo.:	Parks School of Business—Technical Division, Denver
D.C.:	Lewis Hotel-Motel School, Washington
Minn.:	Humboldt Institute, Minneapolis
Minn.:	The McConnell School, Minneapolis
Pa.:	Wilma Boyd Career School, Pittsburgh

Truck Driving

Ore.:	Commercial Driver Training, Portland
Pa.:	Northeastern Training Institute, Fleetville
Wis.:	Diesel Truck Driver Training School, Sun Prairie

Underwater Diving (See Diving)

Upholstery

Pa.:	The Clarissa School of Fashion Design, Pittsburgh
Pa.:	Triangle Institute of Technology, Pittsburgh

Vending Machine Repair (See Coin Operated Machine Repair)

Veterinarian Assisting

Calif.:	Bay City College Dental-Medical Assistants, San Francisco
Calif.:	North-West College of Medical and Dental Assistants, Pomona
Calif.:	North-West College of Medical and Dental Assistants, West Covina
Calif.:	United Health Careers Institute, San Bernardino
Calif.:	Western College of Allied Health Careers, Sacramento
Colo.:	Bel-Rea Institute of Animal Technology, Denver
Ore.:	Portland Paramedical Center, Portland
Pa.:	Median School of Allied Health Careers, Pittsburgh

Vocational Nursing

Calif.:	American Vocational School, Garden Grove
Calif.:	American Vocational School, Los Angeles
Calif.:	Casa Loma Institute of Technology, Pacoima
Calif.:	College of California Medical Affiliates, San Francisco
Calif.:	United Health Careers Institute, San Bernardino

Watchmaking and Repair

Ill.:	Gem City College—School of Horology, Quincy

Water

Mo.:	Water & Wastewater Technical School, Neosho
Pa.:	Triangle Institute of Technology, Pittsburgh

Welding

Ariz.:	Phoenix School of Welding, Phoenix
Calif.:	California Trade Technical School, Long Beach
Calif.:	Fresno Technical College, Fresno
Calif.:	Modern Welding Trade School, Anaheim
Calif.:	Modern Welding Trade School, Downey
Calif.:	South Bay Trade School, San Diego
Calif.:	Welding Trade School, San Jose
Colo.:	Certified Welding School, Denver
Conn.:	Hartford Modern School of Welding, Hartford
Conn.:	Technical Careers Institute, Milford
Md.:	Airco Technical Institute, Baltimore
Minn.:	Dunwoody Industrial Institute, Minneapolis
Mo.:	Ranken Technical Institute, St. Louis
Mo.:	Urban Technical Center, St. Louis
N.J.:	General Technical Institute, Linden
N.Y.:	Airco Technical Institute, Brooklyn
Ohio.:	Airco Technical Institute, Cleveland
Ohio:	Akron Testing Laboratory & Welding School, Barberton
Ohio:	Hobart School of Welding Technology, Troy
Ohio:	Technichron School of Welding, Cincinnati
Okla.:	Sooner Mechanical Trade School, Oklahoma City
Okla.:	Tulsa Welding School, Tulsa
Pa.:	Breeden School of Welding, Whitehall
Pa.:	Dean Institute of Technology, Pittsburgh
Pa.:	New Castle School of Trades, Pulaski
Pa.:	Technician Training School, McKees Rocks
Pa.:	Washington Institute of Technology, Washington
Tenn.:	Nashville Auto Diesel College, Nashville
Texas:	American Trades Institute, Dallas
Texas:	Industrial Trade School, Dallas

X-Rays

Calif.:	Medical Training Institute, Mission Hills
Pa.:	Franklin School of Sciences & Arts, Philadelphia

A GEOGRAPHIC LISTING OF ACCREDITED SCHOOLS

Schools are listed alphabetically under the heading of their respective states. To the right of each listing is the "weeks to complete" column. This tells you how many weeks are normally required to complete the course on a full-time or part-time basis. If the number of weeks required is flexible, depending on student progress, minimum and maximum course times are given—"8/12" means eight to twelve weeks.

After each school name, the reader is given the full address, the name of a school official, the telephone number, the date of founding, and usage of the school by public and governmental agencies. Abbreviations for these offices:

VA	Veterans Administration
VR	Office of Vocational Rehabilitation
INS	Immigration and Naturalization Service for Foreign Students
BIA	Bureau of Indian Affairs

	Length in Weeks	Full Time	Part Time
ALABAMA			
Herzing Institute			
1218 South 20th Street, Birmingham 35205			
Ray T. DeArmond, *Director*			
(205) 322-5506, 1965, VA, VR, INS			
Data Processing & Computer Programming		—	36
Systems and Advance Programming		48	—
Keypunch		8	16/24
Keypunch and Computer I/O Control		24	—
Medical Secretary/Transcriptionist		36	36
United Electronics Institute			
2717 Seventh Avenue South, Birmingham 35233			
Hubbard N. Stone, *Director*			
(205) 323-5816, 1963, VA, VR, INS			
Electronics Technology		91	—
Basic Electronics, Radio & TV		80	—
ARIZONA			
Academy of Drafting			
1202 North Scottsdale Road, Tempe 85281			
Francis J. Cody, *President*			
(602) 967-7813, 1969, VA, VR, INS, BIA			
Drafting (11 Areas of Major)		26/52	86
Mathematics for Drafting		13	—
Arizona Automotive Institute			
6829 North 46th Avenue, Glendale 85301			
P. A. Sandblom, *President*			
(602) 934-7273, 1968, VA, VR, INS, BIA			
Automotive Mechanics		48	—
Drafting		48	—
Arizona College of Medical/Dental/Legal Careers			
4020 North 19th Avenue, Phoenix 85015			
James D. Keener, *Director*			
(602) 277-1451, 1967, VA, VR, BIA			
Medical Assisting		28	—
Dental Assisting		26	—
Respiratory Therapy		46	—
Operating Room Technician		32	—

	Full Time	Part Time
Arizona College of Medical/Dental/Legal Careers		
2354 E. Broadway, Tucson 85719		
Rexine Wetherbee, *Director*		
(602) 622-4851, 1970, VA, VR, INS, BIA		
Dental Assisting	24	—
Medical Assisting	28	—
Respiratory Therapy Technician	46	—
Ron Bailie School of Broadcast		
1830 North Central, Phoenix 85004		
Mike Scott, *Director*		
(602) 257-0303, 1970, VA, VR, BIA		
Announcing	28	—
Electronics Theory	20	—
Announcing & Electronics	48	—
Blair College of Medical and Dental Assistants		
1005 W. Southern Ave., Mesa 85202		
C. Loran Lee, *Director*		
(602) 833-1110, 1968, VA, VR, BIA		
Medical Assistant	28	56
Dental Assistant	24	48
Dental Laboratory Technician	36	72
The Bryman School		
1112 East McDowell Road, Phoenix 85006		
S. W. Rotstein, *Director*		
(602) 258-5901, 1970, VA, VR		
Medical Assisting	28	—
Dental Assisting	28	—
Medical Reception	16	—
DeVry Institute of Technology		
4702 North 24th Street, Phoenix 85016		
F. Roger Hess, *President*		
(602) 956-8806, 1967, VA, VR, INS, BIA		
Electronics Engineering Technology	108/144	—
Electronics Technician	72	—
Phoenix Institute of Technology		
2555 East University Drive, Phoenix 85034		
Ray Sevy, *Director*		
(602) 267-1183, 1970, VA, VR, INS		
Electronics Technology	48	—
Basic Electronics		
Radio and Television	48	—
Architectural Drafting		
and Design	48	—
Automotive Electronic		
Diagnostic Analysis and		
Air Conditioning	24	—
Phoenix School of Welding		
403 S. First Avenue, Phoenix 85003		
Dan A. Buseman, *Administrator*		
(602) 252-7304, 1962, VA, VR, INS, BIA		
Oxy-Acetylene Welding	7	14
Electric Arc Welding	9	17
Plate Welding I	16	31
Flux Cored Wire Welding	1	2
Gas Tungsten Arc Welding	4	7
Gas Metal Arc Welding	1	2
General Welding I	26	52
Preparatory Pipe Welding I	14	27
Pipe Welding	5	10
Principles of Welding	—	16
Intermediate Welding I	17	34
General Pipe Welding I	31	62
Intermediate Pipe Welding I	19	37
Advanced Pipe Welding I	22	44
Plate Welding II	24	47
General Welding II	34	68
Preparatory Pipe Welding II	22	43

	Full Time	Part Time
Intermediate Welding II	25	50
General Pipe Welding II	39	78
Intermed. Pipe Welding II	27	53
Advanced Pipe Welding II	30	60
The Refrigeration School		
3216 East Washington Street, Phoenix 85034		
Ola Lee Loney, *Director*		
(602) 275-7133, 1965, VA, VR, BIA		
Air Conditioning and Refrigeration		
Service Mechanics	20	33
Universal Technical Institute		
3121 West Weldon Avenue, Phoenix 85017		
Robert I. Sweet, *President*		
(602) 264-4164, 1965, VA, VR, INS, BIA		
Complete Auto Mechanics	24	33¼
Automatic Transmissions	9	—
Diesel Engines	9	18
Auto-Diesel Mechanics	33	51½
Refrigeration, Air Conditioning & Heating	27	54

ARKANSAS

	Full Time	Part Time
United Electronics Institute		
7723 Asher Avenue, Little Rock 72204		
Russell Murdoch, *Director*		
(501) 562-5051, 1969, VA, VR, INS		
Electronics Technology	84	—

CALIFORNIA

	Full Time	Part Time
Academy of Art College		
625 Sutter Street, San Francisco 94102		
Richard A. Stephens, *President*		
(415) 673-4200, 1929, VA, VR, INS, BIA		
BFA in Fine Arts	120	240
BFA in Advertising Design	120	240
BFA in Illustration	120	240
BFA in Photography & Film	120	240
Airline Schools Pacific		
6043 Hollywood Boulevard, Hollywood 90028		
Marsha Toy, *President*		
(213) 462-3211, 1948, VA, VR, INS, BIA		
Transportation Management	26	52
Airline Schools Pacific		
191 South "E" Street, San Bernardino 92401		
Darlene M. Powers, *Director*		
(714) 885-3857, 1968, VA, VR, INS, BIA		
Transportation Management	26	52
Airline Schools Pacific		
1520 State Street, Santa Barbara 93101		
Ledyard M. Baxter, *Director*		
(805) 965-5264, 1969, VA, VR, INS, BIA		
Air Transportation Agent,		
Management & Operations	26	52
American Business College—Technical Division		
5952 El Cajon Boulevard, San Diego 92115		
Frank E. Hollar, *President*		
(714) 582-1319, 1959, VA, VR, INS, BIA		
Computer Programming	24	—
Data Processing Assistant	24	—
Keypunch Operations	12	—
Airline—Travel Agency Careers	24	—
Hotel-Motel Careers	16	—
Home Appliance Repair	24	—

	Length in Weeks	Full Time	Part Time
Office Machine Repair		24	—
PBX Receptionist		16	—
Auto Mechanic		24	—
Air Conditioning/Refrigeration/Heating		27	—
Architectural Drafting		24	36
Electronic Drafting		24	36
Mechanical Drafting		24	36
Civil Engineering/Drafting		27	—
Drafting/Technical Illustration		24	—
Building Maintenance Technology		24	—

American College of Paramedical Arts and Sciences
1600 North Broadway, Santa Ana 92706
William J. Anthony, *Director*
(714) 547-0305, 1972, VA, VR, INS

	Length in Weeks	Full Time	Part Time
Inhalation Therapy Technician		50	88
Operating Room Technician		36	65
Emergency Medical Technician		34	63
Nursing Assistant		5	8
Ward Clerk		—	8
Lawyer's Assistant		—	52

American Vocational School
12881 Knott St., Suite 103, Garden Grove 92641
William J. Pruitt, *President*
(714) 898-6761, 1969, VA, VR, INS

	Full Time	Part Time
Respiratory Therapy Tech.	44	—
Operating Room Tech.	50	—
Medical Transcribing	26	—
Vocational Nursing	49	—

American Vocational School
198 South Alvarado Street, Los Angeles 90057
William J. Pruitt, *President*
(213) 413-3390, 1965, VA, VR, INS, BIA

	Full Time	Part Time
Vocational Nursing	49	—
Nursing Assistant	10	—
Respiratory Therapy Technician	44	—
Medical Secretary	39	—
Medical Transcriber	26	—
Operating Room Technician	50	—
Hemodialysis Technician	45	—

Andon College—Vocational Health Careers
1414 North Winchester Boulevard, San Jose 95128
Donald J. Bogue, *President*
(408) 244-8777, 1970, VR, BIA

	Full Time	Part Time
Medical Assistant	28	—
Medical Lab. Assistant	28	—
Medical Receptionist	16	24
Med. Admin. Assistant	28	—
Nurses Aide	11-12	12
Dental Assistant	16	16/19
Dental Assistant (R.D.A.)	28	—
Dental Admin. Asst.	28	—

Associated Technical College
1670 Wilshire Boulevard, Los Angeles 90017
Ronald Quam, *Director*
(213) 484-2444, 1968, VR, INS, BIA

	Full Time	Part Time
Medical Assisting	24	—
Dental Assisting	11	—
Emergency Medical Technician I	8	—

B & J Aviation
8283 Billy Mitchell Drive, Santee 92071
Fred Breise, *Vice-President*
(714) 448-2212, 1945, VR, INS

	Full Time	Part Time
Private Pilot	7-10	14-20
Commercial Pilot	14-20	28-40
Instrument Rating	7-10	14-20
Multi-Eng Rating	2-3	4-6

	Full Time	Part Time
Flight Instructor-Airplane	7-10	14-20
Flight Instructor-Instrument	7-10	14-20
Airline Transport Pilot	7-10	14-20

Ron Bailie School of Broadcast
420 Taylor, San Francisco 94102
Del Chapman, *Director*
(415) 441-0707, 1969, VA, VR, INS

	Full Time	Part Time
Announcing, Production, Copywriting	28	—
Electronics Theory (First Class FCC License)	20	—
Combo-Announcing, Electronic Theory	48	—

Bauder College, Specializing in Fashion Careers
641 Howe Avenue, Sacramento 95825
William J. Kettle, *President*
(916) 927-2936, 1969, VA, INS, BIA

	Full Time	Part Time
Fashion Design	64	—
Fashion Merchandising	64	—
Interior Design	64	—

Bay City College Dental-Medical Assistants
661 Geary Street, San Francisco 94102
Sarah A. Davis, *President*
(415) 776-1667, 1959, VA, VR, INS, BIA

	Full Time	Part Time
Nurses Aide-Male Orderly	12	—
Medical Receptionist	14	—
Medical Assistant	28	—
Dental Assistant	17	—
EKG Technician	15	—
Medical Lab Assistant	26	—
Crown & Bridge Dental Lab	26	—
Ceramics & Porcelain	26	—
Partial Dentures	26	—
Full Mouth Dentures Dental Lab.	52	—
Veterinarian Med. Asst.	24	30

Bay-Valley Technical Institute
3520 De La Cruz Boulevard, Santa Clara 95050
Keith P. Binkle, Jr., *Director*
(408) 248-7400, 1964, VA, VR, INS, BIA

	Full Time	Part Time
General Electronics Technician	36	60
Communications Technology	48	76
Computer Maintenance Technology	48	76
Television Technology	48	76
Electronics Technology II	60	108
Drafting Detailer	—	36
Electronics Drafting	36	60
Mechanical Drafting	36	60
Electro-Mechanical Drafting	60	108
Electronics Trainee	26	—
Electronics Assembly	26	—
Digital Principles	5	10

The Bryman School
1120 North Brookhurst Street, Anaheim 92801
W. A. (Bill) Marsters, *Director*
(714) 778-6500, 1969, VA, VR, INS

	Full Time	Part Time
Medical Assisting	28	34
Dental Assisting	20	24
Medical Office Management	16	19

The Bryman School
20835 Sherman Way, Canoga Park 91306
Jule Goldberg, *Director*
(213) 887-7911, 1970, VA, VR, INS, BIA

	Full Time	Part Time
Medical Assisting	28	40
Dental Assisting	28	45
Medical Office Management	12	19

	Length in Weeks	Full Time	Part Time
The Bryman School			
3633 Long Beach Boulevard, Long Beach 90807			
Janet Hutchins, *Director*			
(213) 426-8388, 1968, VA, VR, INS			
Medical Assisting	28	–	
Dental Assisting	28	–	
Medical Reception	16	24	
The Bryman School			
12340 Santa Monica Boulevard, Los Angeles 90025			
Jules Rosenblatt, *Director*			
(213) 826-7881, 1962, VA, VR, INS, BIA			
Medical Assisting	28	38	
Dental Assisting	28	45	
Medical Office Management	16	21	
The Bryman School			
1017 Wilshire Boulevard, Los Angeles 90017			
Betty Smith, *Director*			
(213) 381-6011, 1969, VA, VR, INS			
Medical Assisting	28	45	
Dental Assisting	28	45	
Medical Office Management	16	25	
The Bryman School			
8505 North Hart Avenue, Rosemead 91770			
Frank R. Haberkorn, *Director*			
(213) 573-5470, 1965, VA, VR, INS, BIA			
Medical Assisting	28	46	
Dental Assisting	20	32	
Medical Office Management	16	25	
The Bryman School			
731 Market Street, San Francisco 94103			
Fred Smith, *Director*			
(415) 777-2500, 1967, VA, VR, INS, BIA			
Medical Assisting	28	44	
Medical Reception	12	20	
Dental Assisting	28	44	
The Bryman School			
1015 Naglee Avenue, San Jose 95128			
Jean Knight, *Director*			
(408) 275-8800, 1970, VA, VR, INS, BIA			
Medical Assisting	24	–	
Dental Assisting	12	–	
Medical Office Management	12	–	
The Bryman School			
1212 West Artesia Boulevard, Torrance 90504			
Michael A. Newman, *Director*			
(213) 542-6951, 1970, VA, VR, INS			
Medical Assisting	28	40	
Dental Assisting	28	40	
Medical Reception	16	24	
California College of Dental Training			
110 South Spring Street, Los Angeles 90014			
J. Serin, *Director*			
(213) 622-2371, 1959, VA, VR, INS			
Dental Technology	34	68/102	
California Trade Technical School			
1633 Long Beach Boulevard, Long Beach 90813			
Edward L. Konkol, *Director*			
(213) 591-5671, 1969, VA, VR, INS, BIA			
Air Conditioning & Refrigeration	27	54	
Auto Body & Fender Repair	17	34	
Auto Body Repair, Master	40	80	
Auto Painting & Refinishing	12	24	
Auto Mechanics, Master	40	80	
Auto Tune-up & Electrical	12	24	

	Length in Weeks	Full Time	Part Time
Auto Brakes & Front End	12	24	
Automatic Transmissions	16	32	
Automobile Air Conditioning	8	16	
Combination Welding	26	52	
Acetylene Welding	8	16	
Arc Welding	8	16	
Tungsten Inert Gas Welding (TIG)	6	12	
Metal Inert Gas Welding (MIG)	4	8	
Electronics Technician	48	96	
Communications	36	72	
Communications License Preparation	8	16	
Electronics Fabrication & Inspection	6	12	
Color Television Technician	40	80	
Electronic-Mechanical Drafting	26	52	
Business Machine Service	40	80	
Insurance Clerk	24	48	
Medical Records Clerk	26	52	
Hospital Admitting Clerk	21	42	
Ward Clerk	21	42	
Casa Loma Institute of Technology			
12502 Van Nuys Boulevard, Pacoima 91331			
Albert M. Elton, *Executive Director*			
(213) 899-1975, 1966, VA, VR, INS			
Dental Technology	104	–	
Licensed Vocational Nursing	52	–	
Respiratory Therapy Technician	52	–	
Respiratory Therapist	78	–	
Attorney Assistant	52	–	
College of California Medical Affiliates			
214 Van Ness Avenue, San Francisco 94102			
James K. Martin, *President*			
(415) 863-8200, 1963, VA, VR, INS, BIA			
Licensed Vocational Nursing (LVN)	52	–	
Respiratory Therapy Technician	52	–	
Orthopaedic Assistant	16	–	
Operating Room Technician	42	–	
Practical Nurse/Orderly	–	9	
Medical Assistant	26	–	
Dental Assistant	26	–	
Dental Lab Technician	46	–	
Computer Learning Center of Los Angeles			
3130 Wilshire Boulevard, Los Angeles 90010			
Bill G. Clutter, *Director*			
(213) 386-6311, 1957, VA, VR, INS, BIA			
Computer Career Program	26	43.3	
Condie College of Business and Technology			
4340 Stevens Creek Boulevard, San Jose 95129			
Marion A. Condie, *President*			
(408) 984-8811, 1968, VA, VR, INS, BIA			
Programming Technology	30	50	
Digital Computer Operations	18	30	
Key Punch Operator	6	10	
Electronic Technology	30	62	
Data Entry Secretary	18	30	
Control Data Institute			
1780 West Lincoln Avenue, Anaheim 92801			
A. A. Scafe, *Director*			
(714) 635-2770, 1966, VA, VR, INS			
Computer Programming and Operations	22	48/56	
Computer Technology	25	42	
Control Data Institute			
5630 Arbor Vitae, Los Angeles 90045			
Donald E. Scherer, *Director*			
(213) 642-2345, 1966, VA, VR, INS, BIA			
Computer Technology	26	42	
Computer Programming & Operations	22	36	
Business Machine Service	26	36	

	Length in Weeks	Full Time	Part Time
Control Data Institute			
71 O'Farrell Street, San Francisco 94102			
Howard E. Hyden, *Director*			
(415) 421-5793, 1953, VA, VR, INS			
Computer Technology	25		42
Computer Programming and Operations	23/26		36
Business Machine Service	21		35
Dental Technology Institute			
969 North Tustin Street, Orange 92667			
F. David Gardner, *Director*			
(714) 997-3052, 1972, VA, VR, INS			
Full/Partial Dentures	26		52
Crown & Bridge	26		52
Dental Ceramics	5		10
Electronic Technical Institute			
8477 Aero Drive, San Diego 92123			
A. E. Stillman, *Executive Director*			
(714) 278-1711, 1955, VA, VR, INS, BIA			
Electronic Engineering Technology	—		156
Radio-Television Technician	34		68
Computer Systems Technician	44		88
Fresno Technical College			
2575 North Blackstone Avenue, Fresno 93703			
John W. Hatch, *President*			
(209) 226-5330, 1958, VA, VR, INS, BIA			
Electronics-Electronic Technician	52		65
Electronics—Radio Television	52		65
Electronics—Mobile Communications			
Equipment Technician	52		65
Engineering Technology—Drafting			
& Surveying	52		65
Refrigeration-Air Conditioning			
& Appliance Technician	48		72
Automotive Technician	48		72
Certified and Production Welding	26		—
Galen College of Medical and Dental Assistants			
1325 North Wishon, Fresno 93728			
Beth Esquivel, *President*			
(209) 264-9726, 1967, VA, VR, INS, BIA ·			
Medical Assisting	28		—
Dental Assisting	24		—
Medical-Dental Receptionist	24		—
Gemological Institute of America			
1660 Stewart Street, Santa Monica 90404			
Richard T. Liddicoat, Jr., *President*			
(213) 829-2991, 1931, VA, VR, INS			
Graduate Gemologist Resident Program	23/26		—
Jewelry Design Resident Program	7		—
Diamond Appraisal Class	1		—
Gem Identification Class	1		—
Diamond Setting Class	2		—
Jewelry Repair Class	2		—
Jewelry Design Class	1		—
International Career Academy			
5612 Van Nuys Boulevard, Van Nuys 91401			
Robert P. Menslage, *Director*			
(213) 989-4462, 1962, VA, VR, INS			
Travel and Transportation Agent	12		30
Travel Counsellor	—		12½
Travel and Transportation Operations	31		—
Air Transport Operations and			
Communications	19		—
Hotel-Motel Management	26		—

	Length in Weeks	Full Time	Part Time
Lawton School for Medical and Dental Assistants			
430 Cambridge Avenue, Palo Alto 94306			
H. N. Hudson, *Director*			
(415) 328-4646, 1967, VA, VR, INS, BIA			
Dental Assistant		16	—
Medical Assistant		27	—
Medical Office Management		12	—
Lawton School			
619 West 17th Street, Santa Ana 92706			
Beverly Howard, *Administrator*			
(714) 541-4461, 1967, VA, VR, INS, BIA			
Medical Assistant		28	34
Dental Assistant		16	21
Medical Office Receptionist		16	19
Long Beach College of Medical & Dental Assistants			
4439 Atlantic Avenue, Long Beach (Bixby Knolls) 90807			
George Andre, *Director*			
(213) 422-0481, 1966, VA, VR, BIA			
Medical Assisting		39	—
Dental Assisting		39	—
Medical Training Institute			
14935 Rinaldi Street, Suite 602, Mission Hills 91345			
C. R. Howe, *Administrator*			
(213) 365-3987, 1966, VA, VR, INS, BIA			
Medical Assisting		25	—
Inhalation Therapy		52	—
X-ray Assistant		11	—
Laboratory Assistant		24	—
Medical Receptionist		24	—
Medical Transcriber		24	—
Merrick Studios Academy of Dramatic Arts			
870 North Vine Street, Hollywood 90038			
Laurence Merrick, *Administrator*			
(213) 462-8444, 1960, VA, VR, INS			
Professional Actor		150	300
Motion Picture & Television Directing		150	300
Motion Picture & Television Producing		150	300
Cinematography		150	300
Film Editing		150	300
Modern Welding Trade School			
1740 Orangethorpe Park, Anaheim 92801			
James Bollenbacher, *Director*			
(714) 879-1053, 1960, VA, VR, INS, BIA			
Basic Arc & Acetylene Welding		13	26
Heliarc Welding		3	6
Advanced Welding		10	20
Combination Welding		26	52
Welding & Structural Blueprint Reading		26	52
Structural Blueprint Reading		4	8
Modern Welding Trade School			
9722 East Firestone Boulevard, Downey 90241			
James M. Johnson, *Director*			
(213) 923-9489, 1954, VA, VR, INS, BIA			
Basic Arc & Acetylene Welding		13	26
Heliarc Welding		3	6
Advanced Welding		10	20
Combination Welding		26	52
Welding & Structural Blueprint Reading		26	52
Structural Blueprint Reading		4	8
National Career Institute			
214 Van Ness Avenue, San Francisco 94102			
Alex E. Sims, *President*			
(415) 626-6757, 1962, VA, VR, INS, BIA			
Architectural, Structural, Civil, Mechanical,			
Piping, Electrical Drafting			
Basic		18	50

	Length in Weeks	Full Time	Part Time
Intermediate		40	—
Advanced		52	—
Electronic Technology		52	—
First Class FCC Licensing		6	—

National Technical Schools
4000 South Figueroa Street, Los Angeles 90037
L. J. Rosenkranz, *President*
(213) 234-9061, 1905, VA, VR, INS, BIA

	Length in Weeks	Full Time	Part Time
Color Television & Hi-Fi Servicing		—	78
Electronics		—	78
Basic Automotive Mechanics		—	13
Advanced Engine Diagnosis		—	13
Automotive Air Conditioning		—	17
Brakes, Wheel Alignment & Safety Service		—	22
Automotive Transmission Mechanics		—	26
Engine Tune-up		—	39
Engine Tune-up and Dynamometer Diagnosis		—	52
Automobile Service Mechanics		—	65
Diesel Mechanics		—	69
Machine Shop		—	26
Technical Drafting		—	26
General Automobile & Diesel Mechanics		—	65
Refrigeration & Air Conditioning Servicing		—	52
Tool & Die Making		—	52
Technical Design Drafting		—	52
Electronics Technology		60	—
Radio, Hi-Fi & Television Servicing		52	—
Automotive Mechanics		39	—
Automotive Technology		47	—
Automotive Mechanics & Diesel Engines		52	—
General Machine Shop		26	—
Air Conditioning & Refrigeration		30	—
Industrial Drafting		17	—
Practical Tool & Die Making		39	—
Design Drafting		30	—
Associate Degree in Electronics Technology		69	—
Associate Degree in Automotive Technology & Diesel Engines		69	—
Associate Degree in Computer Technology		69	—
Automotive Technology (Spanish)		47	—
Radio, Hi-Fi and TV (Spanish)		52	—
General Automobile Mechanic (Spanish)		—	78
Color TV and Hi-Fi (Spanish)		—	78

North-West College of Medical and Dental Assistants
134 West Holt Avenue, Pomona 91768
Mrs. Jeanne Fewkes, *Director*
(714) 623-1552, 1972, VA, VR

	Length in Weeks	Full Time	Part Time
Medical Assisting		28	—
Medical Receptionist		24	—
Medical Insurance Specialist		24	—
Medical Transcriber		24	—
Ward Clerk		10	—
Dental Assisting		28	—
Dental Receptionist		14	—
Veterinary Assisting		28	—

North-West College of Medical and Dental Assistants
121 West Garvey Avenue, West Covina 91790
Marsha Fuerst, *Director*
(213) 962-3495, 1966, VA, VR, BIA

	Length in Weeks	Full Time	Part Time
Dental Assisting		28	—
Dental Receptionist		14	—
Medical Assisting		28	—
Medical Receptionist		24	—
Medical Insurance Specialist		24	—
Medical Transcriber		24	—
Hospital Unit Secretary or Ward Clerk		24	—
Veterinary Assisting		24	—
Inhalation Therapy Technician		38	—

Oakland College Dental and Medical Assistants
388-17th Street, Oakland 94612
Sarah Davis, *President*
(415) 832-6955, 1961, VA, VR, INS, BIA

	Length in Weeks	Full Time	Part Time
Medical Assistant		28	—
Dental Assistant		17	—
Medical Lab. Assistant		26	—
EKG Technician		15	—
Crown & Bridge Dental Tech.		26	—
Full Mouth Denture, Dental Tech.		52	—
Ceramic & Porcelain Dental Tech.		26	—
Nurses' Aide		10	—
Male Orderly		10	—
Medical Receptionist		14	—

Pacific College of Medical & Dental Assistants
4411 30th Street, San Diego 92116
Ben Ferber, *President*
(714) 280-5005, 1966, VA, VR, INS, BIA

	Length in Weeks	Full Time	Part Time
Medical Assisting		28	34
Medical Reception		16	18
Dental Assisting		16	20

Pacific Travel School
610 East 17th Street, Santa Ana 92701
J. R. McClure, *Director*
(714) 543-6655, 1963, VA, VR, INS

	Length in Weeks	Full Time	Part Time
Travel & Transportation Systems		26	50
Air Transportation Agent		—	29
Travel Agency Operation		13/26	26

Practical Schools
1650 Babbitt Avenue, Anaheim 92805
Marlyn B. Sheehan, *President*
(714) 634-4565, 1968, VA, VR, INS, BIA

	Length in Weeks	Full Time	Part Time
Electronics I, II & III		39	74
Rental Yard Equipment Training		26	49
Auto Air Conditioning		—	6
Custodial Science Management		—	8
Air Conditioning and Refrigeration		13	25
Air Conditioning, Refrigeration, Kitchen and Laundry Appliances		26	49
Kitchen and Laundry Appliances		13	25

Rosston School of Men's Hair Design
225 E. Third Street, Long Beach 90802
Roy W. Nixon, *Manager*
(213) 437-6427, 1972, VA, VR, BIA

	Length in Weeks	Full Time	Part Time
Barbering		40	75

Louise Salinger Academy of Fashion
101 Jessie Street, San Francisco 94105
Louise Salinger, *President*
(415) 362-8059, VA, VR, INS, BIA

	Length in Weeks	Full Time	Part Time
Dress Designing		72/96	144/192
Millinery		36/48	72/96
Fashion Design		72/96	144/192

San Diego College for Medical and Dental Assistants
5952 El Cajon Boulevard, San Diego 92115
Frank E. Hollar, *President*
(714) 582-1319, 1959, VA, VR, BIA

	Length in Weeks	Full Time	Part Time
Medical Assistant		24	—
Dental Assistant		16	—
Nurses Aide-Male Orderly		12	—
Medical Receptionist		24	—
Medical Secretary		36	—
Optometric Receptionist/Assistant		24	—
Dental Receptionist		24	—

San Jose Institute of Paramedical Careers
2145—The Alameda, San Jose 95113
Francine Adams, *Director*
(408) 249-2690, 1962, VA, VR, INS, BIA

	Length in Weeks	Full Time	Part Time
Medical Assistant	28	—	
Dental Assistant	16	—	
Medical Receptionist	12	—	
EKG Technician	12	—	
Medical Lab Assistant	26	—	
Crown and Bridge Technician	26	—	
Full Denture Technician	52	—	
Nurses Aide—Male Orderly	8	—	

Sequoia Automotive Institute
2425 Leghorn Street, Mountain View 94040
Daniel J. Heffernan, *Director*
(415) 964-5400, 1962, VA, VR, BIA

	Full Time	Part Time
General Automotive Mechanics	28	56
Automotive Brake & Wheel	7	35
Automotive Transmission	7	35
Automotive Air Conditioning	7	35
Automotive Tune-up	7	35

Sierra Academy of Aeronautics
Oakland International Airport, Oakland 94614
Norris N. Everett, *President*
(415) 568-6100, 1966, VA, INS, BIA

	Full Time	Part Time
Aviation English/English Language	12/24	—
Pilot Preparatory	5	—
Flight Engineer Preparatory	8	—
Private Pilot	6	12/18
Commercial/Instrument Pilot	17	30/50
Multi-Engine Pilot	2	4
Seaplane-Commercial Added	2	4
Flight Instructor-Airplane	5	10
Flight Instructor-Instrument	4	8
Flight Engineer-B-727	11	—
Flight Engineer-B-707	11	—
Airline Transport Pilot-Single Engine	4	8
Airline Transport Pilot-Multi-Engine	4	8
Type Rating-Sabreliner	3	—
Type Rating-Boeing 727	5/9	—
Type Rating-Boeing 707	5/9	—
Helicopter-Commercial Added	6	12
Helicopter-External Load	4	8
Helicopter-Flight Instructor	5	10
Helicopter-Airline Transport Pilot	6	12

South Bay Trade School
2146 Main Street, San Diego 92113
Gene R. Golliet, *President*
(714) 232-4232, 1960, VA, VR, INS, BIA

	Full Time	Part Time
Air Conditioning and Refrigeration	26	52
Auto Body Repair	30	60
Auto Frame Repair	8	16
Auto Air Conditioning	6	12
Auto Brake & Wheel Alignment	8	16
Auto Machinist	16	32
Auto Engine Overhaul	18	36
Auto Parts Counterman	26	52
Auto Tune-Up	12	24
Automatic Transmission	15	30
General Mechanic	53	106
Auto Air Conditioning—Foreign	6	12
Auto Brake & Wheel Alignment—Foreign	8	16
Auto Engine Overhaul—Foreign	18	36
Auto Machinist—Foreign	16	32
Auto Tune-Up—Foreign	12	24
Automatic Transmission—Foreign	15	30
Combination Mechanic—Foreign	48	96
General Mechanic—Foreign	60	120
Auto Paint and Refinishing	26	52
Architectural Drafting	30	60

	Length in Weeks	Full Time	Part Time
Architectural-Mechanical Drafting	20	4	
Civil Engineering Drafting	26	5	
Construction Blueprint Reading	4		
Industrial Blueprint Reading	4		
Electro-Mechanical Drafting	21	4	
Industrial Drafting	45	9	
Marine Architectural Drafting	51	10	
Mechanical Drafting	29	5	
Structural Steel Detailing	20	4	
Technical Illustrating	22	4	
Pipefitting	14	2	
Pipefitter/Welder	40	8	
Aircraft & Structural Assembler	4		
Sheet Metal	17	3	
Shipfitting	15	3	
Shipfitter/Welder	25	5	
Shipwright	17	3	
Arc Welding	5	1	
Combination Welding	16	3	
Inert Gas Welding	5	1	
Metal Inert Gas Welding	3		
Pipe Welding	26	5	
Shipyard Arc Welding	11	2	
Steel Burning	4		
Machine & Tool Design	30	6	

Southern California College of Medical and Dental Careers
1717 South Brookhurst Street, Anaheim 92804
Marvin Barab, *Executive Director*
(714) 635-3450, 1964, VA, VR, INS

	Full Time	Part Time
Medical Assistant	28	2
Dental Assistant	28	2
Medical Receptionist	16	2
Crown & Bridge Dental Lab	26	6
Denture Dental Lab	26	6
Crown, Bridge, and Denture	44	11
Porcelain Dental Lab	—	1
Orthodontic Lab	—	1
Crozat Lab	—	1
Emergency Medical Technician	28	

Southland College of Medical-Dental-Legal Careers
8022 East Florence Avenue, Downey 90240
Betty Jean Mocciaro, *Director*
(213) 869-1001, 1971, VR, INS

	Full Time	Part Time
Medical Assisting	29	
Dental Assisting	24	
Legal Secretary	24	

Southland College of Medical and Dental Careers
15610 South Crenshaw Boulevard, Gardena 90249
Fred Sferrazzo, *Director*
(213) 770-0162, 1967, VA, VR, INS, BIA

	Full Time	Part Time
Medical Assisting	28	
Medical Transcriber	16	
Dental Assistant	24	
Inhalation Therapy Technician	46	
Dental Laboratory Technician	36	

Southland College of Medical, Dental and Legal Careers
6363 Wilshire Boulevard, Los Angeles 90048
Dr. Paul Simpson, *Director*
(213) 655-2375, 1961, VA, INS, BIA

	Full Time	Part Time
Dental Laboratorty Technician	36	
Medical Assistant	37	
Dental Assistant	36	
Respiratory Therapy Technician	46	
Medical Transcriber	26	
Operating Room Technician	40	
Hospital Ward Clerk	24	
Nurses Assistant	8	
Legal Scretary	24	

	Full Time	Part Time
Length in Weeks		

Southland College of Medical-Dental-Legal Careers
512 West Beverly Boulevard, Montebello 90640
Lyn Frazier, *Director*
(213) 723-1672, 1962, VA, VR, INS, BIA

	Full Time	Part Time
Medical Assisting	33	–
Medical Secretary	24	–
Dental Assisting	30	–
Inhalation Therapy Technician	46	–
Dental Laboratory Technician	36	–
Legal Secretary	24	–

Transportation Training Corporation
4204 Atlantic Avenue, Long Beach 90807
Randy M. Erickson, *Vice-President*
(213) 426-8841, 1962, VA, VR, INS

	Full Time	Part Time
Travel & Transportation Agent	26	5?
Travel Agent	14	14
Air Freight Sales & Service	7	17½

United Health Careers Institute
1571 North "E" Street, San Bernardino 92405
Robert J. Sedlak, *Director*
(714) 884-8891, 1967, VA, VR, INS, BIA

	Full Time	Part Time
Medical Assistant	32	–
Dental Assistant	28	–
Medical Office Receptionist	28	–
Professional Office Assistant	18/26	–
Emergency Medical/Intensive Care Technician	28	–
Veterinary Assistant	32	–
Vocational Nurse	50	–
Equivalency Vocational Nurse	42	–
Pharmacology for L.V.N.	–	9

Valley College of Medical-Dental Assistants
4150 Lankershim Boulevard, North Hollywood 91602
Ben F. Ostergren, *Registrar*
(213) 766-8151, 1956, VA, VR, INS, BIA

	Full Time	Part Time
Medical Assistant	28	28
Dental Assistant	28	28
Licensed Vocational Nurse	50	–
Respiratory Therapy Technician	40	48
Optical Dispensing	–	25

Welding Trade School
765 Coleman Avenue, San Jose 95110
Donald R. Forth, *Director*
(408) 297-3150, 1966, VA, VR, BIA

	Full Time	Part Time
Combination General & Pipe Welding	26	52
General Welding	16	32
Production Welding	12	24

Western College of Allied Health Careers
4000 El Camino Avenue, Sacramento 95821
Robert F. Annenberg, *Director*
(916) 481-1922, 1967, VA, VR, INS, BIA

	Full Time	Part Time
Dental Assisting	28	38
Medical Assisting	28	38
Medical Office Management	16	19
Animal Health Assistant	36	–
Medical Office Management/ Dental Assisting	40	53

Western College of Medical and Dental Assistants
5434 Van Nuys Boulevard, Van Nuys 91401
Y. Parker, *Director*
(213) 783-6520, 1964, VR, INS, BIA

	Full Time	Part Time
Medical Assisting	24	–
Dental Assisting	13	–

COLORADO

Automation & Training Universal
425 Lincoln Street, Denver 80203
Lincoln A. Salem, *President*
(303) 744-3381, 1964, VA, VR, INS, BIA

	Full Time	Part Time
Keypunch Operator, Clerical	4	8
Tabulating Machine Operator	5	10
Computer-Peripheral Equip. Operator	10	20
Digital Computer Operator	20	40
Detail Computer Programmer	20	40
Computer Programmer	30	60
Systems Programmer	40	80
Scientific Programmer	10	20
Architectural Drafting	32	64
Machine Drafting	32	64
Electronic Drafting	32	64

Ron Bailie School of Broadcast
816 Acoma, Denver 80204
Dennis G. Johnson, *Director*
(303) 573-1040, 1972, VA, VR, INS

	Full Time	Part Time
Announcing Program	28	–
Electronics Theory Program	20	–
Announcing-Electronics Theory Program	48	–

Bel-Rea Institute of Animal Technology
9870 East Alameda, Denver 80231
Nolan C. Rucker, D.V.M., *Director*
(303) 366-2639, 1971, VA, VR

	Full Time	Part Time
Animal Technology	60/72	–

Certified Welding School
2565 South Broadway, Denver 80210
Gordon Bay, *President*
(303) 733-4607, 1966, VA, VR, BIA

	Full Time	Part Time
Combination Weldor Program #1	17	34
Combination Weldor Program #1A	27	54
Combination Weldor Program #2	19½	39
Combination Weldor Program #2A	31	62

Colorado Aero Tech
10851 West 120th Avenue, Broomfield 80020
Richard J. Blair, *President/Director*
(303) 466-1714, 1965, VA, VR, INS, BIA

	Full Time	Part Time
Combination Airframe and Powerplant Maintenance Technician	60	–

Colorado College of Medical and Dental Assistants
445 Grant, Denver 80203
John P. Tromly, *Director*
(303) 778- 8681, 1967, VA, VR

	Full Time	Part Time
Dental Assistant	28	–
Medical Assistant	36	–

Colorado School of Trades
1575 Hoyt Street, Lakewood 80215
John T. Snyder, *Director*
(303) 233-4697, 1947, VA, VR, INS

	Full Time	Part Time
Gunsmithing	69	92

Denver Automotive and Diesel College
460 South Lipan Street, Denver 80223
Ted C. Stone, *Director*
Toll-Free (800) 525-8956, 1963, VA, VR, INS, BIA

	Full Time	Part Time
Automotive Technician	24	48
Body Fender and Painting	24	48
Diesel	12	24

	Length in Weeks	Full Time	Part Time

Denver Institute of Technology
2250 South Tejon Street, Englewood 80110
R. Wade Murphree, *President*
(303) 922-8101, 1953, VA, VR, INS, BIA

	Full Time	Part Time
Electronics Engineering Technician	48	—
General Electronics Technician	48	—
General Auto Mechanics	36	72
Automotive-Parts Counterman	12	24
Motorcycle Maintenance & Repair	12	24
Air Conditioning, Refrigeration & Heating Servicing	24	48
Architectural-Structural Drafting	48	72
Civil Drafting	48	72
Machine Drafting	48	72
Piping Drafting	48	72
Technical Illustration	48	72

Electronic Technical Institute
1070 Bannock Street, Denver 80204
Mary R. Roland, *President*
(303) 222-2503, 1959, VA, VR, INS, BIA

	Full Time	Part Time
Television Technician	52	—
Electronics Technician	52	—
Electronics Technology	104	—
FCC License Preparation	9	—

National Camera Technical Training Division
2000 West Union Avenue, Englewood 80110
Samuel L. Love, *President*
(303) 789-1893, 1952, VA, VR, INS, BIA

	Full Time	Part Time
Photo Equipment Technician (Repairman)	50	100
Basic Skill Camera Technician (Repairman)	26	52
Basic Movie Equipment Technician (Repairman)	16	32

Parks School of Business-Technical Division
1370 Pennsylvania Street, Denver 80203
C. L. Davis, *Director*
(303) 832-9696, 1904, VA, VR, INS, BIA

	Full Time	Part Time
Medical Assistant	48	—
Travel and Transportation Business	24	—

CONNECTICUT

Chester Institute for Technical Education
2945 Main Street, Stratford 06497
W. L. Brown, *Executive Director*
(203) 375-4463, 1966, VA, VR, INS

	Full Time	Part Time
Mechanical and Electronic Design Drafting and Engineering Technology	86	184
Architectural and Civil Design Drafting and Engineering Technology	86	184
Introductory Graphics	—	16
Electro-mechanical Print Reading	—	16
Architectural Print Reading	—	16
Technical Illustration Fundamentals	—	10
Mechanics of Printed Circuit Boards and Electronic Packaging	—	10
Project Management Techniques	—	10
Basic Drafting Techniques	—	25
Mechanical Drafting Fundamentals	—	25
Machinery and Power Linkage Drafting	—	25
Electronic Drafting	—	25
Wood Frame Drafting	—	25
Steel and Masonry Drafting	—	25
Mechanical and Electrical Construction Drafting	—	25

Connecticut School of Electronics
586 Boulevard, New Haven 06519
Kenneth A. Titus, *President*
(203) 624-2121, 1947, VA, VR, INS

	Full Time	Part Time
Electronic Technology	98	—
Electronic Technician	—	148
Algebra Refresher	—	4

Hartford Modern School of Welding
184 Ledyard Street, Hartford 06114
Robert L. Annecharico, *President*
(203) 249-7576, 1971, VA

	Full Time	Part Time
Combination Arc Welding W-122	325	—
Combination Arc Welding W-123	324	—
Certified Pipe Welding	120	—
Advanced Layout Course	20	—

School of the Hartford Ballet
308 Farmington Avenue, Hartford 06105
Enid Lynn, *Director*
(203) 525-9396, 1960, INS

	Full Time	Part Time
Teacher Training Program	64	Max: 160

Paier School of Art
Six Prospect Court, Hamden 06511
Edward T. Paier, *President*
(203) 777-3851, 1946, VA, VR, INS

	Full Time	Part Time
Advertising	136	272
Illustration	136	272
Fine Arts	136	272
Interior Design	102	102
Photography	68	136
Technical Illustration	—	68

Porter School of Drafting and Design
P.O. Box 330, 2123 Silas Deane Highway, Rocky Hill 06067
W. L. Brown, *Executive Director*
(203) 529-2519, 1945, VA, VR, INS

	Full Time	Part Time
Mechanical & Electronic Design Drafting & Engineering Technology	86	184
Architectural & Civil Design Drafting & Engineering Technology	86	184
Introductory Graphics	—	16
Electro-mechanical Print Reading	—	16
Architectural Print Reading	—	16
Technical Illustration Fundamentals	—	10
Mechanics of Printed Circuit Boards & Electronic Packaging	—	10
Project Management Techniques	—	10
Basic Drafting Techniques	—	25
Mechanical Drafting Fundamentals	—	25
Machinery & Power Linkage Drafting	—	25
Electronic Drafting	—	25
Wood Frame Drafting	—	25
Steel and Masonry Drafting	—	25
Mechanical & Electrical Construction Drafting	—	25

Technical Careers Institute
80 Erna Avenue, Milford 06460
Bradley R. Baran, *Director*
(203) 877-1279, 1970, VA, VR, INS, BIA

	Full Time	Part Time
Welding	16	—
Automotive Mechanics	37	83
Air Conditioning/Refrigeration	37	83
Major Appliance Repair	25	52

DISTRICT OF COLUMBIA

Lacaze Academy—Technical Division
710 14th Street, N.W., Washington 20005
Daniel Grossman, *Director*
(202) 347-6868, 1948, VA, VR, INS

	Full Time	Part Time
Engineering Drafting Technology	36	96
TV-Radio Servicing	30	65

Lewis Hotel-Motel School
2301 Pennsylvania Avenue, N.W., Washington 20037
Joseph L. Ferrare, *President*
(202) 333-4692, 1916, VA, VR, INS, BIA

	Full Time	Part Time
Hotel/Restaurant Management	24/26	48/50

	Length in Weeks	Full Time	Part Time
Food/Beverage Management		12/14	24/26
Front Office & Resident Management Operations		12/14	24/26
International Travel and Secretarial		30	—

Lincoln Technical Institute
7800 Central Avenue, Washington 20027
Louis R. Hernandez, *Director*
(301) 336-7250, 1960, VA, VR, INS

	Full Time	Part Time
Automotive Technology	36	112½
Engine Tune-up	12	37½
Automatic Transmissions	8	25
Auto Air Conditioning	4	12½
Air Conditioning, Refrigeration and Heating	40	150
Heating System Service	12	37½

FLORIDA

Art Institute of Fort Lauderdale
3000 East Las Olas Boulevard, Fort Lauderdale 33316
Mark K. Wheeler, *President*
(305) 463-3000, 1968, VA, VR, INS

	Full Time	Part Time
Advertising Design	96	—
Interior Design	96	—
Fashion Illustration	96	—
Photography	96	—
Fashion Merchandising	72	—

Bauder Fashion College
300 Biscayne Boulevard Way, Miami 33131
Maria Kettle Floyd, *Director*
(305) 371-1508, 1963, VA, VR, INS

	Full Time	Part Time
Fashion Merchandising & Interior Design	35	—
Fashion Merchandising (Associate degree)	70	—
Interior Design (Associate degree)	70	—

Brown Institute
111 N.E. 44th Street, Fort Lauderdale 33334
Ty Mack, *Director*
(305) 772-0280, 1969, VA, VR, INS, BIA

	Full Time	Part Time
First Class FCC License	10	14
Radio-TV Broadcasting	30	40

Charron Williams College—Paramedical Division
2100 West Flagler Street, Miami 33135
Irving Goldstein, *President*
(305) 642-4601, 1951, VA, VR, INS

	Full Time	Part Time
Medical Assistant	24	48
Clinical Laboratory Technician	64	128
Medical Transcriber	16	—
Medical Secretary	24	—
Dental Technician	48	96

FlightSafety International
P.O. Box 2708, Municipal Airport, Vero Beach 32960
James T. Ueltschi, *Manager*
(305) 567-5178, 1966, VA, INS

	Full Time	Part Time
Private Pilot	4-5	—
Commercial Pilot	12	—
Instrument Rating	4-5	—
Multi-Engine Rating	1-2	—
Flight Instructor—Airplane Rating	4-5	—
Flight Instructor—Instrument Rating	3-4	—
Airline Transport Pilot	4	—

Garces Commercial College
1301 S.W. First Street, Miami 33135
Pelayo G. Garces, *Director*
(305) 643-1044, 1961, VA, VR, INS

	Full Time	Part Time
Architectural Drafting	82	—
Mechanical Drafting	74	—

	Length in Weeks	Full Time	Part Time
Interior Decoration		78	—
Computer Programming and Operation		91	—
Medical Secretary		104	—

International Fine Arts College
1737 North Bayshore Drive, Miami 33132
Edward Porter, *President*
(305) 373-4684, 1965, VA, VR, INS

	Full Time	Part Time
Associate degree in Fashion and Merchandising	72	—
Associate degree in Interior Design	72	—

International Technical Institute
2602 North 43rd Street, Tampa 33605
Larry J. Nero, *Director*
(813) 621-3566, 1970, VA, VR, INS

	Full Time	Part Time
Air Conditioning & Refrigeration Technology	36	—
Auto Mechanics	50	—
Auto Mechanics & Diesel	63	—
Diesel Engine Mechanics	13	—
Air Conditioning & Refrigeration Mechanics	—	50
Automotive & Diesel Mechanics	—	50

Tampa Technical Institute
1005 East Jackson Street, Tampa 33602
D. John Benanti, *President*
(813) 223-1637, 1948, VA, VR, INS

	Full Time	Part Time
Computer Engineering Technology	72	—
Electronic Engineering Technology	60	—
Architectural Drafting & Design	72	—
Architectural Drafting Technology	60	—
Structural Drafting & Design	72	—
Structural Drafting Technology	60	—
Mechanical Drafting Technology	72	—
Technical Illustration	72	—

United Electronics Institute
303 West Platt Street, Tampa 33606
M. B. Robbins, *President*
(813) 253-6078, 1967, VA, VR, INS

	Full Time	Part Time
Electronics Technology	99	79

GEORGIA

Academy of Professional Drafting
1655 Peachtree Street, N.E., Atlanta 30309
Vida G. Roberts, *Director*
(404) 874-5278, 1967, VA, VR, INS

	Full Time	Part Time
Electro Mechanical Drafting	40	52
Machine Drawing	40	52
Electrical Drafting	40	52
Architectural Drafting	40	52
Advanced Architectural Drafting	40	52
Technical Illustrating	20	26
Blueprint Reading & Estimating	40	52

Art Institute of Atlanta
3376 Peachtree Street, N.E., Atlanta 30326
E. Wade Close, Jr., *President*
(404) 266-1341, 1949, VA, VR, INS

	Full Time	Part Time
Commercial Art	72/96	—
Photography	72/96	—
Interior Design	96	—
Fashion Merchandising	72	—
Fashion Illustration	72/96	—
Fashion Design	72/96	—

Atlanta College of Medical and Dental Assistants
1280 West Peachtree Street, N.E., Atlanta 30309
Fred W. Rich, *President*
(404) 873-1701, 1961, VA, VR, INS

	Full Time	Part Time
Medical Laboratory Technician	52	—
Dental Laboratory Technician	52/78	—

Length in Weeks	Full Time	Part Time
Medical Assisting	36	54
Dental Assisting	28	52
Medical-Dental Receptionist/Secretary	28	52

Bauder Fashion College
3355 Lenox Street, N.E., Atlanta 30326
Maria Kettle Floyd, *Director*
(404) 237-7573, 1954, VA, VR, INS

Length in Weeks	Full Time	Part Time
Fashion Merchandising & Interior Design	33	—
Double Major (Fashion Merchandising & Modeling)	33	—
Fashion Merchandising major (Second Year)	33	—
Interior Design major (Second Year)	33	—

The Bryman School
1285 West Peachtree, Atlanta 30309
Robert A. Smith, *Director*
(404) 876-6741, 1971, VR

Length in Weeks	Full Time	Part Time
Medical Assistant	28	46
Dental Assistant	20	32
Medical Office Management	16	25

Control Data Institute
3330 Peachtree Road, N.E., Atlanta 30326
I. D. Bill Williams, *Director*
(404) 261-7700, 1968, VA, VR, INS

Length in Weeks	Full Time	Part Time
Computer Technology	25	42
Computer Programming & Operations	26	36

DeVry Institute of Technology
828 West Peachtree Street, N.W., Atlanta 30308
H. B. Overton, *President*
(404) 892-8611, 1969, VA, VR, INS

Length in Weeks	Full Time	Part Time
Electronics Technician	72	—
Electronics Engineering Technology	108	—

IDAHO

Aero Technicians
P.O. Box 7 Rexburg-Madison County Airport, Rexburg 83440
Eldon C. Hart, *President*
(208) 356-4446, 1973, VA, VR, INS

Length in Weeks	Full Time	Part Time
Aviation Maintenance Technician	50	—
Private Pilot	4/20	—
Commercial Pilot	15/60	—
Instrument Rating	4/15	—
Flight Instructor	4/15	—
Instrument Flight Instructor	3/6	—
Multi-engine Rating	2/4	—
Airline Transport Rating	2/8	—
Aerial Applicator	4/20	—
Helicopter	Vairable	—

ILLINOIS

Allied Institute of Technology
1020 South Wabash Avenue, Chicago 60605
Albert L. Molter, *Director*
(312) 427-3915, 1929, VA, VR

Length in Weeks	Full Time	Part Time
Automotive Technology	30	45

American Academy of Art
220 South State Street, Chicago 60604
I. Shapiro, *Director*
(312) 939-3883, 1923, VA, VR, INS, BIA

Length in Weeks	Full Time	Part Time
Art Fundamentals	40	80
Figure Drawing	40	80
Advertising Design	40	80
Illustration	40	80
Lettering and Design	40	80
Photography	80	—
Architectural Rendering	40	80

Length in Weeks	Full Time	Part Time
Oil Painting	40	80
Watercolor	40	80
Interior Design	—	80
Fashion & Merchandise Illustration	40	—

The Bryman School
140 South Dearborn, Chicago 60603
Jerome E. Jaros, *Director*
(312) 368-4911, 1968, VR, INS

Length in Weeks	Full Time	Part Time
Medical Assisting	28	44
Dental Assisting	20	44
Medical Office Management	16	—

Control Data Institute
200 North Michigan Avenue, Chicago 60601
James E. Cobis, Sr., *Director*
(312) 454-6888, 1957, VA, VR, INS

Length in Weeks	Full Time	Part Time
Computer Technology	25	40
Computer Programming and Operations	21.7	38
Business Machines Service	20.8	33

Coyne American Institute
1235 West Fullerton Avenue, Chicago 60614
H. H. Katz, *Director*
(312) 935-2520, 1899, VA, VR, INS, BIA

Length in Weeks	Full Time	Part Time
Electrical Maintenance	36	36
Air Conditioning, Refrigeration & Heating	36	36
Industrial Electronics	48	48
Drafting	36	—

DeVry Institute of Technology
3300 North Campbell, Chicago 60618
Samuel R. Edmonds, *President*
(312) 929-8500, 1931, VA, VR, INS, BIA

Length in Weeks	Full Time	Part Time
Bachelors of Electronics Engineering Technology	144	—
Electronics Engineering Technology (Associate Degree)	108	—
Electronics Technician	72	—
Television and Radio	—	96
Computer Technology	—	96
Radio-Television, Electronics Instrumentation and Controls, and Electronics Communications	—	120
Radio-Television, Electronics Instrumentation and Controls, Electronic Communications, and Computer Technology	—	144

Electronics Technical Institute
37 South Wabash, Chicago 60603
Harold M. Rabin, *President*
(312) 332-3727, 1950, VA, VR, INS, BIA

Length in Weeks	Full Time	Part Time
Electromechanical Computer Engineering Technology (Associate Degree)	72	—
Electronics Technology	50	106
Color TV-Radio Servicing	26	48/56
Electronic Servicing	26	56
Drafting Technology	26	56

Gem City College—School of Horology
700 State Street, Quincy 62301
Warner W. Johnson, *Director*
(217) 222-0391, 1886, VA, VR, INS

Length in Weeks	Full Time	Part Time
Watchmaking & Repairing	60	—
Clock Repairing	6	—
Engraving	12	—
Advanced Engraving	12	—
Jewelry Diamond-Setting	12	—
Jewelry Designing & Manufacturing	12	—
Jewelry Store Management	116	—
Complete Horologist	114	—

	Length in Weeks	Full Time	Part Time
Greer Technical Institute			
7320 West Agatite Avenue, Norridge 60656			
George W. Cates, *Director*			
(312) 625-1535, 1902, VA, VR, INS, BIA			
Automotive Diesel Technology		40	80
Automotive Technology		30	60
Diesel & Gasoline Power Plant			
Specialist		25	50
Refrigeration, Air Conditioning			
& Heating		30	60
Automotive Body & Fender Repair		20	40
Ray-Vogue School			
750 North Michigan Avenue, Chicago 60611			
Wade Ray, *Director*			
(312) 787-5117, 1916, VA, VR, INS, BIA			
Commercial Art		80	—
Interior Design		80	—
Fashion Art		80	—
Dress Design		80	—
Photography		40	—
Fashion Merchandising		40	—
Display		40	—
Robert Morris School			
College Avenue, Carthage 62321			
R. McCartan, *President*			
(217) 357-2121, 1972, VA, VR, INS			
Medical Assisting		30	—
Dental Assisting		36	—

INDIANA

	Length in Weeks	Full Time	Part Time
Indiana Barber College			
536 East Washington Street, Indianapolis 46219			
Kenneth L. Fleener, *Director*			
(317) 356-8222, 1959, VA, VR			
Barber Science		38	50
ITT Technical Institute			
1 South Lincoln Park Drive, Evansville 47714			
Alphonse W. Guimont, *Center Director*			
(812) 479-1441, 1959, VA, VR, INS, BIA			
Electronic Service Technician		—	50
Industrial Electronics		—	40
Electronic Technology		50	—
Electronics Engineering Technology		100	—
Motorcycle Mechanics		—	26
Data Processing and Computer Programming		26	—
ITT Technical Institute			
415 Profit Drive, Fort Wayne 46808			
W. Lauer, *Director*			
(219) 484-4107, 1967, VA, VR, INS			
Electronics Engineering Technology		100	—
Architectural Engineering Technology		100	—
ITT Technical Institute			
720 East 38th Street, Indianapolis 46218			
Donald L. Hendrickson, *Director*			
(317) 545-2231, 1956, VA, VR, INS, BIA			
Air Conditioning, Heating & Refrigeration		50	—
Architectural Engineering Technology		100	—
Electronics Engineering Technology		100	—
Electronics Technology		50	50
Lincoln Technical Institute			
201 Stadium Drive, Indianapolis 46202			
Gary Updike, *Assistant Director*			
(317) 632-5553, 1961, VA, VR, INS			
Automotive and Diesel Truck Technology		70	—
Diesel and Truck Technology		52	—
Automotive Technology		50	—

	Length in Weeks	Full. Time	Part Time
Scientific Engine Tune-up		15	30
Diesel		10	20
Transmissions		10	20
Air Conditioning		5	10
Truck Drive Trains & Chassis		10	20
Midwestern College of Industrial Arts &			
Sciences, 130 East Lewis, Fort Wayne 46802			
Martin F. Pane, *Director*			
(219) 424-1610, 1956, VA, VR, INS			
Tool and Die Design		108	—
Plastics Mold Design		—	48
Professional Careers Institute			
5310 East 38th Street, Indianapolis 46218			
Harold N. Weiss, *Director*			
(347) 545-7291, 1967, VA, VR, INS			
Medical Assistant		32	38
Dental Assistant		32	53
Paramedical Office			
Management		28	30

IOWA

	Length in Weeks	Full. Time	Part Time
Academy of Radio and Television Electronics			
1304 State Street, Bettendorf 52722			
Chuck Hamilton, *Director*			
(319) 359-7571, 1971, VA, VR			
Modern Broadcasting		16	—
Communications Technology		16	—
Electronics Technology		48	—
Modern Broadcasting/FCC Licensing		24	—
Television Servicing/FCC Licensing		24	—
Iowa School of Men's Hairstyling			
603 East 6th Street, Des Moines 50316			
Bert B. Millis, *Owner*			
(515) 244-0971, 1899, VA, VR			
Barber		47	—
Lincoln Technical Institute			
2501 Vine Street, West Des Moines 50265			
William S. Clark, *Director*			
(515) 225-8433, 1965, VA, VR, INS			
Automotive/Diesel Technology		65	—
Automotive Technology		50	—
United Electronics Institute			
1105 Fifth Street, West Des Moines 50265			
Harley Homewood, *Director*			
(515) 274-1720, 1964, VA, VR, INS			
Electronics Technology		91	—
Basic Electronics, Radio & TV		80	—

KANSAS

	Length in Weeks	Full. Time	Part Time
Bryan Institute			
3216 East Douglas, Wichita 67208			
Harry W. Dickerson, *President*			
(316) 685-2284, 1968, VA, VR, INS, BIA			
Computer Programming		32	—
Keypunch		12	—
Medical Assisting		25	—
Dental Assisting		25	—
Climate Control Institute			
2425 East Douglas, Wichita 67211			
Dean E. Newberry, *President*			
(316) 686-7355, 1971, VA, VR, INS, BIA			
Air Conditioning-Heating-Refrigeration		26	47

	Length in Weeks	Full Time	Part Time
Electronic Computer Programming Institute 3600 Topeka Boulevard, Topeka 66611 Ralph G. Denny, *Director* (913) 266-3180, 1968, VA, VR, INS, BIA			
Computer Programming and Data Processing	20/22		32
Electronic Computer Programming Institute 300 West Douglas, Wichita 67202 Walter S. Johnson, *Director* (316) 263-0276, 1968, VA, VR, INS, BIA			
Computer Programming	54		54
Wichita Automotive Institute 4011 East 31st South, Wichita 67210 John S. Poston, *President* (316) 682-6548, 1964, VA, VR, INS, BIA			
Technology of Auto Mechanics— Engine Overhaul & Rebuilding, Tune-up, Electrical, Carburetion, Electrical Trouble Shooting & Air Conditioning Automatic Transmissions, Suspension Systems, Brakes, Alignment & Drivelines	48		—
Service Writer	18		—
Automotive Parts Counter Person	24		—
Auto Body, Frame and Painting	48		—
Wichita Technical Insitute 942 South West Street, Wichita 67213 Paul D. Moore, *President* (316) 943-2241, 1954, VA, VR, INS			
Electronics Technology	104		208
Electronic Communications	85		170
Industrial Electronics and Automation	85		170
Consumer Electronics Servicing	68		136

KENTUCKY

	Length in Weeks	Full Time	Part Time
Institute of Electronic Technology 1301 Broadway, Paducah 42001 Hal Brown, *President* (502) 444-9676, 1964, VA, VR, INS			
Electronic Engineering Technology	100		—
Louisville Technical Institute 3101 Bardstown Road, Louisville 40205 William F. Robinson, II, *Director* (502) 456-6509, 1961, VA, VR, INS			
Design Drafting	48		72
Engineering Technology	—		60
United Electronics Institute 3947 Park Drive, Louisville 40216 W. O. Reidinger, *Director* (502) 448-5304, 1946, VA, VR, INS			
Electronics Technology	91		—
Basic Electronics, Radio & TV	80		—
Medical Assistant	48		—
Medical Lab Technician	72		—

LOUISIANA

	Length in Weeks	Full Time	Part Time
CBM Education Center 2840 Florida Boulevard, Baton Rouge 70802 John W. Brewer, *Executive Director* (504) 343-9254, 1969, VA, VR, INS			
D.P. 101 Keypunch Verifier	6		—
D.P. 111 Operations	16		—
D.P. 112 Programming	29		—
D.P. 113 Oper/Prog	29		—
D.P. 201 Office Spec.	30		—
D.P. 201-S Office Spec.	44		—
D.T. 100 Basic & Advanced	16		<
D.T. 200 Basic & Advanced	32		-
Med. Sec. Rec.	32		-
Nurses Assistant/Ward Clerk	32		-
Paramedical Career Academy 745 Laurel Street, Baton Rouge 70802 Jim E. Hodges, *Administrator* (504) 383-5601, 1971, VA, VR			
Nurse's Assistant	17		28
Doctor's Assistant	21		38
Ward Clerk	23		38
Medical Receptionist	34		56
Emergency Medical Technician	31		51
R.E.T.S. Training Center 4141 Washington Avenue, New Orleans 70125 M. J. LaRue, *Director* (504) 822-2020, 1964, VA, VR, INS			
Electronics Engineering Technology	72		—
Advanced Solid State	50		—

MARYLAND

	Length in Weeks	Full Time	Part Time
Airco Technical Institute 121 Kane Street, Baltimore 21224 James H. Ethridge, *Administrator* (301) 633-4300, 1972, VA, VR, INS			
Combination Welding	13		2
Shipyard Welding	13		2
Shipfitting	13		2
Comprehensive Welding	26		<
Arundel Institute of Technology 5101 Andard Avenue, Baltimore 21226 Manfred Bloch, *Director* (301) 355-1100, 1969, VA, VR, INS			
Communications & Computer Electronics	48		96
Architectural (Drafting) Technology	48		96
Lincoln Technical Institute 3200 Wilkens Avenue, Baltimore 21229 Ralph W. Crews, *Director* (301) 646-5480, 1961, VA, VR, INS			
Automotive Technology	45		<
Auto Mechanics	30		7
Scientific Engine Tune-up	15		3
Automatic Transmissions	10		2
Automotive Air Conditioning	5		1
Maryland Drafting Institute 2045 University Boulevard East, Langley Park 20783 C. B. Sawyer, *Director of Administration* (301) 439-7776, 1968, VA, VR, INS			
Engineering Drafting Technology	48		96
Architectural Drafting Technology	36		72
Mechanical Drafting Technology	36		72
Specialized Architectural Drafting	—		54
Specialized Mechanical Drafting	—		54
Maryland Medical Secretarial School 441-449 North Potomac Street, Hagerstown 21740 David G. Drawbaugh, Jr., *Director* (301) 739-2670, 1938, VA, VR			
Medical Secretarial	80		<
Technical Medical Stenographic	62		<
The Medix School 32 West Road, Baltimore 21204 Jack F. Tolbert, *President* (301) 821-5222, 1969, VA, VR			
Medical Assisting	28		4
Dental Assisting	16		3
Medical/Dental Receptionist	16		3

	Length in Weeks	Full Time	Part Time
Professional Institute of Commercial Art			
4020 Clarks Lane, Baltimore 21215			
Mary Fleck Wise, *Owner-Director*			
(301) 358-6311, 1965, VA, VR, INS			
Basic Commercial Art, Fashion			
Illustration, and Advertising	52	104	
Cartooning	16	32	
Animation	20	40	
Production	12	24	
R.E.T.S. Electronic School			
511 Russell Street (Balto.-Wash. Pkwy.), Baltimore 21230			
H. V. Leslie, *President*			
(301) 727-6863, 1956, VA, VR, INS			
Electronic Engineering Technology	96	–	
Practical Electronics Servicing	48	–	
Color TV Servicing	–	52	
TESST Electronic School			
5114 Baltimore Avenue, Hyattsville 20781			
Wayne Moore, *Administrator*			
(301) 864-5750, 1968, VA, VR, INS			
TESST TWO (Engineering Technician)	100	–	
Solid State Electronics Analyst	–	60	
Digital Electronic Concepts and			
Applications	–	20	
Introduction to Solid State			
Electronics	–	10	

MASSACHUSETTS

	Length in Weeks	Full Time	Part Time
The Art Institute of Boston			
700 Beacon Street, Boston 02215			
William H. Willis, Jr., *Director*			
(617) 262-1223, 1912, VA, VR, INS			
Advertising Design	102	–	
Illustration	102	–	
Photography	102	–	
Painting	102	–	
Sculpture	102	–	
Printmaking	102	–	
Ceramics	102	–	
Technical Illustration	–	68	
Cartooning	–	68	
Associated Technical Institute			
19 Dover Street, Somerville 02144			
Brian Matza, *Director*			
(617) 625-7700, 1972, VA, VR, INS			
Air Conditioning and Refrigeration	50	–	
Air Conditioning and Refrigeration			
(modified)	74	–	
Refrigeration and Air Conditioning Servicing	–	50	
The Bryman School			
623 Boylston Street, Brookline 02146			
Maritza Samoorian, *Director*			
(617) 232-6035, 1970, VR, INS			
Dental Assisting	20	32	
Medical Assisting	28	46	
Medical Office Management	16	25	
Control Data Institute			
20 North Avenue, Burlington 01803			
Larry F. Clark, *Director*			
(617) 272-4070, 1965, VA, VR, INS			
Computer Technology	25	42	
Computer Programming & Operations	26	36	
Digital Computer Operations	20	26	

	Length in Weeks	Full Time	Part Time
Coyne Electrical and Technical School			
100 Massachusetts Avenue, Boston 02115			
Francis J. Hickey, *Director*			
(617) 267-3015, 1896, VA, VR, INS			
Practical Electricity with Industrial			
Electronics, Electrical Layout,			
Estimating and Drafting	78	–	
Practical Electricity with Industrial			
Electronics	–	78	
National Electrical Code Course	–	13	
East Coast Aero Technical School			
Hanscom Field, Box 426, Lexington 02173			
John T. Griffin, *President*			
(617) 274-6400, 1932, VA, VR, INS			
Airframe & Powerplant Technician Training	75	–	
ITT Technical Institute			
45 Spruce Street, Chelsea 02150			
William C. Fennelly, *Center Director*			
(617) 889-3600, 1936, VA, VR, INS			
Drafting	48	–	
Automotive Mechanics	41	–	
Leland Powers School			
452 Beacon Street, Boston 02115			
Donald V. Baker, III, *President*			
(617) 247-1300, 1904, VA, VR, INS, BIA			
Radio TV Broadcasting	30	–	
Theatre Acting	30	–	
Massachusetts Radio and Electronics School			
271 Huntington Avenue, Boston 02115			
Frederick J. Aloi, Director			
(617) 266-1010, 1899, VA, VR, INS			
Electronic Technician	50	–	
Electronic Service Technician			
Radio & TV Servicing	–	50	
Solid State & Digital Electronics	–	25	
New England Appliance Service School			
1018 Commonwealth Avenue, Boston 02215			
Darrell C. Hoag, *Director*			
(617) 232-8875, 1966, VA, VR, INS			
Appliance Repair including			
Refrigeration & Air Conditioning	26	82	
New England School of Art and Design			
28 Newbury Street, Boston 02116			
J. W. S. Cox, *President*			
(617) 536-0383,-0460,-0461,-0494, 1923, VA, VR, INS			
Foundational Year	32	–	
Graphic Design	64	–	
Environmental Design	64	–	
Fine Arts	64	–	
Fashion Illustration	64	–	
Northeast Broadcasting School			
282 Marlborough Street, Boston 02116			
Victor S. Best, *President*			
(617) 267-7910, 1962, VA, VR, INS			
Radio-TV Broadcasting	30	30	
Northeast Institute of Industrial Technology			
41 Phillips Street, Boston 02114			
John W. Hoffman, *President*			
(617) 523-2813, 1942, VA, VR, INS			
Refrigeration and Air Conditioning Technology	45	60	
Electronics Technology	45	60	
Drafting and Design Technology	45	60	
Architectural Drafting	–	30	
Electronic-Electrical Drafting	–	30	
Piping Drafting	–	30	

	Length in Weeks	Full Time	Part Time
Automatic Oil Heating		6	30
Electronics Instrumentation		–	15
Electrical Technology		45	60

R.E.T.S. Electronic School
965 Commonwealth Avenue, Boston 02215
Henry J. Renzi, *Director*
(617) 783-1197, 1958, VA, VR, INS

	Full Time	Part Time
Electronic Technician	72	–

Sylvania Technical School
63 Second Avenue, Waltham 02154
Lewis W. Snow, *Director*
(617) 890-7711, 1970, VA, VR, INS

	Full Time	Part Time
Computer Electronics	24	58
Communications Electronics	30	72
Radio/Television Electronics	30	72

United Technical School
17-23 Morgan Street, Springfield 01107
John M. Dooley, *President*
(413) 733-0081, 1964, VA, VR

	Full Time	Part Time
Auto Mechanics	38	65
Auto Body	30	84
Scientific Tune-up	–	40
Automatic Transmissions	–	40
Auto Air Conditioning	–	40

Vesper George School of Art
44 Saint Botolph Street, Boston 02116
Fletcher P. Adams, *President*
(617) 267-2045, 1924, VA, VR, INS

	Full Time	Part Time
Basic Art	32	–
Commercial Art	64	–
Interior Design	64	–
Fine Arts	64	–

MICHIGAN

Allied Careers Institute
637 East Eight Mile Road, Hazel Park 48030
Richard E. LaDuke, *President*
(313) 543-0432, 1938, VA, VR, INS, BIA

	Full Time	Part Time
Industrial Technology—First Term (Time & Motion Study)	13	40
Industrial Technology—Second Term (Process & Cost Estimating)	13	40
Design Technology—First Term	20	40
Design Technology—Second Term	19	40
Machine Tool Making—First Term	14	52
Machine Tool Making—Second Term	14	52
Mathematics, Drafting & Tool Design	–	52
Mathematics, Drafting & Die Design	–	52
Industrial Blueprint Reading	–	25
Basic Shop Mathematics	–	10
Mechanical Drafting & Basic Shop Mathematics	–	40

Carnegie Institute of Detroit
200 Park Avenue Building, Detroit 48226
James F. McEachern, *Administrative Director*
(313) 963-2774, 1947, VA, VR, INS

	Full Time	Part Time
Medical Assistant	48	–
Medical Laboratory Assistant	–	48
Medical Receptionist-Secretary	24	–

Control Data Institute
23775 Northwestern Highway, Southfield 48075
F. R. Martin, Sr., *Director*
(313) 444-1044, 1967, VA, VR, INS

	Full Time	Part Time
Computer Technology	25	41.6
Computer Programming and Operations	26	36.1

Detroit Engineering Institute
2030 Grand River, Detroit 48226
F. E. Lamb, *President*
(313) 961-7540, 1910, VA, VR, INS

	Full Time	Part Time
Mechanical Engineering Technology	108	150
Design Engineering Technology	108	150
Air Conditioning, Refrigeration and Heating Servicing	50	90
Temperature Engineering Technology	72	104
Technical Illustration	72	104

Detroit Institute of Aeronautics
Willow Run Airport, Ypsilanti 48197
Lee R. Koepke, *President*
(313) 483-3758, 1969, VA, VR, INS

	Full Time	Part Time
Airframe Course	42	84
Powerplant Course	43	86
Airframe & Powerplant Course	64	128

Flint Institute of Barbering
3214 Flushing Road, Flint 48504
John L. Ayre, *President*
(313) 234-2741, 1925, VA, VR

	Full Time	Part Time
Barbering and Men's Hairstyling	52	–

Institute of Computer Technology
14650 West Eight Mile Road, Oak Park 48237
Harry M. Borcherding, *Director*
(313) 967-1107, 1964, VR, INS

	Full Time	Part Time
Data Processing Generalist	39	82
Advanced Data Processing Specialist	77	162
Computer Programming	26	54
Special Languages Electives	28	57
Seminar Topics Electives	50	103
Keypunch Operation	5	8
Data Control	3	7
Data Librarian	1	2
Console Operation	4	9

Kendall School of Design
1110 College, N.E., Grand Rapids 49503
Phyllis Danielson, *President*
(616) 451-2886, 1928, VA, VR, INS, BIA

	Full Time	Part Time
Advertising Design	90	–
Furniture Design	90	–
Illustration	90	–
Interior Design	90	–

Michigan Career Institute
14486 Gratiot Avenue, Detroit 48205
Richard N. Diggs, *President*
(313) 372-0404, 1965, VA, VR, INS

	Full Time	Part Time
Advanced Auto Mechanics	48	90
Basic Auto Mechanics	36	60
Engine Tune-up	18	30
Automatic Transmissions	12	30
Automotive Air Conditioning	–	20
Diesel Mechanics	18	30
Motorcycle Mechanics	12	30

MoTech Automotive Education Center
35155 Industrial Road, Livonia 48150
W. R. DeBusk, *Manager*
(313) 522-9510, 1973, VA, VR

	Full Time	Part Time
Automotive Mechanics	50	–
Auto Body Repair	26	–

R.E.T.S. Electronic School
1625 East Grand Boulevard, Detroit 48211
Laurence R. Howard, *President*
(313) 925-5600, 1935, VA, VR, INS, BIA

	Full Time	Part Time
Electronic Engineering Technology	108	–
Specialized Electronics Servicing	50	–
Color Television Servicing	52	–

	Length in Weeks	Full Time	Part Time
R.E.T.S. Electronic School			
823 28th Street, S.W., Wyoming 49509			
David L. Withers, *President*			
(616) 538-3170, 1956, VA, VR			
Electronic Engineering Technology	36	–	
Color Television Servicing	–	52	
United Electronics Institute			
3013 Eastern Avenue, S.E., Grand Rapids 49508			
Kyle Hickam, *Director*			
(616) 452-1458, 1968, VA, VR			
Electronics Technology	84	–	

MINNESOTA

	Length in Weeks	Full Time	Part Time
Brown Institute			
3123 East Lake Street, Minneapolis 55406			
Richard C. Brown, *Director*			
(612) 721-2481, 1946, VA, VR, INS, BIA			
Radio-TV Broadcasting	40	54	
Advanced Television	8	10	
FCC License	16	–	
Computer Programming	25	50	
Electronics Technology 220	98	160	
Electronics Technology 440	84	140	
Communication Technology	62	100	
Computer Technology	62	100	
Bio-Medical Electronics Technology	62	100	
Color TV Technology	62	100	
Audio Recording Technology	62	100	
Control Data Institute			
1001 Washington Avenue North, Minneapolis 55401			
N. L. Blaede, *Director*			
(612) 339-8282, 1965, VA, VR, INS, BIA			
Computer Technology	25	42	
Computer Operations	16	–	
Computer Programming and Operations	22	36	
Dunwoody Industrial Institute			
818 Wayzata Boulevard, Minneapolis 55403			
John P. Walsh, *President*			
(612) 374-5800, 1914, VA, VR, INS, BIA			
Air Conditioning Technology	72	–	
Architectural Drafting	72	–	
Auto Body Repair & Painting	72	–	
Automobile Mechanics	72	–	
Baking	40	–	
Electrical Construction & Maintenance	72	–	
Computer Technology	72	–	
Electronics Technology	72	–	
Civil Technology and Land Surveying	72	–	
Machine—Tool, Die, and Mold Making	72	–	
Machine Drafting and Design	72	–	
Printing	72	–	
Refrigeration & Appliance Repair	72	–	
Sheet Metal	72	–	
Welding	72	–	
Elkins Institute			
4103 East Lake Street, Minneapolis 55406			
S. R. Gardiner, *Director*			
(612) 721-1687, 1964, VA, VR, INS, BIA			
Radio Licensing	–	8	
Radio Broadcasting	–	16	
Radio Broadcasting-Licensing	–	24	
Radio-Television Repair	–	24	
Radio Operator Licensing—Radio-			
Television Repair	–	32	
Fundamentals of Professional Photography	–	24	
Photographic Retouching and Spotting	–	8	

	Length in Weeks	Full Time	Part Time
Humboldt Institute			
2201 Blaisdell Avenue, South, Minneapolis 55404			
Robert T. Wilson, *Director*			
(612) 339-9287, 1895, VA, VR, INS, BIA			
International Travel & Secretarial	30	–	
Travel & Transportation Management	30	36	
Dental Laboratory Technician	48	–	
Lakeland Medical-Dental Academy			
1402 West Lake Street, Minneapolis 55408			
S. L. Troup, *President*			
(612) 827-3876, 1958, VA, VR, INS, BIA			
Medical Laboratory Technician	48	–	
Medical Assistant-Receptionist	32	–	
Dental Assistant-Receptionist	32	–	
The McConnell School			
1030 Nicollet Avenue, Minneapolis 55403			
William McKay, *President*			
(612) 335-4238, 1937, VA, VR, INS			
Travel Career Training	12/28	–	
Minneapolis Drafting School			
3407 Chicago Avenue, Minneapolis 55407			
Robert X. Casserly, *Director*			
(612) 824-8321, 1961, VA, VR, INS, BIA			
Architectural & Structural Drafting	30	60	
Architectural & Structural Drafting	60	120	
Mechanical & Electronic Drafting	30	60	
Mechanical & Electronic Drafting	60	120	
Minnesota Institute of Medical and Dental Assistants			
2915 Wayzata Boulevard, Minneapolis 55405			
Etta C. Erickson, *Director*			
(612) 374-2742, 1968, VA, VR, INS			
Medical Assistant	32	–	
Dental Assistant	28	–	
Medical Secretary	20	–	
Northwest Technical Institute			
7600 Highway # 7, Minneapolis 55426			
Norris Nelson, *President*			
(612) 933-2233, 1957, VA, VR, INS			
Engineering Drafting and Design	64	–	
Structo-Architectural Drafting & Design	64	–	
Northwestern Electronics Institute			
3800 Minnehaha Avenue, South, Minneapolis 55406			
Clifford L. Larson, *President*			
(612) 721-2469, 1930, VA, VR, INS, BIA			
Associate in Electronics Technology Degree	96	–	
Computer Technician	72	–	
Radio-Television Technician	72	–	
Industrial Electronics Technician	60	–	
Digital Electronics Specialist	–	96	
Electronics Technician	–	144	
Television Specialist	–	96	

MISSISSIPPI

	Length in Weeks	Full Time	Part Time
Phillips College—Technical Division			
1920 Pass Road, Gulfport 39501			
John C. Miller, *Director*			
(601) 863-2803, 1927, VA, VR			
Electronic Engineering Technology	66/72	132/144	
Phillips College—Technical Training Division			
528 North State Street, Jackson 39201			
Nan Thompson, *Director*			
(601) 969-3202, 1973, VR			
Electronics Engineering Technology	72	–	

	Length in Weeks	Full Time	Part Time
MISSOURI			
Aero Mechanic School			
838 Richards Road, Municipal Airport, Kansas City 64116			
Richard I. Schauble, *Director*			
(816) 221-8111, 1946, VA, INS			
Powerplant Mechanic Course	43	–	
Airframe Mechanic Course	43	–	
Powerplant and Airframe Mechanic Course	70	–	
Bailey Technical School			
3750 Lindell Boulevard, St. Louis 63108			
Merlyn W. Cooper, *Director*			
(314) 533-8700, 1936, VA, VR, INS			
Automotive Technology	41	–	
Diesel Technology	26	–	
Automotive/Diesel Technology	61	–	
Engineering Drafting	50	–	
Architectural Engineering Technology	100	–	
Basic Institute of Technology			
1600 S. Kingshighway, St. Louis 63110			
James A. Zoeller, *Director*			
(314) 771-4307, 1936, VA, VR, INS			
Video Engineering Technology	72	–	
Electronic Engineering Technology	84	–	
Computer Engineering Technology	108	–	
Air Conditioning, Refrigeration, and Heating	48	–	
Drafting & Design Technology	48	–	
Bryan Institute			
5841 Chippewa, St. Louis 63109			
C. Larkin Hicks, Jr., *Director*			
(314) 752-4371, 1970, VA, VR, INS			
Medical Assisting	25	–	
Dental Assisting	25	–	
Control Data Institute			
3694 West Pine Boulevard—Des Peres Hall, St. Louis 63108			
Amir Niknejadi, *Director*			
(314) 534-8181, 1958, VA, VR, INS			
Computer Terminal Technology	27	45	
Computer Programming & Operations	26	36	
Electronic Computer Programming Institute			
611 West 39th Street, Kansas City 64111			
Norman E. Capps, *Director*			
(816) 561-7758, 1966, VA, VR, INS, BIA			
Data Processing & Computer Programming	20/22	32	
Data Preparation, Emphasis on Keypunch	4/6	–	
Electronic Institute			
6000 Independence Avenue, Kansas City 64125			
James Miller, *Managing Director*			
(816) 231-4262, 1953, VA, VR, INS, BIA			
Communications & Industrial Technology	52	–	
Practical Electronics	–	38	
Solid State Servicing	38	76	
Electrical and Mechanical Production	10	–	
Digital Electronics	–	48	
Gradwohl School of Laboratory Technique			
3514 Lucas Avenue, St. Louis 63103			
Stanley Reitman, M.D., *Director*			
(314) 533-9250, 1920, VA, VR, INS, BIA			
Comprehensive Medical Laboratory Technician Course	52	–	

	Length in Weeks	Full Time	Part Time
Kansas City College of Medical and Dental Assistants			
2928 Main—Penn Park Medical Center, Kansas City 64108			
B. Robinson, *Director*			
(816) 531-5223, 1967, VA, VR, INS, BIA			
Medical Assistant	28	36	
Dental Assistant	20	29	
Medical Receptionist	12	–	
Physicians Lab	12	–	
Mid Continent Aviation School of Aeronautics			
836 Richards Road, Kansas City 64116			
James Baker, *President*			
(816) 221-8111, 1968, VA, VR, INS, BIA			
Airframe and Powerplant Mechanics	70	–	
Missouri Institute of Technology			
1644 Wyandotte Street, Kansas City 64108			
C. R. LeValley, *President*			
(816) 421-5852, 1931, VA, VR, INS, BIA			
Bachelor of Science Degree in Electronics Engineering Technology	135	–	
Associate Degree in Electronics Engineering Technology	105	–	
Electronics Technician	75	–	
Missouri School for Doctors' Assistants & Technicians			
10121 Manchester Road, St. Louis 63122			
Susan Day, *Administrative Director*			
(314) 821-7700, 1963, VA, VR, INS			
Medical Laboratory Technician	51	–	
Dental Laboratory Technician	50	–	
Advanced Dental Laboratory Technician	50	–	
Medical Office Assistant	12	–	
Medical Office & Lab Assistant	12	24	
Registered Medical Assistant	26	38	
Doctors' Office Management	14	–	
Dental Operating Assistant	18	–	
Dental Operating & Lab Assistant	18	34	
Administrative Dental Assistant	32	48	
Ranken Technical Institute			
4431 Finney Avenue, St. Louis 63113			
R. L. Garrett, *Director*			
(314) 371-0233, 1907, VA, VR, INS, BIA			
Architectural Design Drafting & Structural Technology	72	–	
Automotive Maintenance Technology	72	–	
Carpentry	72	–	
Electronics/Communications & Computer Tech.	72	–	
Industrial Electricity-Electronics Tech.	72	–	
Machine Shop Technology	72	–	
Mechanical Design Drafting & Engineering Technology	72	–	
Plumbing	72	–	
Refrigeration/Air Conditioning & Heating Technology	72	–	
Automobile Body Repair	–	36	
Welding (Combination Gas and Arc)	–	36	
Diesel Gasoline Engine Mechanics and Diesel Electric Systems	–	48	
Urban Technical Center			
3854 Washington, St. Louis 63108			
John C. Vatterott, *President*			
(314) 534-2586, 1969, VA, VR			
Building Service Technician #780	26	–	
Combination Welding	24	–	
Contemporary Welding	14	–	
Production Welding	14	–	
Nurse Aide-Orderly	8	–	

	Length in Weeks	Full Time	Part Time
ater & Wastewater Technical School			
O. Box 370, Neosho 64850			
onald F. Layton, *President*			
417) 451-2786, 1959, VA, VR, INS, BIA			
Basic Course	48		–
Advanced Course	12		–

MONTANA

	Length in Weeks	Full Time	Part Time
Montana Auto College			
18 First Avenue, North, Great Falls 59401			
arryl Meyer, *President*			
406) 761-7550, 1968, VA, VR, BIA			
Automotive Technician	36		–
Engine Rebuilding	9		–
Standard & Automatic Transmissions	9		–
Electrical, Carburetion, Tune-up	9		–
Front-end, Chassis, & Brakes	9		–
Small Engines & Motorcycles		–	5
Auto Parts Counterman	24		48
Engines		–	15
Automatic Transmissions		–	15
Front-end Alignment		–	5
Tune-up		–	10

NEBRASKA

	Length in Weeks	Full Time	Part Time
Electronic Computer Programming Institute			
404 Farnam Street, Omaha 68102			
Lee Frink, *Director*			
02) 345-1300, 1966, VA, VR, INS			
Data Processing and Computer Programming	26		52
Gateway Electronics Institute			
001 South 24th, Omaha 68107			
B. Weddington, *President*			
02) 734-4420, 1971, VA, VR			
Electronics Technology	48		80
Omaha College of Health Careers			
1 South 32nd Avenue, Omaha 68131			
illiam J. Stuckey, *President*			
02) 342-1818, 1967, VA, VR, INS			
Medical Assistants	32		–
Dental Assistants	36		–
Radio Engineering Institute			
01 South 24th Street, Omaha 68107			
B. Weddington, *President*			
02) 734-4420, 1945, VA, VR, INS, BIA			
Industrial Electronics		–	48
Consumer Electronics		–	48
Electronic Technician		–	74
Universal Technical Institute			
2 Capitol Avenue, Omaha 68102			
an Abdouch, *Director*			
02) 345-2422, 1946, VA, VR, INS, BIA			
Automotive Mechanics	32		–
Auto Body Repair & Painting	32		–
Refrigeration and Air Conditioning-			
Part I	32		72
Advanced Air Conditioning & Heating-			
Part II	20		40

NEVADA

	Length in Weeks	Full Time	Part Time
American School of Diamond Cutting			
0 Main Street, Gardnerville 89410			
onard Ludel, *Director*			
02) 782-2646, 1967, VA, VR, INS			
Beginners	40		–
Journeyman's	40		–
Advanced	40		–

	Length in Weeks	Full Time	Part Time
Education Dynamics Institute			
2635 North Decatur Boulevard, Las Vegas 89108			
Lee Wilder, *President*			
(702) 648-1522, 1961, VA, VR, BIA			
Real Estate Principles		–	10
Real Estate Law		–	10
Commercial and Domestic Air Conditioning,			
Refrigeration and Heating Service	26		38
Fashion Merchandising Institute of Nevada			
1456 East Charleston Boulevard, Las Vegas 89104			
Bernie Lenz, *Director*			
(702) 382-3143, 1970, VA, VR, BIA			
Fashion Merchandising	40		80
Professional Fashion Sales	24		56
Nevada Gaming School			
3100 Sirius Road, Las Vegas 89102			
A. W. Morgan, *President*			
(702) 873-2345, 1973, VA, VR			
Coin Machine Mechanics			
Training Program	26		32½

NEW JERSEY

	Length in Weeks	Full Time	Part Time
Brick Computer Science Institute			
525 Highway 70, Bricktown 08723			
Edward Zapp, *Director*			
(201) 477-0975, 1970, VA, VR, INS			
Computer Operator 360/370	8		16
System 3—Computer Operating or Programming	4		8
System 32—Computer Operating or Programming	4		8
Data Processing Equipment Repair	30		60
Data Processing Equipment Repair			
Preparatory	8		16
Keypunch (Basic)	6		10
Keypunch (System 3 Data Recorder)	2		4
Data Entry—(CRT)	3		5
Office Products Repair	24		50
Programmer Basic	24		50
Systems Analyst	27		58
Medical Secretarial	24		48
Legal Secretarial	24		48
The Bryman School			
Branco Estates Center, Route 18, East Brunswick 08816			
Robert E. Zoba, *Director*			
(201) 249-9383, 1966, VA, VR, INS			
Medical Assisting	30		–
Dental Assisting	20		–
Medical Office Management	17		–
Chubb Institute for Computer Technology			
51 John F. Kennedy Parkway, Short Hills 07078			
Peter C. Enander, *School Director*			
(201) 379-7083, 1967, VA, VR, INS			
Computer Programming	21		63
DeVry Technical Institute			
479 Green Street, Woodbridge 07095			
Robert Bocchino, *President*			
(201) 964-1500, 1969, VA, VR, INS			
Electronics Engineering Technical	108		–
Electronics Technician	72		–
Electronic Computer Programming Institute			
177 Duncan Avenue, Jersey City 07306			
John D. Thompson, *President*			
(201) 435-8955, 1968, VA, VR, INS			
Data Processing and Computer Programming	26		47/57
Loss Prevention/Security	16		29

Length in Weeks	Full Time	Part Time
Electronic Computer Programming Institute		
152 Market Street, Paterson 07505		
John Tinnesz, *President/Director*		
(201) 523-1200, 1964, VA, VR, INS		
Data Processing and Computer Programming	26	45
Keypunch Operation	3/7	5/9
Empire Technical School		
576 Central Avenue, East Orange 07018		
Bernard F. Rodgers, *Director*		
(201) 675-0565, 1965, VA, VR, INS		
Computer Programming	26	62
Loss Prevention/Security	16	29
Medical Secretary/Transcriptionist	30	42
General Technical Institute		
1118 Baltimore Avenue, Linden 07036		
Gregory G. Sytch, Jr., *President-Director*		
(201) 486-0150, 1953, VA, VR, INS		
Acetylene Welding	2	5
Acetylene Welding, Maint.	4	10
Acetylene Welding, Certification Pipe	12	30
Electric Welding	2	5
Electric Welding, Maint.	4	10
Electric Welding, Certification Plate	9	22
Electric Welding, Certification Pipe	10	24
Electric Low Hydrogen, Certification Plate	2	5
Electric Low Hydrogen, Certification Pipe	2	5
Heli Arc Tig Welding	1½	3
Heli Arc Tig Welding	4	10
Sigma Mig Welding	½	1½
Flux Core Innershield	1	4
X-Ray Qualification	2	5
Blue Print Reading	3	—
Lincoln Technical Institute		
6901 Route 130 N at Bethel Avenue, Pennsauken 08110		
R. G. DelliSante, *Director*		
(609) 665-3010, 1957, VA, VR, INS		
Air Conditioning/Refrigeration	30	75
Electronics Technology	87	—
Drafting Technology	104	—
Architectural Drafting Technology	104	—
Electronics Servicing	52	—
Electronics Technician	—	40
Architectural Drafting	52	150
Mechanical Drafting	52	150
Lincoln Technical Institute		
2299 Vauxhall Road, Union 07083		
William A. Hart, *Director*		
(201) 964-7800, 1946, VA, VR, INS		
Automotive-Diesel Technology	60	—
Automotive Technology	45	—
Auto Mechanics	—	75
Scientific Tune-up	—	37½
Diesel Engines	—	37½
Automatic Transmissions	—	25
Automotive Air Conditioning	—	12½
Air Conditioning, Refrigeration and Heating Technology	52	—
Air Conditioning, Refrigeration and Heating Systems	40	125
Air Conditioning, Refrigeration Servicing	32	100
Heating System Service	12	37½
Lyons Institute		
16 Springdale Road, Cherry Hill 08003		
John T. Roney, *Director*		
(609) 424-5800, 1960, VA, VR, INS, BIA		
Medical Lab. Technician	50	—
Dental Technician	66	118
Medical Assistant	40	—

Length in Weeks	Full Time	Part Time
Medical Assisting	—	43
Dental Assistant	24	43
Medical Lab. Techniques	—	43
Digital Computer Elec.	27	64
Radio Television Elec.	34	80
Air Conditioning/Refrigeration Servicing	30	71
Lyons Institute		
10 Commerce Place, Clark 07066		
Elaine Landesberg, *Director*		
(201) 684-2197, 1957, VA, VR, INS		
Electric Wiring	33	66
Medical Laboratory Technician	50	—
Medical Assistant	40	43
Medical Laboratory Techniques	—	43
Dental Assistant	24	43
Dental Laboratory Technician	66	118
Lyons Institute		
342 Main Street, Hackensack 07601		
Hal Warren, *Director*		
(201) 488-3790, 1970, VA, VR, INS		
Medical Laboratory Technician	50	—
Assistant Medical Laboratory Technician	—	43
Medical Assistant	40	—
Medical Assisting	—	43
Dental Technician-Comprehensive	66	118
Dental Assistant	40	43
Electrical Wiring	33	66
Lyons Institute		
900 Broad Street, Newark 07102		
Michael DuBroff, *Executive Director*		
(201) 642-3420, 1952, VA, VR, INS		
Medical Laboratory Technician	50	—
Assistant Medical Laboratory Technician	—	43
Medical Assistant	40	—
Dental Technician-Comprehensive	66	118
Dental Assistant	26	43
Electrical Wiring	33	66
Drafting	—	72
The Plaza Technical Institute		
Garden State Plaza—Routes 17 & 4, Paramus 07652		
Edward Frank, *Director of Admissions*		
(201) 843-8500, 1947, VA, VR, INS		
Architectural Drafting	40	80
Electro-mechanical I	40	80
Electronics Engineer	104	104
Radio-TV Electronic	50	78
Computer Technician	50	78
Teterboro School of Aeronautics		
80 Moonachie Avenue, Teterboro 07608		
Anthony DiStefano, *Director*		
(201) 288-6300, 1947, VA, VR, INS		
Airframe & Powerplant Mechanic Course	89	—
Comprehensive Radio-TV and Electronic Course	104	—

NEW MEXICO

Length in Weeks	Full Time	Part Time
AAA College—Technical Division		
525 San Pedro, N.E., Albuquerque 87108		
Noel Cudd, *President*		
(505) 265-5904, 1965, VA, VR, INS, BIA		
Drafting	48	—
Fashion Merchandising	96	—
Medical Secretarial	84	—
Medical Transcriber	52	—
Medical Receptionist	48	—

	Length in Weeks	Full Time	Part Time
Coronado Technical Institute			
225 San Pedro N.E., Albuquerque 87108			
Arthur Russell, *President*			
(505) 255-2360, 1962, VA, VR, BIA			
Architectural Drafting	30/48		99
Civil Engineering Drafting	26/42		86
Electro-Mechanical Drafting	33/52		108
Office Machines Repair	9/12		16
North American Technical Institute			
1606 Central Avenue, S.E., Albuquerque 87106			
Walter L. Johnston, *President*			
(505) 247-1448, 1957, VA, VR, INS, BIA			
Associate Degree in Electronic			
Engineering Technology	96		180

NEW YORK

	Length in Weeks	Full Time	Part Time
Advanced Career Training			
8 West 40th Street, New York 10018			
Carolynn Welton, *President*			
(212) 695-6770, 1966, VA, VR, INS, BIA			
Medical Assistant	24		48
Dental Assistant	24		48
Medical Lab Technician	43		83
Medical Asst./Secretary	26		52
Electrocardiograph Tech	10		—
Advanced Training Center			
2829 Sheridan Drive, Tonawanda 14150			
Frederic J. Rambuss, *Director*			
(716) 835-4410, 1965, VA, VR, INS, BIA			
Computer Programming Course 370	24		52
Radio/TV Broadcasting Course 325	24		34
Key Punch Course 80	4		8.3
Computer Technology Course 910	52		—
Airco Technical Institute			
620 Degraw Street, Brooklyn 11217			
N. Michael Terzian, *Director*			
(212) 596-7777/8, 1971, VA, VR, INS, BIA			
Combination Welding & Related			
Vocational Services	13		26
Shipfitting & Related Vocational Services	13		26
Combination Welding	13		26
Oxy-Fuel Gas Welding, Brazing & Cutting	2		4
Basic Arc Welding	6		12
Advanced Arc Welding	4		8
Metal Inert Gas (MIG) Welding	2		4
Tungsten Inert Gas (TIG) Welding	2		4
TIG For Beginners	3		6
Pipewelding I	4		8
Pipewelding II	4		8
Shipfitting	13		26
Comprehensive Welding	26		52
Allen School for Physicians Aides			
88-50 165th Street, Jamaica 11432			
Daniel W. Bien, *Director*			
(212) 291-2200, 1961, VA, VR, INS			
Medical Laboratory Technology	52		—
Medical Office Assistant	26		—
Dental Office Assistant	16		—
Histology Technician	—		20
Blood Bank Technician	—		20
Electrocardiograph (ECG) Technician	—		12
Hematology Technician	—		20
Electroencephalograph (EEG) Technician	—		12

	Length in Weeks	Full Time	Part Time
Apex Technical School			
222 Park Avenue South, New York 10003			
John Cann, *President*			
(212) 674-5544, 1961, VA, VR, INS			
Refrigeration & Air Conditioning	26		52
Radio & Television Technology	26		52
Major Home Appliances	26		52
Stationary Engineer License	—		23
Refrigeration Machine Operator License	—		23
Custodian Engineer	—		24
Stationary Fireman	—		12
Air Pollution Control Techniques	—		8
Berk Trade School			
384 Atlantic Avenue, Brooklyn 11217			
Irving Berk, *Director*			
(212) 855-5603, 1940, VA, VR, INS			
Comprehensive Plumbing	25		62½
Air Conditioning & Domestic Refrigeration	25		62½
Air Conditioning & Refrigeration			
Service & Application Engineering	50		125
Careerco School for Paraprofessionals			
847 James Street, Syracuse 13203			
Allan Apple, *President*			
(315) 472-7501, 1969, VA, VR, INS, BIA			
Medical Assisting	16		—
Dental Assisting	16		—
Dental Lab Technician	52		—
Medical Lab Technician	54		—
Vending Machine Repairman	26		—
Control Data Institute			
105 Madison Avenue, New York 10016			
James A. Cantrell, *Director*			
(212) 481-1680, 1967, VA, VR, INS			
Computer Technology	25		42
Computer Programming and Operations	26		36
Business Machine Service	26		52
Culinary Institute of America			
P.O. Box 53, Hyde Park 12538			
Henry Ogden Barbour, *President*			
(914) 452-9600, 1946, VA, VR			
A.O.S. Degree in Culinary Arts	72		—
Eastern School for Physicians' Aides			
85 Fifth Avenue, New York 10003			
Henry Young, *Director*			
(212) 242-2330, 1936, VA, VR, INS			
Medical Receptionist	20		20
Medical Transcriber	15		25
Basic Medical Assistant	30		38
Medical Assistant	48		—
Medical Secretary	48		—
Medical Laboratory Technician	48		98
Pediatric and Geriatric Care	15		15
Hematology for Medical Technicians	7		15
Blood Bank and Serology Technician	4		8
Bacteriology for Medical Technicians	8		16
Clinical Chemistry for Medical Technicians	9		19
Histology for Medical Technicians	4		8
Sales Concepts	4		4
Electrocardiograph Technician	3		15
Medical Field Orientation	5		—
Blood Bank and Hematology Technician	11		23
Empire Technical School			
137 North Franklin Street, Hempstead 11550			
Barbara C. Kamholtz, *Director*			
(516) 538-7766, 1973, VA, VR, INS			
Loss Prevention/Security	16		30

	Length in Weeks	Full Time	Part Time
Empire Technical School			
350 Fifth Avenue, New York 10001			
Jay R. Stevens, *Director*			
(212) 563-3100, 1956, VA, VR, INS			
Data Processing and System 360-370			
Computer Programming		–	29
Loss Prevention/Security		16	29
Computer Programming and Introduction			
to Operations		28	–
Customer Engineering for			
Electric Typewriter		26	52
5-H Acres School of Riding			
RD #4, Kinney Gulf Road, Cortland 13045			
Blanche Hendrickson Davis, *Owner*			
(607) 753-0329, 1963, INS			
Riding Instructor Course		62	–
French Fashion Academy			
600 Madison Avenue, New York 10022			
John Klamar, *Director*			
(212) 421-7770, 1966, VA, VR, INS			
Fashion Design & Clothing Construction		40	80
Germain School of Photography			
225 Broadway, New York 10007			
Dr. Milton W. Willenson, *Director*			
(212) 964-4550, 1947, VA, VR, INS, BIA			
Commercial Photography		14	23
Portrait Illustration & Lighting		8	13
Color Photography		12	29
General Professional Career Photography		34	65
Comprehensive Photography		35	70
Motion Picture Photography		20	25
Ektacolor Printing		7	16
Dye Transfer Printing		8	20
Photo Journalism		–	10
Creative Photo Communications		–	10
Medical & Scientific Photography		–	25
Camera Repair & Mechanics		12	43
Negative Retouching		8	20
Oil Coloring		6	12
Airbrush Techniques		8	20
Color Transparency Retouching		–	30
Video Tape Techniques		–	10
Fashion Photography		–	10
Darkroom Craftmanship		–	10
Advertising Illustration		–	10
Industrial Photography		–	10
Advanced Film Editing		–	10
Sound & Music for Films		–	10
Animation		–	10
Script Writing for Films		–	10
Economics of Films		–	10
Art of Film Communications		–	10
Creative Workshop in Advanced Film Production		–	10
A.S. Degree (In Cooperation with			
St. John's University)		34	–
B.F.A. Degree (In Cooperation with			
St. John's University)		34	30
International School of Dog Grooming			
243 East 58th Street, New York 10022			
Ben Stone, *Director*			
(212) 593-1231, 1972, VA, VR			
Basic Course in Dog Grooming		8	16
Advanced Course in Dog Grooming		12	24
Comprehensive Dog Grooming		26	52

	Length in Weeks	Full Time	Part Time
Island Drafting & Technical Institute			
128 Broadway, Amityville 11701			
Joseph P. DiLiberto, *President*			
(516) 691-8733, 1957, VA, VR, INS, BIA			
Mechanical Drafting		34	72
Architectural Drafting		34	72
Electronic Drafting		34	72
Refresher Mathematics		15	36
Electronic Wiring, Assembly and Testing		9	20
Basic Electronics		21	50
Blueprint Reading		3	9
Radio Television Servicing		30	70
Kerpel School of Dental Technology			
37 West 65th Street, New York 10023			
Julius A. Kerpel, *Director*			
(212) 362-4702, 1933, VA, VR, INS			
Comprehensive Course in Dental Technology		59	83
Gold Course		47	65
Ceramic Course		39	56
Acrylic Course		35	47
Denture Course		17	26
Adv. Precision Attachment Course		35	47
Adv. Orthodontic Course		22	30
Porcelain Course		21	29
Theories and Techniques of Oral Implantology		12	15
Laboratory Institute of Merchandising			
12 East 53rd Street, New York 10022			
Adrian G. Marcuse, *President*			
(212) 752-1530, 1939, VA, VR, INS			
Fashion Merchandising Associate Degree			
in Occupational Studies (AOS)		74	–
Mandl School for Medical and Dental Assistants			
175 Fulton Avenue, Hempstead 11550			
Belle Edelson, *Director*			
(516) 481-2774, 1963, VA, VR, INS			
Medical Assistant		43	–
Dental Assistant		16	24
Medical Secretary		43	–
Laboratory Techniques		–	43
Dental Techniques		–	26
Mandl School for Medical and Dental Assistants			
254 West 54th Street, New York 10019			
Fredric Hirsch, *Director*			
(212) 247-3434, 1924, VA, VR, INS			
Medical Assistant		43	–
Dental Assistant		16	24
Medical Secretary		43	–
Laboratory Techniques		43	–
Electrocardiograph		–	19
Histology		–	14
Medical Terminology & Transcription		–	15
Mayer School of Fashion Design			
64 West 36th Street, New York 10018			
Herbert Mayer, *Director*			
(212) 563-3636, 1937, VA, VR, INS			
Designing		37	84/168
Patternmaking		9	41
Dressmaking		10.5	48
Draping		3	14
Pattern Grading		3	15
Fashion Drawing		10.8	51
Fashion Workshop		8	36.5
Suit & Coat Patternmaking		9	41
Sportswear Patternmaking		5	23
Children's Clothes Patternmaking		5	23
Lingerie Patternmaking		5	23
Brushup or Refresher		2	9.5

	Length in Weeks	Full Time	Part Time
Albert Merrill School			
21 West 60th Street, New York 10023			
Oscar Schapira, *Director*			
(212) 246-7130, 1967, VA, VR, INS			
Computer Programming		26	52
Data Processing Technician		26	52
New York Institute of Dietetics			
154 West 14th Street, New York 10011			
Helen S. Doneger, *Director*			
(212) 675-6655, 1935, VA, VR, INS			
Dietetics		52	87
Food Supervision		26	52
Dietetics & Food Management		52	—
Food Cost Control		—	16
Catering I		—	12
Catering II		—	12
Artistic Cake Decorating		—	12
Pastry & Cake Baking		—	18
Dietetic Technician		69	—
Commercial Cooking & Catering		26	—
New York School for Medical and Dental Assistants			
116-16 Queens Boulevard, Forest Hills 11375			
E. Richard Schwabach, *President*			
(212) 793-2330, 1966, VA, VR, INS			
Dental Assistant		16	—
Medical Assistant		16	—
Physician's Office Assistant		12	24
Medical Lab Technician		50	—
Hematology Technician		—	18
Electrocardiography Technician		—	8
Medical Lab Techniques		—	38
New York School of Computer Technology			
200 West 51st Street, New York 10019			
Beverly Kossove, *Director*			
(212) 265-6390, 1965, VA, VR, INS			
Computer Programming		26	48
The New York School of Dog Grooming			
248 East 34th Street, New York 10016			
Sam Kohl, *President*			
(212) 685-3776, 1960, VA, VR, INS, BIA			
Basic Course		6	10/30
Advanced Course		12	20/60
Comprehensive		24	40/120
Kennel Management		6	—
Printing Trades School			
222 Park Avenue South, New York 10003			
Edwin G. Jenkins, *Director*			
(212) 675-0505, 1906, VA, VR, INS			
Complete Photo Offset Printing Course		33½	66½
Offset Photography		10	20
Offset Stripping		8½	16½
Offset Platemaking		3½	6½
Combination Course: Photography, Stripping and Platemaking		21½	43½
Offset Presswork		11½	23½
Offset Press, Jr.		5	10
Offset Press, Sr.		6½	13½
Color Separation Photgraphy		10	20
Alphatype Photo-Typesetting Course		10	20
IBM Selectric Typing Course		10	20
Mechanical Paste-Up & Typositor Course		10	20
Combination Course, Jr.: Photography, Stripping, Platemaking & Jr. Presswork		26½	53½
Combination-Typography Course Selectric Typing, Alphatype Photo-Typesetting, Mechanical Paste-Up & Typositor		30	60

	Length in Weeks	Full Time	Part Time
PSI Institute			
151 West 51st Street, New York 10019			
Frank Christiana, *Director*			
(212) 977-9800, 1959, VA, VR, INS			
Data Processing & Computer Programming Technology		26	52
Digital Electronics & Computer Technology		26	52
Computer Operators Course		—	8
High School Equivalency Test Preparation		—	6
Riverside School of Aeronautics			
Riverside Airport, P.O. Box 444, Utica 13503			
Gloria L. Santucci, *Director*			
(315) 736-5241, 1966, VA, VR, INS, BIA			
Aviation Maintenance Technician Course (Airframe & Powerplant Ratings)		50	—
Suburban Technical School			
175 Fulton Avenue, Hempstead 11550			
Annette Robb, *Director*			
(516) 481-6660, 1970, VA, VR, INS			
Digital Computer Technology		30	60
Radio/Television Electronics		30	60
Syracuse School of Automation			
847 James Street, Syracuse 13203			
Allan Apple, *President*			
(315) 472-7501, 1968, VA, VR, INS, BIA			
Computer Programming/Systems Concepts		27	56
Data Processing Machine Operations		—	27
Keypunch Operations		5	5
Computer Technology/Electronics		34	68
Technical Career Institutes			
320 West 31st Street, New York 10001			
Nathan Buch, *Director, Resident School*			
(212) 594-4000, 1909, VA, VR, INS, BIA			
Electronics Technology Program		117	—
Electronics Circuits and Systems Program		78	208
Electronics Circuits Program		39	104
Radio-Television and Electronics Servicing Program		39	—
Air Conditioning and Refrigeration Servicing Program		39	—
Digital Computer Electronics Program		—	26
Radio and Color TV Servicing Program		—	52
Home and Auto Air-Conditioning and Refrigeration Program		—	65
Communications Electronics and FCC License Program		—	78
Color TV Servicing Program		—	13
Preparatory Program		13/26	—
Preparatory Mathematical Program		—	13
Solid State Servicing Program		—	26
Tobe-Coburn School for Fashion Careers			
851 Madison Avenue, New York 10021			
Avon Lees, Jr., *President*			
(212) 879-4644, 1937, VA, INS			
Fashion Retailing and Promotion Associate Degree in Occupational Studies, (A.O.S.)		72	—
Traphagen School of Fashion			
257 Park Avenue South, New York 10010			
Wanda Wdowka, *Director*			
(212) 673-0300, 1923, VA, VR, INS			
Fashion Design & Illustration (1st year)		30	—
Fashion Design & Illustration (2nd year)		30	—
Fashion Design & Illustration (3rd year)		30	—
Clothing Construction & Design (1st year)		30	—
Clothing Construction & Design (2nd year)		30	—
Interior Design & Decoration		30	—
Advanced Clothing Construction		—	15

	Length in Weeks	Full Time	Part Time
Patternmaking, Draping & Sketching		—	24
Patternmaking, Draping for Design		—	15
Draping for Design I		—	8
Dressmaking, Fitting, Finishing & Tailoring		—	8
Fashion Design & Illustration		—	6
Draping for Design		—	6
Patternmaking & Grading		—	6
Dressmaking, Tailoring & Finishing		—	6
Interior Design & Decoration		—	6

NORTH CAROLINA

National School of Heavy Equipment
Moore's Chapel Road (P.O. Box 8529) Charlotte 28208
Fred W. White, *President*
(704) 394-0371, 1955, VA, VR, INS, BIA

	Length in Weeks	Full Time	Part Time
Bulldozer, Self-Propelled Scraper	3		—
Motor Grader	3		—
Crane, Clamshell, Backhoe, Dragline, Hydraulic Excavator	6		—
Bulldozer, Self-Propelled Scraper, Motor Grader	5		—
Construction Equipment Diesel Mechanic	6		—
Backhow, Crawler, Wheel Loader	3		—

Piedmont Aerospace Institute
Smith Reynolds Airport, Winston-Salem 27102
Henry F. Murray, *Executive Director*
(919) 767-5271, 1966, VA, VR, INS

	Full Time	Part Time
Aeronautical Maintenance Technology (AAS Degree)	60/72	—
Electro Mechanical Technology (AAS Degree)	60/72	—
Aircraft Maintenance Technology—Avionics	96	—
Aircraft Maintenance Technician	60	—
Avionics Technician	54	—

OHIO

Airco Technical Institute
1361 East 55th Street, Cleveland 44103
Thomas Chevako, *Administrator*
(216) 431-1050, 1968, VA, VR, INS, BIA

	Full Time	Part Time
Basic Metal Arc Welding	6	12
Advanced Metal Arc Welding	6	12
Oxy-Acetylene Welding, Brazing and Cut	4	8
Metal Inert Gas Welding	2	4
Tungsten Inert Gas Welding	2	4
Blueprint Reading	1	2
Combination Welding	13	26
Comprehensive Welding	26	52

Akron Testing Laboratory & Welding School
1550 West Waterloo Road, Barberton 44203
Eula Smerglia, *Director*
(216) 753-2260, 1953, VA, VR

	Full Time	Part Time
Electric Arc-Plate & Structural	3.3	6.2
Electric Arc-Pipe with Certification	2.7	4.4
Gas Welding—OxAcetylene	1.2	2.4
Heli-Arc T.I.G.	1	2
Short-Arc M.I.G. (semi-auto)	1	2
Dual Shield-Flux-Cored (semi)	1.75	3.3
Beginners Welder Blue-Print	5	5
Adv. Welder Blue-Print Reading	13	13
Combination Welding Course	13	26
Trade & Technical Welding	24/25	—

A.T.E.S. Technical School
2076-86 Youngstown-Warren Road, Niles 44446
M. E. Riley, *President*
(216) 652-9919, 1954, VA, VR

	Full Time	Part Time
Electronic Engineering Technology (Associate Degree)	80	—
Electronic Technology	—	115
Engineering Drafting	—	67
Television Servicing	—	56
Industrial Mathematics	—	15
Refrigeration & Air Conditioning Service	—	52
Auto Air Conditioning	—	20
Solid State Electronics	—	30

Control Data Institute
15401 Detroit Avenue, Lakewood 44107
Al R. Swinney, *Director*
(216) 228-7800, 1968, VA, VR, INS

	Full Time	Part Time
Computer Terminal Technology	27	44
Computer Programming and Operations	26	36

Cooper School of Art
2341 Carnegie Avenue, Cleveland 44115
Howard Hammerlund, *Administrator*
(216) 241-1486, 1936, VA, VR, INS, BIA

	Full Time	Part Time
Communications Design Major	99	150
Design Illustration Major	99	150
Fashion Illustration Major	99	150
Painting & Printmaking Major	99	150
Photography Major	99	150
Production Artist Prog.	—	56
Professional Photography Prog.	—	56

Electronic Technology Institute
5111 West Tuscarawas Avenue, Canton 44708
E. J. Hunter, *President*
(216) 477-6261, 1929, VA, VR, INS, BIA

	Full Time	Part Time
Electronic Engineering Technology	88	168
Industrial-Communication Electronics	88	168
Electronic Servicing	—	50
Industrial Servicing	—	50
FCC License Preparation	—	40
Transistors, Solid State Devices	—	25

Electronic Technology Institute
4300 Euclid Avenue, Cleveland 44103
A. Jablonski, *President*
(216) 391-9696, 1929, VA, VR, INS, BIA

	Full Time	Part Time
Electronic Engineering Technology	88	132
Industrial-Communication Electronics	88	147
Electronic Servicing	—	50
Industrial Electronics	—	50
FCC License Preparation	—	40
Transistors, Solid State Devices	—	25
Data Processing & Advanced Computer Programming	25	78½

Hobart School of Welding Technology
Trade Square East, Troy 45373
Russell E. Simmons, *Superintendent*
(513) 339-6215, 1930, VA, VR, INS

	Full Time	Part Time
Shielded Metal-Basic	4	—
Shielded Metal-Advanced	4	—
Shielded Metal-Arc Pipe Basic	2	—
Shielded Metal-Arc Pipe Advanced	4	—
Oxyacetylene Welding & Cutting	2	—
Gas Tungsten-Arc	2	—
Gas Tungsten-Arc Pipe	2	—
Plasma-Arc	1	—
Gas Metal Arc Basic	2	—
Gas Metal Arc Advanced	2	—
Gas Metal Arc Pipe	2	—
Welding Teachers Refresher	2	—

Length in Weeks	Full Time	Part Time
Welding For Artists	3	—
Welding Symbols & Blueprint Reading	.3	—
Welding Technology for Supervisors and Engineers	1	—
Welding Inspection & Quality Control	1	—
Welding Inspection Preparation For AWS Inspector Certification	2	—
Welding Equipment, Troubleshooting and Repair	1	—

International Broadcasting School
6 South Smithville Road, Dayton 45431
Don Gingerich, *President*
(513) 258-8251, 1968, VA, VR, INS

Broadcasting	17	26

ITT Technical Institute
4920 Northcutt Place, Dayton 45414
Russell E. Hartzell, *President*
(513) 278-8286, 1935, VA, VR, INS

Architectural Engineering Technology	100	—
Electronics Engineering Technology	100	—
Tool Engineering Technology	100	—
Electronics Technology	50	—
Industrial Drafting Technology	50	—

ITT Technical Institute
224 Superior Street, Toledo 43604
Calvin F. Harding, *Director*
(419) 241-7208, 1924, VA, VR, INS

Air Conditioning, Heating & Refrigeration	50	100
Architectural Drawing	—	150
Electronics Technology	—	75

National School of Meat Cutting
33-37 North Superior Street, Toledo 43604
Albert T. Grasley, *President*
(419) 242-2281, 1923, VA, VR, INS, BIA

Meat Cutting, Meat Merchandising and Self Service Meats	8	—

Northwestern Business College-Technical Center
1441 North Cable Road, Lima 45805
Loren R. Jarvis, *President*
(419) 227-3141, 1920, VA, VR

Automotive Technician Training	48	96
Automotive Technology (Associate Degree)	72	144
Auto-Diesel Mechanics	72	144
Auto-Diesel Technology (Associate Degree)	96	192

Ohio Diesel Technical Institute
1421 East 49th Street, Cleveland 44103
Julius A. Brenner, *President*
(216) 523-1717, 1970, VA, VR, INS, BIA

Diesel Engine Tractor Trailer Mechanics	38	—

Ohio Institute of Photography
3 South Jefferson Street, Dayton 45402
C. Terry Guthrie, *President*
(513) 228-2763, 1971, VA, VR

General Applied Photography	56/70	84/98
Photo Lab Technician	42/56	56/70
Commercial Photography	56/70	84/98
Portraiture Photography	56/70	84/98
Scientific and Technical Photography	56/70	70/98

Ohio Institute of Technology
1350 Alum Creek Drive, Columbus 43209
R. A. Czerniak, *President*
(614) 253-7291, 1952, VA, VR, INS

Bachelor of Electronics Engineering Technology	144	—

Length in Weeks	Full Time	Part Time
Associate of Electronics Engineering Technology	108	—
Electronics Technician	72	—

Ohio School of Broadcast Technique
3940 Euclid Avenue, Cleveland 44115
Bill Clark, *General Manager*
(216) 391-1111, 1969, VA, VR

Broadcast-Announcing	8	13
FCC First Class License Preparation	9	15

Ohio Visual Art Institute
124 East Seventh Street, Cincinnati 45202
James E. Price, *Director*
(513) 241-4338, 1947, VA, VR, INS

Business Art	80	120
Fine Art	80	120
Photography	80	—
Interior Design	—	30

Para Professional Institute
4550 Indianola Avenue, Columbus 43214
Barbara K. Conley, *Director*
(614) 263-1841, 1966, VA, VR, INS

Data Processing and Advanced Computer Programming	25	45
Data Processing and Computer Programming	19	34
Loss Prevention/Security	25	45

R.E.T.S. Tech Center
116 Westpark Road, Dayton 45459
Edward D. Benore, *President*
(513) 433-3410, 1965, VA, VR, INS

Associate Degree—Electronic Engineering Technology	72	—
Applied Electronic Technology	48	—
Climate Control Technology	36	—

Technichron School of Welding
2917 Colerain Avenue, Cincinnati 45225
Lee Spievack, *Director*
(513) 541-1470, 1942, VA, VR

Oxy-Acetylene Welding and Cutting	7½	15
Basic Shielded Metal-Arc Welding	12	23
Advanced Shielded Metal-Arc Welding	7	14
Allied Subjects (Theory, Basic Metallurgy, And Blueprint Reading)	2½	5
Gas Tungsten Arc Welding	1	2
Gas Metal Arc Welding (Semi-Automatic)	1/3	1
Shielded Metal Arc Pipe Welding	3	5
Gas Metal Arc Pipe Welding (Semi-Automatic)	1½	3

Toledo Medical Educational Center
5321 Southwyck Boulevard, Toledo 43614
Robert Lownsbury, *President*
(419) 865-2361, 1970, VA, VR, INS

Medical Assistant	26	—
Dental Assistant	26	—
Dental Laboratory Tech.	36	—

United Electronics Institute
1225 Orlen Avenue, Cuyahoga Falls 44221
Victor C. Richard, *Director*
(216) 923-9959, 1966, VA, VR

Electronics Technology	84	—
Basic Electronics, Radio & TV	80	—

Virginia Marti School of Fashion Design
11308 Detroit Avenue, Cleveland 44102
Virginia Marti, *Director*
(216) 281-8584, 1966, VA, VR, INS, BIA

Basic Sewing	24	96
Couturier Dressmaking	24	96
Fashion Design	48	192

	Length in Weeks	Full Time	Part Time
West Side Institute of Technology			
9801 Walford Avenue, Cleveland 44102			
Richard I. Pountney, *Director*			
(216) 651-1656, 1958, VA, VR, INS, BIA			
Associate Degree in Environmental Technology	78	—	
Associate Degree Instrumentation Technology	78	—	
Building Engineer	52	—	
Air Conditioning Serviceman (Heating)	—	78	
Air Conditioning & Refrigeration Mechanic (Heating & Advanced Air Conditioning)	—	104	
Steam Plant Operation (Stationary Engineer)	—	52	
Refrigeration System Operation and Repair	—	52	
Youngstown College of Business and Professional Drafting			
2720 Market Street, Youngstown 44507			
Michael D. Cruse, *Director*			
(216) 788-2419, 1967, VA, VR, INS			
Industrial Drafting & Design Tech.	36	72	
Mechanical Drafting & Design Tech.	72	—	
Structural Drafting & Design Tech.	72	—	

OKLAHOMA

	Length in Weeks	Full Time	Part Time
American Flyers			
P.O. Box 3241, Airpark Branch, Ardmore 73401			
Reed Pigman, *President*			
(405) 223-4020, 1939, VA, VR, INS, BIA			
Private Pilot	6/8	—	
Commercial Pilot	12/18	—	
Flight Instructor	5	—	
Instrument Rating	5/9	—	
Instrument Instructor Airplane	2	—	
Airplane Transport Pilot (Plus S&MEL)	5/7	—	
Multi-Engine	2	—	
Flight Engineer	10/12	—	
Aerobatic	1	—	
Bryan Institute			
1203 South Boulder, Tulsa 74119			
Bonita Mahannah, *Director*			
(918) 587-1591, 1972, VA, VR			
Medical Assistants	25	—	
Dental Assistants	25	—	
Sooner Mechanical Trade School			
1100 West Main Street, Oklahoma City 73106			
Robert L. Cain, *President*			
(405) 235-8683, 1965, VA, VR, INS, BIA			
Refrigeration & Air Conditioning	26	52	
Combination Welding	16	43	
Basic Arc Welding	—	24	
Complete Pipe Welding	14	40	
Plumbing	26	52	
Electrical	26	52	
Related Trades	82	169	
Southwest Automotive School			
1520 South Central, Oklahoma City 73125			
Charles W. Locke, *General Manager*			
(405) 632-7785, 1963, VA, VR, BIA			
Complete Automotive	39	78	
Automobile Mechanics	27	54	
Industrial Machinist	39	78	
Paint and Body Repair	39	78	
Automatic Transmissions	12	24	

	Length in Weeks	Full Time	Part Time
Spartan School of Aeronautics			
8820 East Pine Street, Tulsa 74151			
V. M. Setterholm, *President*			
(918) 836-6886, 1928, VA, VR, INS, BIA			
Aviation Maintenance Technician	68		
Powerplant Technician	44		
Airframe Technician	44		
Aviation Instrument/Electronics Technician	80		
Aviation Electronics Technician	48		
Aviation Instrument Technician	64		
Mechanical Instrument Technician	20		
Industrial Testing and Inspection Technician	16		
Aviation Technician	108		
Private Pilot	8/20		
Commercial Pilot	4/12		
Instrument Rating	5/18		
Flight Instructor (airplane)	5/16		
Instrument Flight Instructor	4/8		
Multi engine Rating	2/6		
Seaplane Rating	1/6		
Airline Transport Rating	3/12		
Commercial Helicopter Category	2/8		
Helicopter Flight Instructor	3/8		
Helicopter Agricultural Applicator	4/8		
Helicopter External Load	1/4		
Tulsa Welding School			
3038 Southwest Boulevard, Tulsa 74107			
Noel E. Adams, *President*			
(918) 587-6789, 1949, VA, VR, INS, BIA			
Combination Welding	16	3	
Refinery & Industrial Pipe	11	2	
Pipeline Welding	10	2	
Plate & Structural (Only)	5	1	
Refinery & Industrial Pipe (Only)	4		
Pipeline Welding (Only)	4		
United Electronics Institute			
3020 North Stiles Avenue, Oklahoma City 73105			
Truman Smith, *Director*			
(405) 528-2731, 1969, VA, VR, INS			
Electronics Technology	108		
Basic Electronics, Radio and Television	80		

OREGON

	Length in Weeks	Full Time	Part Time
Bassist Institute			
923 Southwest Taylor Street, Portland 97205			
Donald H. Bassist, *President*			
(503) 228-6528, 1964, VA, VR, INS, BIA			
Buying and Merchandising	40		
Interior Decorating	80		
Apparel Design	80		
Commercial Driver Training			
2416 North Marine Drive, Portland 97217			
Louis S. Friton, *President*			
(503) 285-7542, 1962, VA, VR, BIA			
Transport Operator	5		2
North Pacific Dental College, Training Auxiliary Personnel			
917 S.W. Oak Street, Portland 97205			
Donald R. McCauley, *President*			
(503) 222-1769, 1954, VA, VR, INS, BIA			
Dental Technician	40		
Crown & Bridge	16		
Dental Chairside Assistant	16		
Dental Office Management	16		
Dental Assistant and Office Management	28		

	Length in Weeks	Full Time	Part Time
Oregon Career Institute			
2118 S.W. Fifth, Portland 97201			
Walter R. Peterson, *Director*			
(503) 226-1241, 1966, VA, VR, INS			
Business Data Processing	36		48
Portland Paramedical Center			
520 S.W. Hall, Portland 97201			
John H. Engel, *Director*			
(503) 222-3801, 1970, VA, VR, INS, BIA			
Clinical Medical Assistants	28		44
Administrative Medical Assistants	24		40
Dental Assistants	28		44
Animal Health Assistant	34		–
Medical Office Management	16		24
United Electronics Institute			
10521 North Lombard Street, Portland 97203			
Burt MacShara, *Director*			
(503) 286-8208, 1971, VA, VR			
Electronics Technology	91		–
Basic Electronics, Radio & TV	80		–

PENNSYLVANIA

	Length in Weeks	Full Time	Part Time
American Institute of Drafting			
1616 Orthodox Street, Philadelphia 19124			
Lester S. Klein, *Director*			
(215) 288-8200, 1966, VA, VR, INS			
Electro-mechanical Drafting	44		88
Architectural Drafting	44		88
Electro-mechanical Drafting &			
Design Tech.	88		–
Architectural Drafting Technology	88		–
Drafting Technology	88		–
Architectural Blueprint Reading	–		27
Mechanical Blueprint Reading	–		27
Steel Detailing	22		–
Drafting for Apprentices	–		40
Antonelli School of Photgraphy			
1210 Race Street, Philadelphia 19107			
Joseph B. Thompson, *Vice President*			
(215) 563-8558, 1938, VA, VR, INS			
Photography Professional Standard Diploma	90		120
Photgraphy Professional Advanced Diploma	135		180
Art Institute of Philadelphia			
1818 Cherry Street, Philadelphia 19103			
Philip Trachtman, *Director*			
(215) 567-7080, 1966, VA, VR, INS			
Commercial Art	96		–
Fashion Illustration	96		–
Interior Design	96		–
Art Institute of Pittsburgh			
526 Penn Avenue, Pittsburgh 15222			
John A. Johns, *President*			
(412) 471-5651, 1921, VA, VR, INS, BIA			
Visual Communications			
(AST Degree Program)	96		–
Fashion Illus. (AST Degree Program)	96		80
Interior Design (AST Degree Program)	96		80
Photography/Multi-Media (AST Degree Program)	36		80
Automotive Training Center			
Pickering Creek Industrial Park, 114 Pickering Way, Exton 19341			
Harry A. Fields, *Director*			
(215) 363-6716, 1917, VA, VR, INS			
Automotive Maintenance	54		–
General Automotive Service			
Technology	72		–

	Length in Weeks	Full Time	Part Time
Specialized Automotive Service Technology			
Transmission Major	72		–
Specialized Automotive Service Technology			
Engine Rebuilding Major	72		–
Specialized Automotive Service Technology			
Engine Diagnosis & Emmission Control Major	72		–
Specialized Automotive Service Technology			
Front End Major	72		–
Diesel Technology	81		–
Diesel Technology-Fuel Injection Major	90		–
Collision Reconditioning Technology	63		–
Berean Institute—Technical Division			
1901 West Girard Avenue, Philadelphia 19130			
Lucille P. Blondin, *Executive Administrator*			
(215) 763-4833, 1899, VA, VR, INS			
Basic Communications	–		80
Electronics—Basic	–		40
Electronics—Advanced	–		40
Electronics Technology	80		–
Refresher & unit courses in all areas	–		20
Wilma Boyd Career School			
On The Plaza, Chatham Center, Pittsburgh 15219			
Wilma Boyd, *President*			
(412) 391-2584, 1968, VA, VR, INS			
Airline and Travel Agency	12		26
Breeden School of Welding			
3578 MacArthur Road, Whitehall 18052			
Robert K. Wiswesser, *Administrator*			
(215) 437-9720, 1968, VA, VR, INS			
Complete Shop Welding	60		120
Special Shop Welding	33		66
General Shop Welding	17		34
Standard Shop Welding	6		12
Inert Gas Arc Welding	2		4
Oxygen and Acetylene Welding & Cutting	2		4
Diagnostic Welding	2		4
Blueprint Reading for Welders	–		5
Complete Shop Welding	25		50
Advanced Pipe Welder Qualification	2		4
Flux Cored Arc Welding	2		4
Career Educational Institute—Technical Division			
1200 Walnut Street, Philadelphia 19107			
Martin Austin, *Director*			
(215) 546-3377, 1966, VA, VR, INS, BIA			
Computer Programming Trainee	15		48
Keypunch	6		10
Data Processing Machine Repair	15		48
The Clarissa School of Fashion Design			
107 Sixth Street, Fulton Bldg., Pittsburgh 15222			
M. J. R. Narcisi, *President*			
(412) 471-4414, 1950, VA, VR, INS			
Fashion Design Course	67		320/384
Dressmaking-Swatch Construction	12		58/70
Patternmaking	13		67/80
Women's Fashion Design	20		100/120
Women's Tailoring	5		25/30
Chair Covering-Drapery Making	10		50/60
Millinery	5		25
Men's Garment Design Course	64		333/400
Men's Tailoring	16		80/96
Men's Knit	5		25/30
Dean Institute of Technology			
1501 W. Liberty Avenue, Pittsburgh 15226			
John R. Dean, *President*			
(412) 531-4433, 1947, VA, VR, INS			
Mechanical Drafting	60		120
Architectural Drafting	60		120

	Length in Weeks	Full Time	Part Time
Structural Drafting		60	120
Structural Design		85	170
Electrical Drafting		60	120
Tool & Die Design		85	170
Metallurgical Technician		60	120
Electrical Technician		60	120
Industrial Electricity		50	100
House Wiring		50	100
Welding V Combination		24	48
Welding I Oxyacetylene		5	10
Welding Arc		7	14
Welding III Pipe		4	8

Electronic Institute
1660-80 South Cameron Street, Harrisburg 17104
William Margut, *Director*
(717) 236-5422, 1959, VA, VR

	Length in Weeks	Full Time	Part Time
Electronic & Computer Technology (Associate Degree)		96	—
Drafting & Design Technology (Associate Degree)		96	—
Industrial Electronic Mechanic		48	—
Communications Technician		48	—
Computer Technology		64	—
Electronic Technology		64	—
Structural Drafting		48	—
Engineering Drafting Technology		64	—

Electronic Institute
1402 Penn Avenue, Pittsburgh 15222
Philip Chosky, *President*
(412) 471-3962, 1955, VA, VR, INS

	Length in Weeks	Full Time	Part Time
Electronic & Computer Technology (Associate Degree)		96	—
Drafting & Design Technology (Associate Degree)		96	—

Erie Barber School
902-904 Parade Street, Erie 16503
LeRoy Cameroni, *President*
(814) 454-2875, 1965, VA, VR

	Length in Weeks	Full Time	Part Time
Barbering & Hairstyling		35	55

Fashion Academy of Pittsburgh
110 Ninth Street, Pittsburgh 15222
Rose E. Casasanta, *Director*
(412) 261-3543, 1961, VA, VR, INS

	Length in Weeks	Full Time	Part Time
Fashion Design and Clothing Construction		66	—
Traditional Tailoring and Clothing Construction		44	—

Franklin School of Sciences & Arts
251 South 22nd Street, Philadelphia 19103
William S. Kalaboke, *Director*
(215) 732-3300, 1919, VA, VR, INS

	Length in Weeks	Full Time	Part Time
Medical Laboratory Technology		96	—
Radiologic Technology		96	—
Medical Assistant		36	48
Dental Assistant		36	—

Gateway Technical Institute
100 Seventh Street, Pittsburgh 15222
Wayne D. Smith, Director
(412) 281-4111, 1908, VA, VR, INS,

	Length in Weeks	Full Time	Part Time
Electronics Technology		80/48	96
Drafting & Design Technology		80/48	96
Air Conditioning & Refrigeration Technology		80/48	96

Greensburg Institute of Technology
302 West Otterman Street, Greensburg 15601
Donna M. Chalfant, *Director*
(412) 837-3330, 1955, VA, VR, INS

	Length in Weeks	Full Time	Part Time
Mechanical Drafting Technology		104	208
Architectural Drafting Technology		104	208
Structural Drafting Technology		104	208
Mechanical Design Technology		52	104
Electronic Technology		104	208
Electrical Technology		104	208
Building Construction Technology		104	208

Hussian School of Art
1300 Arch Street, Philadelphia 19107
Ronald Dove, *President/Director*
(215) 563-5726, 1946, VA, VR, INS

	Length in Weeks	Full Time	Part Time
Commercial Art		136	—
Illustration		136	—
Advertising Design		136	—
Fine Arts		136	—

Ivy School of Professional Art
University Avenue, Pittsburgh 15214
Morris B. Kirshenbaum, *Director*
(412) 323-8800, 1960, VA, VR, INS

	Length in Weeks	Full Time	Part Time
Commercial Art—with majors in:		96	—
Advertising Design, Art Direction and Television			
Story and Advertising Illustration			
Retail Art (Fashion and Merchandise drawing and layout)			
Filmmaking and Animation			
Photography			
Environmental Design (Interior Design; Exposition Design)			
Fine Arts (Painting, Sculpture, Printmaking)			

Lincoln Technical Institute
5151 Tilghman Street, Allentown 18104
Donald R. Frey, *Director*
(215) 395-5891, 1949, VA, VR, INS

	Length in Weeks	Full Time	Part Time
Electronics Technology		87	—
Drafting Technology		104	216
Electronics Servicing		52	—
Electronics Technician		—	26
Architectural Drafting		52	108
Mechanical Drafting		52	108

Lincoln Technical Institute
9191 Torresdale Avenue, P.O. Box 21036, Philadelphia 19114
Alfiero A. Alfieri, *Director*
(215) 335-0800, 1946, VA, VR, INS

	Length in Weeks	Full Time	Part Time
Automotive-Diesel Technology		60	94/188
Automotive Technology		45	70/140
Automotive Mechanics (Basic Course)		30	47/93
Scientific Engine Tune-Up		15	24/47
Diesel Engines		15	24
Automatic Transmissions		15	47
Automotive Air-Conditioning		5	16
		5	16

Lyons Technical Institute
"D" Street & Erie Avenue, Philadelphia 19134
Milton Kochman, *Director*
(215) 426-5500, 1941, VA, VR, INS

	Length in Weeks	Full Time	Part Time
Electrical Wiring		42	85
Electronics Technology		87	—
Drafting Technology		104	216
Electronics Servicing		52	—

	Length in Weeks	Full Time	Part Time
Electronics Technician		–	52
Architectural Drafting		52	108
Mechanical Drafting		52	108
Electronic Computer Technician		–	85

Lyons Technical Institute
67 Long Lane, Upper Darby 19082
Ralph G. Verdieck, *Director*
(215) 734-1323, 1969, VA, VR, INS

	Full Time	Part Time
Digital Computer Electronics	32	64
Radio & Television Electronics	32	64

Maxwell Institute
2512 West Main Street, Norristown 19401
William F. Maxwell, Jr., *President*
(215) 631-1558, 1970, VA, VR, INS

	Full Time	Part Time
Computer Programmer Trainee	16	55
Basic Fortran	–	17
Keypunch	2	4
Systems Analysis and Design	–	20
Diploma Course in Computer Data Processing	36	–
Overview Course in Computer Data Processing	–	6½
Computer Operations	10	36
ANS-COBOL	5½	19
RPG-II	4	14
BAL	4½	16½

Median School of Allied Health Careers
12 Eighth Street, Pittsburgh 15222
Frank I. Gale, *President*
(412) 391-7021, 1958, VA, VR, INS

	Full Time	Part Time
Medical Assistant	38	–
Dental Assistant	38	–
Dental Technician	45	–
Medical Secretary	60	–
Medical-Dental Receptionist	16	–
Animal Health Technician	60	–

National School of Health Technology
Penn Towers Bldg., 2nd Floor, 1819 J.F. Kennedy Boulevard,
Philadelphia 19103
William Lobel, C. D. T., *President/Director*
(215) 561-5020, 1963, VA, VR, INS

	Full Time	Part Time
Dental Laboratory Technician	34	100
Dental Assistant	26	–
Medical Assistant	32	75
Dietetic Assistant	36	75
Respiratory Therapy Assistant	32	67
Medical Laboratory Technician	88	–
Psychiatric Assistant	32	67
Operating Room Technician	32	67
Geriatric Assistant	32	67
E.E.G. Technician Assistant	32	67

New Castle School of Trades
R.D. #1, Pulaski 16143
Joseph L. Clavelli, *Administrator*
(412) 964-2351, 1945, VA, VR, INS

	Full Time	Part Time
Auto Auto Body and Fender Repair	52	104
Automotive Repair	52	104
Fundamentals of Automotive	26	52
Fundamentals of Auto Body	26	52
Electric House Wiring	26	52
Interior Electric Wiring	65	130
Combination Welding	26	52
Health and Food Service Aide	54	–
General Welding	32	–
General Automotive (Mech.)	48	–
General Automotive (Body)	48	–
Building Maintenance	48	–
Electrical Maintenance	48	–
Small Gas Engines	32	–

	Length in Weeks	Full Time	Part Time

Northeastern Training Institute
Box 9, Fleetville 18420
Gregg R. Aversa, *President*
(717) 945-5135, 1968, VA, VR, INS

	Full Time	Part Time
Heavy Equipment Operator	10	–
Tractor Trailer Driver	8	–
Ashphalt Paving Course	6	–
Highway-Bridge Carpenter Helper	6	–
Diesel Mechanic Technician	16	–

Penn Technical Institute
110 Ninth Street, Pittsburgh 15222
Louis A. Dimasi, *Director*
(412) 355-0455, 1947, VA, VR, INS

	Full Time	Part Time
Electronics Technology	91	186

Pennco Tech
3815 Otter Street, Bristol 19007
John A. Hobyak, *President*
(215) 824-3200, 1962, VA, VR, INS, BIA

	Full Time	Part Time
Automotive Gas & Diesel Technology	60	100
Automotive Tune-up & Diagnosis	1	2
Automotive Air-Conditioning	1	2
Automatic Transmission-Ford	1	2
Diesel Servicing	5	10
Front End Suspension & Wheel Alignment	1	2
Carburetion & Fuel Systems	1	2
Basic Level Automobile Mechanics	–	32
Electronic Engineering Technology (Associate Degree)	84	–
Electronic Technician	60	120
Computer Maintenance Technology	48	96
Radio-Television Maintenance Technology	48	96
Fundamentals of Digital Computer Programming	–	24
Applied Digital Computer Programming	–	12

Pennsylvania Institute of Technology
414 Sansom Street, Upper Darby 19082
John C. Strayer; *Director*
(215) 352-7100, 1952, VA, VR, INS

	Full Time	Part Time
Aerospace Engineering Technology	84	175
Architectural Engineering Technology	84	175
Drafting Design Technology	84	175
Electronic Engineering Technology	84	175
Electronics Design Technology	84	175
Mechanical Engineering Technology	84	175
Structural Engineering Technology	84	175
Tool Design Technology	84	175
Construction Supervision	–	72
Civil Engineering Technology	84	175

Philadelphia Offset Printing School
125 South 9th Street, Philadelphia 19107
Jack Rosenfeld, *Director*
(215) 923-9020, 1958, VA, VR, INS, BIA

	Full Time	Part Time
Offset Printing Technology	32	–
Offset Printing II (Elementary Intermediate)	–	24
Offset Printing I (Elementary)	–	8
Camera & Platemaking	–	12

Pittsburgh Barber School
421 East Ohio Street, Pittsburgh 15212
Frank Quinio, *Director*
(412) 321-5457, 1946, VA, VR

	Full Time	Part Time
Barbering	36	56
Men's Advanced Hairstyling	8	–

	Length in Weeks	Full Time	Part Time
Pittsburgh Institute of Aeronautics			
P.O. Box 10897, Pittsburgh 15236			
John Graham, II, *President*			
(412) 462-9011, 1929, VA, VR, INS			
Aeronautical Maintenance Technician	84		—
Airframe & Powerplant Mechanic		—	127
Airframe Mechanic		—	85
Powerplant Mechanic		—	85
Pittsburgh Technical Institute			
717 Liberty Avenue, Pittsburgh 15222			
N. D. Wilcox, *President*			
(412) 471-0985, 1946, VA, VR, INS			
Drafting Technology	60		120
Industrial Engineering Technology	60		120
R.E.T.S. Electronic School			
214 South 69th Street, Upper Darby 19082			
Edmund Leuter, *Director*			
(215) 352-5586, 1958, VA, VR, INS			
Electronic Technician	72		—
Specialized Electronic Servicing	48		—
Practical Industrial Electronics		—	75
Television Servicing, B/W and Color		—	25
Solid State Electronics		—	25
Computer Electronics		—	25
Communications Electronics		—	25
Rosedale Technical Institute			
1402 Penn Avenue, Pittsburgh 15222			
John Binotto, *Director*			
(412) 765-3833, 1949, VA, VR, INS			
Automotive & Diesel Technology	72		144
Technician Training School			
1000 Island Avenue, McKees Rocks 15136			
Richard J. Zaiden, Jr., *Director*			
(412) 771-7590, 1937, VA, VR, INS, BIA			
Air Conditioning I	25		—
Refrigeration II	25		—
Major Appliances III	25		—
Auto Mechanics	40		—
Auto Transmission	33		—
Auto Body (Collision)	33		—
Bricklaying	33		—
Combination Welding	25		—
MotorCycle Mechanics	33		—
Plumbing	50		—
Carpentry	33		—
Tracey-Warner School			
401 North Broad Street, Philadelphia 19108			
Lewis H. Warner, *President*			
(215) 574-0402, 1956, VA, VR, INS			
Fashion Technology (Associate Degree)	60		120
Men's & Women's Clothing Design	60		120
Advanced Original Design	30		—
Fashion Merchandising & Retailing	60		120
Commercial & Retail Operations	30		—
Triangle Institute of Technology			
635-637 Smithfield Street, Pittsburgh 15222			
James R. Agras, *President*			
(412) 281-2013, 1944, VA, VR, INS			
Architectural Drafting & Construction	70		170
Mechanical Drafting & Design	70		170
Advanced Architectural Drafting and Construction	17		42
Advanced Mechanical Drafting and Design	17		42
Structural Drafting	70		170
Advanced Piping Drafting		—	25
Advanced Machine Design & Drafting		—	40

	Length in Weeks	Full Time	Part Time
Advanced Industrial Design & Drafting		—	50
Time Study and Cost Estimating		—	40
Blueprint Reading for Machine Trades		—	17
Blueprint Reading for the Building Trades		—	17
Perspective Drawing		—	17
Air and Water Pollution Technology	70		170
Upholstery	50		170
Upholstery for seats, backs & arms		—	31
Stripping & Springing		—	31
Channeling & Tufting		—	31
Curtains or Draperies		—	17
Slipcovers		—	17
Upholstering fabrics		—	17
Refrigeration, Heating, Ventilation and Air Conditioning	52		70
Vale Technical Institute			
35 North Liberty Street, Blairsville 15717			
John H. McKenrick, *Director*			
(412) 459-9500, 1946, VA, VR, INS			
Automotive Technics and Management	60		—
Auto Mechanics	30		—
Body and Fender Repair	30		—
Washington Institute of Technology			
110 South Main Street, Washington 15301			
Stanley S. Bazant, *Director*			
(412) 222-1942, 1969, VA, VR			
Electronic Technology	63		—
Engineering Drafting	79		158
Combination Welding	24		48
The Williamson Free School of Mechanical Trades			
Middletown Road, Media 19063			
James R. Clemens, *President*			
(215) 566-1776, 1888			
Construction Technology	102		—
Electric Power Technology	102		—
Mechanical Technology	102		—
Interior Planning & Decorating	102		—
Brickmasonry	102		—
Carpentry	102		—
Machinist	102		—
Painting and Decorating	102		—
Power Plant Operating	102		—
York Academy of Arts			
625 East Philadelphia Street, York 17403			
William A. Falkler, *Director*			
(717) 848-1447, 1952, VA, VR, INS			
Commercial Art	108		—
Interior Design	108		—
Fine Arts	108		—

RHODE ISLAND

	Length in Weeks	Full Time	Part Time
New England Technical Institute			
184 Early Street, Providence 02907			
Richard I. Gouse, *President*			
(401) 467-7744, 1940, VA, VR, INS			
Electronics Technician	52		—
Electronics Technology	78		—
Refrigeration Air Conditioning Technician	52		—
Refrigeration Air Conditioning Heating Technician	78		—
Refrigeration Air Conditioning Heating and System Design	93		—
Heating Technician	26		—
Detail Draftsman	52		—
Design Draftsman	104		—
Electrical Technician	52		—
Electronics Servicing	52		—
Refrigeration Air Conditioning Servicing	52		—

Length in Weeks	Full Time	Part Time
Refrigeration Air Conditioning Heating		
Servicing	104	–
Oil Burner Servicing	52	–
Detail Drafting	52	–
Advance Detail-Design Drafting	104	–
Essentials of Electrical Theory and		
Maintenance	52	–
Major Home Appliance Servicing	26	–
Refrigeration Air Conditioning Heating and		
Major Home Appliance Servicing	130	–

Rhode Island School of Electronics
14 Third Street, Providence 02906
Robert E. Obenhaus, *Managing Director*
(401) 861-9664, 1919, VA, VR, INS

	Full Time	Part Time
Electronics Technology	96	96
Electronics Technology (Special Course)	48	–
Radio & Television Servicing	48	96

Rhode Island Trades Shops School
361 Fountain Street, Providence 02903
Jason H. Rubin, *Director*
(401) 331-3008, 1963, VA, VR

	Full Time	Part Time
Auto Mechanics	46	50
Auto Body & Spray Painting	40	40

SOUTH CAROLINA

Nielsen Electronics Institute
1600 Meeting Street, Charleston 29405
Robert R. Nielsen, *President*
(803) 722-2344, 1965, VA, INS

	Full Time	Part Time
Electronics Technology (Associate Degree)	100	125

SOUTH DAKOTA

Nettleton College-Technical Division
9th and Spring Avenue, Sioux Falls 57102
Eugene Reinholt, *President*
(605) 336-1837, 1919, VA, VR, BIA

	Full Time	Part Time
Medical Assistant	60	–

TENNESSEE

Bailey Technical School
554 Adams, Memphis 38103
Kenneth C. Preston, *Director*
(901) 525-4503, 1970, VA, VR

	Full Time	Part Time
Automotive/Diesel Technology	40	53
Automotive Technology	30	41

Nashville Auto Diesel College
1524 Gallatin Road, Nashville 37206
H. O. Balls, *President*
615) 226-3990, 1918, VA, VR, INS

	Full Time	Part Time
Automotive Mechanics	19/24	–
Combined Automobile & Diesel	32/40	–
Combined Arc & Acetylene Welding	10/13	–
Auto Body Repairman	48	–
Combined Auto-Diesel Welding	42/53	–

Tennessee Institute of Broadcasting
2106-A 8th Avenue, South, Nashville 37204
Jerry W. Masters, *Director*
615) 297-5396, 1966, VA, VR, INS

	Full Time	Part Time
Radio Licensing	8	–
Radio Broadcasting–Licensing	16	24

Tennessee Institute of Electronics
3121 Broadway N.E., Knoxville 37917
E. Ray Massengill, *President*
(615) 688-9422, 1947, VA, VR, INS

	Full Time	Part Time
Electronic Specialist	52	104
Electronics Technology	24	50

TEXAS

Aero Technical Institute
3801 Jacksboro Highway, P.O. Box 1916, Wichita Falls 76307
B. J. Brown, *General Manager*
(817) 766-3471, 1968, VA, VR, BIA

	Full Time	Part Time
Aviation Airframe & Powerplant Mechanic	65	130
Avionics-Electronics Technician	48	96

American Trades Institute
1605 North Stemmons, Dallas 75207
Jim Craddock, *President*
(214) 744-4040, 1964, VA, VR, INS, BIA

	Full Time	Part Time
Air Conditioning, Heating and Refrigeration	26	52
Automotive Service Technician	26	52
Combination Welding	26	52
Offset Printing	26	52
Radio-Television Repair	26	52
Commercial-Residential Electrician	–	23
Plumbing		
Basic	–	12
Journeyman	–	14
Master	–	4

Bauder Fashion College
508 South Center Street, Arlington 76010
John Kettle, *President*
(817) 277-6666, 1967, VA, VR, INS

	Full Time	Part Time
Fashion Design	33	–
Fashion Merchandising	33	–
Interior Design	33	–
Fashion Merchandising (2 Year)	66	–
Fashion Design (2 Year)	66	–
Interior Design (2 Year)	66	–

The Bryman School
2404 West Holcombe Boulevard, Houston 77030
G. C. Stewart, *Director*
(713) 666-7411, 1970, VR, INS

	Full Time	Part Time
Medical Assisting	28	34
Dental Assisting	20	24
Medical Office Management	16	19

CBM Education Center
1121 Navarro, San Antonio 78205
Richard Jauregui, *President*
(512) 224-9286, 1968, VA, VR, INS

	Full Time	Part Time
Keypunch/Verifier Operation	4/8	12/24
Computer & Punch Card Equipment		
Concepts & Operation	15	30
Computer Programming	26	52
Computer Operation & Programming	39	78
Medical Receptionist	13	26
Nurses Aide/Male Orderly	14	20

Control Data Institute
8585 North Stemmons Freeway, Dallas 75247
Charles R. Stewart, *Director*
(214) 688-5900, 1967, VA, VR, INS, BIA

	Full Time	Part Time
Computer Technology	25	41.6
Computer Programming/Operations	23.2	38.7

Length in Weeks	Full Time	Part Time

DeVry Institute of Technology
5353 Maple Avenue, Dallas 75235
D. A. Kerr, *President*
(214) 638-6480, 1969, VA, VR, INS, BIA

Bachelor of Science in Electronics		
Engineering Technology	135	—
Associate Degree in Electronics		
Engineering Technology	105	—
Electronics Technician	75	—

Durham's Business College—Technical Division
600 Lavaca, Austin 78767
S. E. Mylum, Jr., *President*
(512) 478-3446, 1936, VA, VR, INS

Electronic Mechanic	26	52
Electronic Technology	39	78
Basic Drafting	26	52
General Drafting	39	78

Hallmark Aero-Tech
1130 99th Street, San Antonio 78214
Richard H. Fessler, *Director*
(512) 924-8551, 1969, VA, VR, INS

Airframe & Powerplant Technician	52	—

Industrial Trade School
7200 Harry Hines Boulevard, Dallas 75235
F. P. Childress, *Director*
(214) 350-8753, 1958, VA, VR, BIA

General Welding	16	32
Combination General & Pipe Welding	26	52
Machine Shop Training	26	49
Radio-Television Technician	26	52
Maintenance Mechanic	22	42

Lincoln Technical Institute
2227 Irving Boulevard, Dallas 75207
J. E. Fambry, *Director*
(214) 631-2780, 1966, VA, VR, INS, BIA

Auto-Diesel Truck Technology	70	—
Automotive Technology	50	—
Basic Automotive Mechanics	30	—
Scientific Engine Tune-up	15	—
Diesel Engines	10	—
Automatic Transmissions	10	—
Diesel & Truck Technology	52	—

Mannequin Manor Fashion Merchandising School
512 North Mesa, El Paso, 79901
Mary Frances Simon, *President*
(915) 533-6311, 1968, VA, VR, INS

Fashion Merchandising-Apparel Major	36	—
Fashion Merchandising-Interior Design		
& Decoration Major	36	—

San Antonio College of Medical and Dental Assistants
505 East Travis Street, San Antonio 78205
Kathleen B. Voigt, *Director*
(512) 224-0756, 1966, VA, VR, INS

Medical Assistant/Clinical/Clerical	32	—
Dental Assistant	24	—
Lab Assistant	15	—
Medical Receptionist/Clerical	16	—

Southwest School of Medical Assistants
115 North Broadway, San Antonio 78205
Stanley H. Dennis, *Director*
(512) 224-2296, 1971, VA, VR

Laboratory Assistant	26	—
Medical Assistant	26	—
Nurse Aide/Male Orderly	9	—

Texas College of Medical & Dental Assistants
4255 L.B.J. Freeway at Midway Road, Suite 242,
Dallas 75234
W. Lanny Tucker, *Director*
(214) 263-6778, 1969, VA, VR, INS, BIA

Medical Assistant	28	—
Dental Assistant	21	—

Texas Institute
Frito-Lay Tower (240-C), Dallas 75235
Stewart W. Swacker, *President/Director*
(214) 357-6522, 1966, VA, VR, INS, BIA

Industry Oriented Data Processor	32	64
Mini-Systems Data Processor	32	64
Data Processor	26	52
Business Oriented Computer Programming	18	36
Common Business Oriented Language (COBOL)	6	12
Assembly Language Programming	7	14
Disk Operating System (DOS)	2	4
Application Programming Workshop	6	12
Computer Operations	11	22
Data Conversion Operator (KEYPUNCH)	15	26

United Electronics Institute
3631 Cedar Springs Road, Dallas 75219
Donald R. White, *Director*
(214) 526-2760, 1968, VA, VR, INS

Electronics Technology	91	—
Basic Electronics, Radio & TV	80	—

Miss Wade's Fashion Merchandising College
Suite M-1000, The Apparel Mart, Dallas 75207
Frank J. Tortoriello, Jr., *President*
(214) 637-3530, 1965, VA, VR, INS, BIA

Fashion Merchandising	48	—
Fashion Design	48	—
Interior Design	48	—

West Texas Barber College
4001 Mockingbird Lane, Amarillo 79109
James Watson, *Vice President*
(806) 355-9426, 1938, VA, VR

Barber Styling	38	76

UTAH

The Bryman School
445 South Third East, Salt Lake City 84111
Kathleen Dixon, *Director*
(801) 521-2830, 1970, VA, VR

Medical Assisting	28	40
Dental Assisting	28	40
Medical Office Management	28	40

Ron Bailie Western School of Broadcast
364 South State Street, Salt Lake City 84111
Paul Droubay, *President*
(801) 355-3632, 1968, VA, VR, BIA

Electronics Theory-First Class		
F.C.C. License	44	—
Announcing	24	—

Salt Lake City College of Medical and Dental Assistants
P.O. Box 15625, 2624 South Main Street, Salt Lake City 84115
H. Max Seal, *Director*
(801) 487-0657, 1966, VA, VR, INS

Medical Assisting	30	—
Dental Assisting	20	—
Medical Receptionist	20	—

VIRGINIA

Computer Learning Center
9401 Lee Highway, Fairfax 22030
Bradford Daggett, *Center Director*
(703) 273-7501, 1967, VA, VR, INS

	Length in Weeks	Full Time	Part Time
Data Processing Program	24		40

Control Data Institute
3717 Columbia Pike, Arlington 22204
John J. Lantzy, *Director*
(703) 979-3450, 1966, VA, VR, INS, BIA

	Length in Weeks	Full Time	Part Time
Computer Programming & Operations	26		54
Computer Technology	26		49

Electronic Computer Programming Institute
416 Janaf Office Building, Norfolk 23502
A. Dreyfus, *Director*
(804) 855-3311, 1965, VA, VR, INS

	Length in Weeks	Full Time	Part Time
Data Processing & Computer Programming	26		75
Advanced Programming (Systems)	8		26
Advanced Programming (Scientific)	8		26
Data Processing & Keypunch	12		–
Computer Electronics	16		50
Computer Systems	12		38
Computer Technology	28		88

Fogg's Technical Institute
Route 1, Hanover 23069
George O. Fogg, *Owner-Director*
(804) 798-4849, 1971, VA, VR

	Length in Weeks	Full Time	Part Time
Automotive Technology	52		–
Nursing Assistance Program	9		–

WASHINGTON

Ron Bailie School of Broadcast
170 Denny Way, Seattle 98109
Ronald L. Bailie, *President*
(206) 682-3696, 1963, VA, VR

	Length in Weeks	Full Time	Part Time
Announcing-Production	28		–
Electronics Theory (1st Class FCC License)	20		–

Ron Bailie School of Broadcast
East 2022 Sprague Avenue, Spokane 99202
Bob Summers, *Director*
(509) 535-1080, 1969, VA, VR

	Length in Weeks	Full Time	Part Time
Announcing-Production	28		–
Electronic Theory	20		–

Divers Institute of Technology
1133 N.W. 45th Street, Seattle 98107
John W. Manlove, *President*
(206) 783-5543, 1968, VA, VR, INS, BIA

	Length in Weeks	Full Time	Part Time
Commercial Diving Course (Air & Mixed Gas)	14		–
Professional Deep Sea Diving Course (Saturation Training)	25		–

J. M. Perry Institute
2011 West Washington Avenue, Yakima 98903
Fred J. Iraola, *Director*
(509) 453-0374, 1941, VA, VR, INS, BIA

	Length in Weeks	Full Time	Part Time
Automotive Technology	92		–
Body & Fender	69		–
Electrical Technology	92		–
Instrumentation & Industrial Electronics	92		–
Machine Technology	92		–
Refrigeration, Air Conditioning & Heating	69		–
Restaurant Cook	47		–
Automotive Parts Counterman	47		69
Major Appliance Servicing	47		–

Spokane Technical Institute
1818½ East Sprague Avenue, Spokane 99202
William L. Bieber, *President*
(509) 535-7771, 1970, VA, VR, BIA

	Length in Weeks	Full Time	Part Time
Electronics Technology Course	52		–
Advanced Television Servicing	12		–
Biomedical Electronics Technician	24		–
Sanitation Technology Course	4		–

Washington Technical Institute
2222 2nd Avenue, Seattle 98121
Carl R. MacDonald, *President*
(206) 682-1911, 1914, VA, VR, INS, BIA

	Length in Weeks	Full Time	Part Time
Electronics Technician	52		96
Television Technician	64		112
Sanitation Technology	6		–
Electronics Assembly	6		–
Bio-Medical Electronics	64		96
Graphic Arts	–		26

WEST VIRGINIA

Huntington Barber College
338 Washington Avenue, Huntington 25701
T. G. Rumler, *President*
(304) 523-6311, 1957, VA, VR

	Length in Weeks	Full Time	Part Time
Barber-Styling	45		–

Meredith Manor School of Horsemanship
Route 1, Waverly 26184
Ronald W. Meredith, *Proprietor*
(304) 679-3128, 1963, VA, INS

	Length in Weeks	Full Time	Part Time
Riding Master	36		–
Riding Instructor	24		–
Camp Instructor	12		–
Riding-Blacksmith	34		–

United Electronics Institute
2345 Chesterfield Avenue, S.E., Charleston 25304
Charles L. Deitz, *Director*
(304) 343-0121, 1968, VA, VR

	Length in Weeks	Full Time	Part Time
Electronics Technology	91		–
Basic Electronics, Radio, TV	80		–

WISCONSIN

Acme Institute of Technology
1122 Washington Street, Manitowoc 54220
William W. Warren, *President*
(414) 682-5615, 1955, VA, VR, INS, BIA

	Length in Weeks	Full Time	Part Time
Industrial Mathematics	4		–
Mechanical Drawing	8		–
Tool Designing	48		–
Die Designing	48		–
Plastics Mold Designing	56		–

Acme Institute of Technology
9235 West Capitol Drive, Milwaukee 53222
William W. Warren, *President*
(414) 463-9070, 1958, VA, VR, INS, BIA

	Length in Weeks	Full Time	Part Time
Industrial Mathematics	4		–
Mechanical Drawing	8		–
Tool Designing	48		–
Die Designing	48		–
Plastics Mold Designing	56		–

Diesel Truck Driver Training School
Highway 151 & Elder Lane, Sun Prairie 53590
Robert Klabacka, *President*
(608) 837-7800, 1963, VA, VR, BIA

	Length in Weeks	Full Time	Part Time
Diesel tractor-trailer semi operation	3		–

	Length in Weeks	Full Time	Part Time
Trans American School of Broadcasting			
811 North First Avenue, Wausau 54401			
Raymond J. Szmanda, *President*			
(715) 842-1000, 1969, VA, VR, BIA			
Broadcasting	33	–	
Wisconsin School of Electronics			
1915 Sherman Avenue, Madison 53704			
Vincent A. Vanderheiden, *President*			
(608) 249-6611, 1948, VA, VR, INS, BIA			
Electronic Technician–Certificate	48	–	
Associate Degree, Electronic Engineering			
Technology	96	–	
Medical Secretary/Transcription	36	–	

	Length in Weeks	Full Time	Part Time
WYOMING			
Wyoming Technical Institute			
Box 906, North of Laramie, Laramie 82070			
Michael K. Schutte, *President*			
(307) 742-3776, 1966, VA, VR, BIA			
Automotive Technician	26	–	
Auto Body and Paint Technician	26	–	
Diesel Technician	26	–	

NATTS 1976-77 DIRECTORY
SUPPLEMENTAL LISTING 1-16-77

*Denotes schools accredited January 16, 1977

*Mr. E. B. Kessler, Director
ABC Trade School
3848 East 39th Street
Tucson, Arizona 85713

Mr. John Wade, Director
American Academy of Broadcasting
726 Chestnut Street
Philadelphia, Pennsylvania 19106

*Mr. William M. Pierce, President
American College of Health & Business Careers
2811 N.W. 36th
Oklahoma City, Oklahoma 73112

*Mr. C. F. Allison, President
Bailey Technical School
5303 East 103rd Street
Kansas City, Missouri 64137

Mr. Tom Summers, Director
Ron Bailie School of Broadcast
1245 South Winchester Boulevard
San Jose, California 95128

Mr. Steven B. Sotraidis, Director of
Administration
Brooks College, Specializing in Fashion
and Design Careers
4825 East Pacific Coast Highway
Long Beach, California 90804

*Mr. Joseph L. Butera, Director
Butera School of Art
111 Beacon Street
Boston, Massachusetts 02116

Ms. Estelle Harman, Director
Estelle Harman Actors' Workshop
522 North La Brea Avenue
Los Angeles, California 90036

*Mr. John Koutavas, Director
Magna Institute of Dental Technology
386 Park Avenue South
New York, New York 10016

*Mr. Jack Y. Kahn, President
Medical Institute of Minnesota
2309 Nicollet Avenue
Minneapolis, Minnesota 55404

Mr. Jack Tolbert, President
The Medix School
1406 Crain Highway South
Glen Burnie, Maryland 21061

*Mrs. Elizabeth Shreffler, Associate
Director
Midwest Institute for Medical
Assistants
111 North Taylor Avenue
Kirkwood, Missouri 63122

*Mr. Louis G. Farber, President
Ohio State College of Barber Styling
195 South High Street
Columbus, Ohio 43215

Mr. Thomas E. Kmetz, Director
Opticians Institute
2020 West Liberty Avenue
Pittsburgh, Pennsylvania 15226

*Ms. Jean Dunn Salata, Director
Progressive Fashion School
406 Euclid Avenue
Cleveland, Ohio 44114

*Mr. W. G. Dubuque, President
The Quincy Technical School
501 North 3rd Street
Quincy, Illinois 62301

*Mr. W. G. Graffeo, General Manager
R.E.T.S. Electronic School
103 Park Avenue
Nutley, New Jersey 07110

Mr. Ross L. Alloway, President
Rosston School of Men's Hair Design
137 South Anaheim Boulevard
Anaheim, California 93815

Mr. Ross L. Alloway, President
Rosston School of Men's Hair Design
717 Pine Avenue
Long Beach, California 90813

Mr. Ross L. Alloway, President
Rosston School of Men's Hair Design
29 West Colorado Boulevard
Pasadena, California 91105

Mr. Ross L. Alloway, President
Rosston School of Men's Hair Design
18452 Sherman Way
Reseda, California 91335

Mr. Ross L. Alloway, President
Rosston School of Men's Hair Design
475 North "E" Street
San Bernardino, California 92401

Mr. Donald C. Jarrell, Director
Southlake College of Dental Technology
4130 East South Street
Lakewood, California 90712

Mr. Stanley Warshaw, President
U.S. School of Professional Paperhanging
16 Chaplin Avenue
Rutland, Vermont 05701

Mr. Phillip J. Hassan, President
Vo-Tech Institute
315 Juan Tabo N.E., P.O. Box 11372
Albuquerque, New Mexico 87112

*Mr. Lewis H. Warner, President
Welder Training & Testing Institute
1741 Woodhaven Drive
Cornwells Heights, Pennsylvania 19020

APPENDIX B: A SAMPLER OF NONACCREDITED SPECIALTY SCHOOLS

In all the skill areas, there are other, nonaccredited schools out there, waiting to be found. Finding these schools is like mushroom gathering: two days after you last looked others have sprouted, the result of a twenty-year dream or a lucky accident that suddenly propelled someone into the private school business.

In this listing are given the names, addresses, and, in some cases, telephone numbers of more than one hundred nonaccredited schools. We have studied their catalogs and think they make sense. Obviously this is not a definitive listing; there are hundreds and hundreds of schools that are not included. This is just a "sampler." The Bibliography contains a list of useful directories for help in finding additional schools and skills.

None of these schools is accredited, although any number of them may seek accreditation in the future. The schools are for you to investigate. We have visited only a few of them.

Small, private specialty schools are sensitive to local and national labor markets; they flourish or wane depending on the quality of their management. Consequently, a few will be out of business by the time you decide to write away for a catalog.

AUCTIONEERING

Fort Smith Auction School
Fort Smith, Arkansas 72901
Tel: (501) 646-1181

The Reisch College of Auctioneering
Mason City, Iowa 50401

Reppert School of Auctioneering
Decatur, Indiana 46733
Tel: (219) 724-3804

Superior School of Auctioneering
P.O. Box 1281
Decatur, Illinois 62525
Tel: (217) 817-3253

AUTO DESIGN

> *H. L. Bosca School of Automotive Body Design*
> *23225 Johnston Avenue*
> *East Detroit, Michigan 48021*

BAKING

> *American Institute of Baking*
> *400 East Ontario Street*
> *Chicago, Illinois 60511*

BANKING AND LAW

> *The Institute for Paralegal Training*
> *13th Floor—401 Walnut Street*
> *Philadelphia, Pennsylvania 19106*
> *Tel: (215) WA 5-0905*

> *Safair Finance Credit Collection Management School*
> *252 West Manchester Avenue*
> *Los Angeles, California 90003*

> *Teller Training Institute*
> *1505 Fourth Avenue, Suite 403*
> *Seattle, Washington 98101*
> *Tel: (206) 624-7450*

BARTENDING

> *Américan Bartenders School*
> *369 Lexington Avenue*
> *New York, New York 10017*

> *Bartender Training Institute*
> *830 Ala Moana Boulevard, Suite 225*
> *Honolulu, Hawaii 96813*
> *Tel: (808) 537-1869*

> *Bartenders School*
> *2211 North 24th Street*
> *Phoenix, Arizona 85008*

The Denver Bartending School
"Denver's Original Bartending School"
706 East 17th Avenue
Denver, Colorado 80203
Tel: (303) 255-7737

Your Host of Hollywood
1645 North La Brea Avenue
Holywood, California 90028
Tel: (213) 874-0120

CAKE DECORATING

Gates School of Cake Decorating
10214 East Beach
Bellflower, California 90706

Prichett's School of Master Cake Decorating
R.F.D. No. 2, Box 173
Dover, New Hampshire 03820
Tel: (603) 868-8869

CANDYMAKING

Philadelphia School of Candymaking
136 South State Road
Upper Darby, Pennsylvania 19082
Tel: (215) HI 6-8228

CHICK SEXING

American Chick Sexing School
168 Prospect Avenue
Lansdale, Pennsylvania 19446

CHILD CARE

Center for Early Education
563 North Alfred Street
Los Angeles, California 90048
Tel: (213) 651-0707

Midwest Montessori Teacher Training Center
1010 West Chicago Avenue
Chicago, Illinois 60622
Tel: (312) CH 3-4586

Montessori Institute of Atlanta
P.O. Box 12054
2461 Peachtree Road, N.E.
Atlanta, Georgia 30305
Tel: (404) 261-2029

CHILD CARE ATTENDANT

New England School for Pediatts
866 Beacon Street
Boston, Massachusetts 02215

CINEMA

Anthropology Film Center
P.O. Box 493
Santa Fe, New Mexico 87501

CLOWN THEATRE

Ringling Bros. and Barnum and Bailey Circus
Solters/Sabinson/Roskin, Inc.—National Press Representatives
62 West 45th Street
New York, New York 10036
Tel: (212) 867-8500

COIN MACHINE REPAIR

Coin Machine Technical Training Institute, Ltd.
123 South Main Street
Fort Morgan, Colorado 80701
Tel: (303) 867-8477

CONSTRUCTION

> *Institute of Design and Construction*
> *141 Willoughby Street*
> *Brooklyn, New York 11201*
> *Tel: (212) UL 5-3661*

COOKING

> *Miss Farmer's School of Cookery*
> *40 Hereford Street*
> *Boston, Massachusetts 02115*

COTTON GRADING

> *Murdock's International Cotton School*
> *805–13 McCall Building*
> *Memphis, Tennessee 38103*

COURT REPORTING

> *Mile Hi Reporting School*
> *6301 West 44th Avenue*
> *Wheat Ridge, Colorado 80033*
> *Tel: (303) 421-3685*

CROP DUSTING

> *Cal-Ag-Aero*
> *Hanford Airport*
> *Hanford, California 93230*
> *Tel: (209) 582-0225*

DEALING

> *Nevada School of Dealing*
> *226 Ogden*
> *Las Vegas, Nevada 89101*
> *Tel: (702) 382-6522*

DRY CLEANING

Gerber's School for Advancement of Drycleaning Skills
3712 West Jefferson Boulevard
Los Angeles, California 90016
Tel: (213) 735-5116

FARM EQUIPMENT REPAIR

Agri-Trade Schools
P.O. Box 2111
Salinas, California 93901

FLORAL DESIGN

Bambi's Floral Trade School
5835–5903 Allen Road
Allen Park, Michigan 48101

Design Floral School
2518 West 29th
Denver, Colorado 80211
Tel: (303) 477-3805

Elva May School of Floral Designing
1500 West Commonwealth Avenue
Fullerton, California 92633
Tel: (714) 525-8464

Everett's School of Floristry
Everett Menkens Artistic Enterprises Inc.
204 Clifton Avenue
Lakewood, New Jersey 08701
Tel: (201) 367-2100

GEM CUTTING

Bethel Hill Lapidary
Rt. 202 and Aquetong Road
New Hope, R.D., Pennsylvania 18938
Tel: (215) 862-5404

GUNSMITHING

> *Colorado School of Trades, Inc.*
> *1545 Hoyt Street*
> *Lakewood, Colorado 80215*
> *Tel:* (303) 233-4697

> *Pennsylvania Gunsmith School*
> *812 Ohio River Boulevard*
> *Avalon*
> *Pittsburgh, Pennsylvania 15202*

HORSEMANSHIP

> *Huntlea Horse Center*
> *Lynnville, Tennessee 38472*
> *Tel:* (615) 527-3387

> *Morven Park International Equestrian Institute*
> *Route 2, Box 8*
> *Leesburg, Virginia 22075*
> *Tel:* (703) 777-2890

> *Williamson School of Horsemanship*
> *P.O. Box 506*
> *Hamilton, Montana 59840*
> *Tel:* (406) 363-2874

> *Windfield Manor School of Horsemanship*
> *Route 1, Box 101*
> *Fargo, North Dakota 58102*
> *Tel:* (701) 293-6323

HORSESHOEING

> *Eastern States Farrier School*
> *R.D. 1, Box 49*
> *Phoenix, New York 13135*
> *Tel:* (315) 695-6232

Martinsville School of Farriery
P.O. Box 1341
Martinsville, Virginia 24112
Tel: (703) 638-1015

Midwest Farrier School
223 Fairground Road
Xenia, Ohio 45385
Tel: (513) 372-9731

Midwest Horse Shoeing School
Maple Avenue, R.R. 3
Macomb, Illinois 61455
Tel: (309) 833-4063

Nebraska Farrier School
Rural Route 1
Lincoln Nebraska 68502
Tel: (402) 432-2639

Oklahoma Farrier's College
Bud and Connie Beaston
Route 1, Box 13
Sperry, Oklahoma 74073

Porterville Horseshoeing School, Inc.
810 North Jaye Street
Porterville, California 93257
Tel: (209) 784-8967

HORTICULTURE

Du Page Horticultural School, Inc.
Box 342
West Chicago, Illinois 60185
Tel: (312) 231-3414

Pacific Tropical Botanical Garden
P.O. Box 340
Lawai, Kauai, Hawaii 96765
Tel: (808) 332-8131

LIE DETECTOR EXAMINER

The Backster School
165 West 46th Street
New York, New York 10036
Tel: (212) 265-6824

John E. Reid and Associates
Suite 700–600 South Michigan Avenue
Chicago, Illinois 60605
Tel: (312) 922-1800

LOCKSMITHING

Lockmasters
Clover Park Professional Building
2425 Clover St.
Rochester, N.Y. 14618
Tel: (716) 244-4750

Universal School of Master Locksmithing, Inc.
P.O. Box 4868
Sacramento, California 95825
Tel: (916) 482-4213

LUMBER INSPECTION

National Hardwood Lumber Association
59 East Van Buren Street
Chicago, Illinois 60605
Tel: (312) 427-2810

MARINE OCCUPATIONS

Merchant Marine School of Seamen's Church Institute of New York
15 State Street
New York, New York 10004
Tel: (212) 269-2710

The National River Academy of the United States of America
Drawer No. 827
Helena, Arkansas 72342
Tel: (501) 338-6701

Pacific Maritime Academy
1739-C Ala Moana
Honolulu, Hawaii 96815

Stewards Training and Recreation, Inc.
4088 Porter Creek Road
Santa Rosa, California 95404
Tel: (707) LI 2-1533; (707) EX 2-1440

MEAT CUTTING

Cut-Wrap-Sell Meat-Cutting School
603 San Juan
Trinidad, Colorado 81082
Tel: (303) 846-2275

Oregon Meat Cutting School
26 North 7th Street
Cottage Grove, Oregon 97424
Tel: (503) 942-5351

Southwestern College of Meat Cutters
1301 South May Avenue
Oklahoma City, Oklahoma 73108
Tel: (405) 681-2633

MEDICAL SPECIALTY

Metropolitan School of Infant and Geriatric Care
175 Fifth Avenue
New York, New York 10010

The North American College of Acupuncture
4584 Fraser Street
Vancouver 10, B.C.
Canada

MOTORCYCLE MECHANICS

American Motorcycle Mechanics School
2840 North Halsted Street
Chicago, Illinois 60657
Tel: (312) 929-0771

American Motorcycle Institute
P.O. Box 2628
Daytona Beach, Florida 32015

West Coast Training Service, Inc.
1125 21st Street
Milwaukie, Oregon 97222
Tel: (503) 659-5181

MULTI-COURSE SCHOOLS

Daryl School of Trades
1531 Vine Street
Philadelphia, Pennsylvania 19102
Tel: (215) LO 3-2484

> *Building Maintenance*
> *Maintenance Electricity*
> *Carpentry*
> *Typewriter Repair*
> *Office Machine Repair*

Southwest Electrical & Mechanical Institute
120 Playmoor
San Antonio, Texas 78210
Tel: (512) 532-5281

> *Building Maintenance*
> *Carpentry*
> *Maintenance Electricity*
> *Typewriter Repair*
> *Office Machine Repair*
> *Electrical Appliance Repair*
> *Small Gasoline Engine Repair*
> *Outboard Motor Repair*

Technical Trades Institute
11 West Vermijo
Colorado Springs, Colorado 80902
Tel: (303) 632-7626

>   *Technical Drawing*
>   *Technical Drafting*
>   *Architectural Drafting*
>   *Civil Eng. Drafting*
>   *Television Technician*
>   *Electronic Technician*
>   *Electronic Service Technician*
>   *Appliance Repair Technician*
>   *Refrigeration/Air Conditioning Technician*
>   *Major Appliance/Refrig./Air Conditioning Technician*

MUSICAL INSTRUMENT REPAIR

>   *Eastern School of Musical Instrument Repair*
>   *1565 Union Avenue*
>   *Union, New Jersey 07083*
>   *Tel: (201) 686-6494*

OFFICE MACHINE REPAIR

>   *Wichita Office Equipment Repair School*
>   *1913 East Central*
>   *Wichita, Kansas 67214*
>   *Tel: (316) 265-6233*

OIL BURNER REPAIR

>   *Oil Heat Institute of Washington*
>   *400 Dexter Avenue North*
>   *Seattle, Washington 98109*
>   *Tel: (206) MA 3-8730*

OUTFITTERS AND GUIDES

Exum Mountain Guide Service and School of
American Mountaineering
Moose Post Office
Wyoming 83012
Tel: (307) 733-2297

The National Outdoor Leadership School
Box AA
Lander, Wyoming 82520
Tel: (307) 332-4381

PIANO TUNING

Emil Fries Piano Hospital and Training Center
2510 East Evergreen Boulevard
Vancouver, Washington 98661
Tel: (206) 693-1511

Perkins School of Piano Tuning & Technology
9901 Lorain Avenue
Cleveland, Ohio 44102
Tel: (216) 631-9485

The Sims School of Piano Technology
P.O. Box 3277
Columbus, Georgia 31903

PRINTING

Ambassador School of Lithography
3141 South Broadway
Englewood, Colorado 80110
Tel: (303) 761-1898

Manhattan School of Printing
88 West Broadway
New York, New York 10007

SADDLE MAKING

Brand's School of Western Saddlery
P.O. Box 748
Ralston, Wyoming 82440
Tel: (307) 754-4336

SIGN PAINTING

Bloomfield School of Signcraft
172 Orange Street
Bloomfield, New Jersey 07003
Tel: (201) 748-2182

Institute of Lettering and Design
1733 West Greenleaf Avenue
Chicago, Illinois 60626

SMALL APPLIANCE REPAIR

New England Appliance Service School, Inc.
1018 Commonwealth Avenue
Boston, Massachusetts 02215
Tel: (617) 232-8875

SURVEYING AND MAPPING

Brinker School of Surveying and Mapping, Inc.
2475 West 26th Avenue
Denver, Colorado, 80211
Tel: (303) 458-6424

TAILORING

Joe D. Cole's Tailoring School
2540 Bradley Road
Baton Rouge, Louisiana 70807

Craft School of Tailoring
933 North Broad Street
Philadelphia, Pennsylvania 19123
Tel: (215) CE 5-2867

Metropolitan School of Tailoring
128 South Paulina Street
Chicago, Illinois 60612

THEATRE

Will-O-Way Apprentice Theatre
775 West Long Lake Road
Bloomfield Hills, Michigan 48013
Tel: (313) MI 4-4418

TRAFFIC CONTROL

Academy of Advanced Traffic
50 Broadway
New York, New York 10004
Tel: (212) WH 3-7160

College of Advanced Traffic
22 West Madison Street
Chicago, Illinois 60602
Tel: (312) 346-8630

UMPIRING

Al Somers School for Umpires
P.O. Box 2041
Daytona Beach, Florida 32015

UPHOLSTERY

Colorado School of Upholstery
1424 Wazee Street
Denver, Colorado 80202
Tel: (303) 623-4500

Fitzgibbons School of Upholstery
11363 S.W. 40th Street
Miami, Florida 33165
Tel: (305) 223-2764

Moch Upholstery School
1001 Ohio Street
Quincy, Illinois
Tel: (217) 224-1673

Portland Upholstery School
7626 N.E. Sandy Boulevard
Portland, Oregon 97213
Tel: (503) 288-7384

Upholstery Trades School
721 Broadway
New York, New York 10003
Tel: (212) OR 7-1680

VIOLIN MAKING

Professional Violin-Making School of America
304 East 2nd South
Salt Lake City, Utah 84111
Tel: (801) 364-3651

WATCHMAKING

Bowman Technical School of Watchmaking, Engraving &
Jewelry Repairing
Duke and Chestnut Streets
Lancaster, Pennsylvania 17602

Etienne School of Watchmaking
818 East Washington Boulevard
Pasadena, California 91104

Houston Technical College
1301 Waugh Drive
Houston, Texas 77019

APPENDIX C: NATIONALLY RECOGNIZED ACCREDITING ASSOCIATIONS FOR SPECIALIZED OCCUPATIONAL PROGRAMS

The following accrediting bodies have been recognized by the United States Commissioner of Education as being reliable authorities concerning the quality of education or training offered by educational institutions or programs.

BUSINESS

(Private junior and senior colleges of business, and private business schools)

Association of Independent Colleges and Schools
Dana R. Hart, Executive Secretary
Accrediting Commission
1730 M Street, N.W.
Washington, D.C. 20036

COSMETOLOGY

(Cosmetology schools and programs)

Cosmetology Accrediting Commission
James Taylor, Executive Director
25755 Southfield Road
Southfield, Michigan 48075

FUNERAL SERVICE EDUCATION

(Independent schools and collegiate departments)
American Board of Funeral Service Education
William H. Ford, Administrator
201 Columbia Street
Fairmont, West Virginia 26554

HOME STUDY EDUCATION

(Private correspondence schools)
National Home Study Council
William A. Fowler, Executive Secretary
Accrediting Commission
1601 18th Street, N.W.
Washington, D.C. 20009

OCCUPATIONAL, TRADE, AND TECHNICAL EDUCATION

(Private trade and technical schools)
National Association of Trade and Technical Schools (NATTS)
William A. Goddard, Secretary
Accrediting Commission
2021 L Street, N.W.
Washington, D.C. 20036

APPENDIX D: CONSUMER ADVICE OFFICES

	STATE APPROVAL AND LICENSING AGENCIES	STATE CONSUMER OFFICES	STATE ASSOCIATIONS
ALABAMA	State Department of Education Division of Vocational Education 845 State Office Building Montgomery, Alabama 36104	Consumer Protection Officer Office of the Governor 138 Adams Building Montgomery, Alabama 36104	
ALASKA	Vocational & Adult Education Department of Education Pouch "F" Juneau, Alaska 99801	Attorney General of Alaska Pouch "K", State Capitol Juneau, Alaska 99801	
ARIZONA	Arizona State Board of Private Technical & Business Schools 1812 West Monroe Phoenix, Arizona 85007 Arizona Veterans Service Commission P.O. Box 6123 Phoenix, Arizona 85005	Attorney General of Arizona 159 State Capitol Building Phoenix, Arizona 85007	Arizona Private School Association P.O. Box 2668 Mesa, Arizona 85204
ARKANSAS	State Approving Agency for Veterans Department of Education Arch Ford Building Little Rock, Arkansas 72201 Vocational Standards Section Department of Education	Attorney General of Arkansas Justice Building Little Rock, Arkansas 72201	

Arch Ford Building
Little Rock, Arkansas 72201

CALIFORNIA	*Southern* State Department of Education 217 West First Street Los Angeles, California 90012 *Northern* Bureau of School Approvals 721 Capitol Mall Sacramento, California 95814	Attorney General of California 500 Wells Fargo Bank Building Sacramento, California 95814	California Association for Private Education 926 J Street Sacramento, California 95814 Santa Clara County Association of Private Schools 1414 North Winchester Boulevard San Jose, California 95128
COLORADO	Proprietary Schools & Veterans Education State Board of Community Colleges & Occupational Education 503 State Service Building 1525 Sherman Street Denver, Colorado 80203	Attorney General of Colorado 104 State Capitol Denver, Colorado 80203	Colorado Private School Association 3501 East First Avenue, Suite One Denver, Colorado 80206
CONNECTICUT	Consultant for Private Schools State Department of Education P.O. Box 2219 Hartford, Connecticut 06115 Veterans Education & Services State Department of Education P.O. Box 2219 Hartford, Connecticut 06115	Department of Consumer Protection State Office Building Hartford, Connecticut 06115	Connecticut Association of Private Schools 2279 Mount Vernon Road Southington, Connecticut 06489

	STATE APPROVAL AND LICENSING AGENCIES	STATE CONSUMER OFFICES	STATE ASSOCIATIONS
DELAWARE	Director of Vocational Education Department of Public Instruction Dover, Delaware 19901	Attorney General of Delaware Public Building Wilmington, Delaware 19801	
DISTRICT OF COLUMBIA	License Branch Department of Economic Development 614 H Street, N.W., Room 308 Washington, D.C. 20001	Department of Economic Development Consumer Retail Credit Division 614 H Street, N.W., Room 306 Washington, D.C. 20001	Chesapeake & Potomac Association of Private Schools 720 Providence Road Towson, Maryland 21204
	Services to Veterans 415 12th Street, N.W. Room 1001 Washington, D.C. 20004		
FLORIDA	State Board of Independent Postsecondary Vocational, Technical, Trade & Business Schools	Consumer Advisor to the Governor Holland Building, 2nd Floor Tallahassee, Florida 32304	Florida State Association of Private Schools 1005 East Jackson Street Tampa, Florida 33602
	490 Barnett Bank Building Tallahassee, Florida 32304		
	State Approving Agency for Veterans Training 1720 South Gadsden Street Tallahassee, Florida 32304		

GEORGIA	Department of Veterans Service One Hunter Street, S.W. Atlanta, Georgia 30334 State Department of Education 312 State Office Building Atlanta, Georgia 30334	Georgia Consumer Services Program 15 Peachtree Street, Room 909 Atlanta, Georgia 30303	Georgia Private School Association P.O. Box 7174 Atlanta, Georgia 30309
HAWAII	Accreditation & Private School Licensing Department of Education 1270 Queen Emma Street Honolulu, Hawaii 96813	Director of Consumer Protection Office of the Governor P.O. Box 3767 Honolulu, Hawaii 96811	
IDAHO	State Approving Agency Department of Education State Office Building Boise, Idaho 83707	Attorney General of Idaho State Capitol Boise, Idaho 83707	
ILLINOIS	State Approving Agency Illinois Veterans' Commission 1229 South Michigan Avenue Chicago, Illinois 60605 Private Business & Vocational Schools 316 South Second Street Springfield, Illinois 62706	Attorney General of Illinois 160 North LaSalle Street Chicago, Illinois 60601	Illinois Federation of Independent Private Schools 1135 West Fullerton Avenue Coyne American Building, Room 600 Chicago, Illinois 60614

	STATE APPROVAL AND LICENSING AGENCIES	STATE CONSUMER OFFICES	STATE ASSOCIATIONS
INDIANA	Indiana Private School Accrediting Commission ISTA Building, Suite 810 150 West Market Street Indianapolis, Indiana 46204	Attorney General of Indiana 219 State House Indianapolis, Indiana 46204	Indiana Association of Private Schools P.O. Box 1665 Indianapolis, Indiana 46202
	Department of Veterans' Affairs 707 State Office Building 100 North Senate Avenue Indianapolis, Indiana 46204		
IOWA	Veterans Education & Training Department of Public Instruction Grimes State Office Building Des Moines, Iowa 50319	Attorney General of Iowa State Capitol Des Moines, Iowa 50319	Iowa Private Specialized Schools Association 2500 Fleur Drive Des Moines, Iowa 50321
KANSAS	Kansas Veterans' Commission 701 Jackson Street Topeka, Kansas 66603	Attorney General of Kansas State House Topeka, Kansas 66612	Kansas Association of Private Career Schools 6211 Beach Wichita, Kansas 67208
	Proprietary Schools State Department of Education 120 East 10th Street Topeka, Kansas 66612		
KENTUCKY	Veterans Education State Department of Education Capitol Plaza Tower, 22nd Floor Frankfort, Kentucky 40601	Attorney General of Kentucky State Capitol Frankfort, Kentucky 40601	

Proprietary School Licensing Unit
Bureau of Vocational Education
Department of Education
Frankfort, Kentucky 40601

LOUISIANA

Proprietary School Commission
State Department of Education
Baton Rouge, Louisiana 70804

Veterans Education & Training
Department of Education
P.O. Box 44064
Baton Rouge, Louisiana 70804

Consumer Affairs and Promotion
Office
Department of Agriculture
P.O. Box 44302, Capitol Station
Baton Rouge, Louisiana 70804

MAINE

Bureau of Vocational Education
Department of Educational &
Cultural Services
29 Chapel Street
Augusta, Maine 04330

Attorney General of Maine
State House
Augusta, Maine 04330

MARYLAND

Business, Trade & Technical
Schools
Baltimore Washington Inter-
national Airport
P.O. Box 8717
Baltimore, Maryland 21240

Attorney General of Maryland
1200 One Charles Center
Baltimore, Maryland 21201

Chesapeake & Potomac
Association of Private Schools
720 Providence Road
Towson, Maryland 21204

	STATE APPROVAL AND LICENSING AGENCIES	STATE CONSUMER OFFICES	STATE ASSOCIATIONS
MASSACHUSETTS	Agent for Veterans Affairs Board of Higher Education Department of Education 182 Tremont Street Boston, Massachusetts 02111 Office of Private Schools Division of Occupational Education Department of Education 182 Tremont Street Boston, Massachusetts 02111	Attorney General of Massachusetts State House Boston, Massachusetts 02133	Massachusetts Association of Private Schools Hanscom Field, Box 426 Lexington, Massachusetts 02173
MICHIGAN	Private Trade Schools Department of Education P.O. Box 420 Lansing, Michigan 48902	Special Assistant to the Governor for Consumer Affairs c/o Department of Licensing 1033 South Washington Street Lansing, Michigan 48910	Michigan Association of Private Schools 1625 East Grand Boulevard Detroit, Michigan 48211
MINNESOTA	Veterans Education Unit Department of Education Capitol Square Building St. Paul, Minnesota 55101 Private Vocational School Unit Special Programs & Services Section Vocational-Technical Division Department of Education Capitol Square Building St. Paul, Minnesota 55101	Attorney General of Minnesota 102 State Capitol St. Paul, Minnesota 55101	Minnesota Association of Private Vocational Schools 160 West Ninth Street St. Paul, Minnesota 55102

MISSISSIPPI	Veterans Affairs Board P.O. Box 22623 637 North President Street Jackson, Mississippi 39205 Mississippi School & College Registration Commission P.O. Box 771 Jackson, Mississippi 39205	Attorney General of Mississippi State Capitol Jackson, Mississippi 39201	
MISSOURI	Veterans Education State Department of Education P.O. Box 480 Jefferson City, Missouri 65101	Attorney General of Missouri Supreme Court Building Jefferson City, Missouri 65101	Missouri Association of Trade and Technical Schools 722 Walnut Kansas City, Missouri 64106
MONTANA	Veterans' Education & Training Department of Public Instruction State Capitol Building Helena, Montana 59601	Consumer Protection Division Office of County Attorney 155 West Granite Street Butte, Montana 59701	.
NEBRASKA	Private Vocational Schools & Veterans Education State Department of Education 233 South 10th Street Lincoln, Nebraska 68505		Nebraska Council of Private Vocational Schools 1660 North Grant Fremont, Nebraska 68025
NEVADA	Professional Standards Branch State Department of Education Carson City, Nevada 89701	Consumer Affairs Division Department of Commerce Room 315, Nye Building 201 South Fall Street Carson City, Nevada 89701	Nevada Association of Private Schools 2635 North Decatur Boulevard Las Vegas, Nevada 89108

	STATE APPROVAL AND LICENSING AGENCIES	STATE CONSUMER OFFICES	STATE ASSOCIATIONS
NEW HAMPSHIRE	Veterans Educational Services Department of Education Division of Postsecondary Education 163 Loudon Road Concord, New Hampshire 03301	Attorney General of New Hampshire State House Annex Concord, New Hampshire 03301	
NEW JERSEY	Bureau of Area Vocational Technical & Private Schools Division of Vocational Education State Department of Education 225 West State Street, P.O. Box 2019 Trenton, New Jersey 08625	Attorney General of New Jersey State House Annex Trenton, New Jersey 08625	Private Career School Association of New Jersey P.O. Box 6832 Journal Square Station, New Jersey 07306
	(for Computer Schools only) Private Business & Correspondence Schools Division of Vocational Education Department of Education 225 West State Street, P.O. Box 2019 Trenton, New Jersey 08625		

NEW MEXICO	Governor's Approval Committee for Veterans' Training State Capitol Building Santa Fe, New Mexico 87501 Private & Postsecondary Schools Department of Education Capitol Building Santa Fe, New Mexico 87501	Attorney General of New Mexico Supreme Court Building, Box 2246 Santa Fe, New Mexico 87501	New Mexico Association of Private Schools 225 San Pedro, N.E. Albuquerque, New Mexico 87108
NEW YORK	Bureau of Occupational School Supervisions State Education Department Albany, New York 12224 *(for schools offering AOS only)* Bureau of Two-year Colleges State Education Department Albany, New York 12224	Attorney General of New York The Capitol Albany, New York 12225	Private Vocational Schools Association 88 West Broadway New York, New York 10007
NORTH CAROLINA	Veterans Education Department of Public Instruction Heart of Raleigh Building Raleigh, North Carolina 27601	Attorney General of North Carolina P.O. Box 629 Raleigh, North Carolina 27602	
NORTH DAKOTA	Private Vocational Schools State Board of Vocational Education 900 East Boulevard Bismarck, North Dakota 58501	Attorney General of North Dakota The Capitol Bismarck, North Dakota 58501	

	STATE APPROVAL AND LICENSING AGENCIES	STATE CONSUMER OFFICES	STATE ASSOCIATIONS
OHIO	State Board of School & College Registration, Room 3646 30 East Broad Street Columbus, Ohio 43215 State Approving Agency for Veterans' Training 240 Parson Avenue, Room 207 Columbus, Ohio 43215	Attorney General of Ohio State House Annex Columbus, Ohio 43215	Ohio Council of Private Colleges & Schools 1441 North Cable Road Lima, Ohio 45805
OKLAHOMA	State Accrediting Agency P.O. Box 53067, Capitol Station Oklahoma City, Oklahoma 73105	Department of Consumer Affairs Lincoln Office Plaza, Suite 74 4545 Lincoln Boulevard Oklahoma City, Oklahoma 73105	Oklahoma Private School Association 8820 East Pine Tulsa, Oklahoma 74151
OREGON	Vocational & Private School Licensing State Department of Education 942 Lancaster Drive, N.E. Salem, Oregon 97310	Attorney General of Oregon 322 State Office Building Salem, Oregon 97310	Oregon Association of Accredited Independent Vocational Schools 2416 North Marine Drive Portland, Oregon 97217 Oregon Private School Association P.O. Box 2721 Portland, Oregon 97208
PENNSYLVANIA	Bureau of Private Schools & Vocational Education Department of Education Harrisburg, Pennsylvania 17126	Attorney General of Pennsylvania 238 Capitol Building Harrisburg, Pennsylvania 17120	Pennsylvania Association of Private School Administrators Box 21036 Philadelphia, Pennsylvania 19114

	State Board of Private Trades Schools P.O. Box 911 Harrisburg, Pennsylvania 17126	
PUERTO RICO	Director of Veterans Education Department of Education Hato Rey, Puerto Rico 00919	Attorney General of Puerto Rico P.O. Box 192 San Juan, Puerto Rico 00902
RHODE ISLAND	Veterans Education State Department of Education Roger Williams Building Providence, Rhode Island 02903	Attorney General of Rhode Island Providence County Court House Providence, Rhode Island 02903
SOUTH CAROLINA	Division of Veterans Education 1429 Senate Street Columbia, South Carolina 29201	Office of Consumer Affairs Governor's Office State House Columbia, South Carolina 29201
SOUTH DAKOTA	Consultant in Guidance & Counseling Human Resources Development Division Department of Public Instruction State Capitol Building Pierre, South Dakota 57501	Attorney General of South Dakota State Capitol Pierre, South Dakota 57501
TENNESSEE	Division of Veterans Education State Department of Education 111 "E" Cordell Hull Building Nashville, Tennessee 37219	Tennessee Association of Proprietary Schools 4711 Old Kingston Pike Knoxville, Tennessee 37919

	STATE APPROVAL AND LICENSING AGENCIES	STATE CONSUMER OFFICES	STATE ASSOCIATIONS
TEXAS	Proprietary Schools & Veterans Texas Education Agency 201 East Eleventh Street Austin, Texas 78701	Attorney General of Texas Supreme Court Building Austin, Texas 78701	Texas Association of Proprietary Schools 8585 North Stemmons, Suite 201 Dallas, Texas 75247
UTAH	Veterans & Vocational Technical Affairs Utah System of Higher Education 1201 University Club Building Salt Lake City, Utah 84111	Attorney General of Utah State Capitol Salt Lake City, Utah 84114	Utah Private School Association 805 East 3300 South Salt Lake City, Utah 84106
VERMONT	Educational Field Services Department of Education Montpelier, Vermont 05602	Attorney General of Vermont State Library Building Montpelier, Vermont 05602	
VIRGINIA	Proprietary School Service State Department of Education P.O. Box 6-Q Richmond, Virginia 23216 Committee on Veterans Education State Department of Education P.O. Box 6-Q Richmond, Virginia 23216	Attorney General of Virginia Supreme Court–Library Building Richmond, Virginia 23219	Chesapeake & Potomac Association of Private Schools 720 Providence Road Towson, Maryland 21204
WASHINGTON	Veterans Education & Training Coordinating Council of Occupational Education 216 Old Capitol Building Olympia, Washington 98504	Attorney General of Washington Temple of Justice Olympia, Washington 98501	Washington Federation of Private Vocational Schools 1923 Fifth Avenue Seattle, Washington 98101

WEST VIRGINIA	Supervisor of Private Schools Department of Education 1900 Washington Street, East Charleston, West Virginia 25305	Attorney General of West Virginia The Capitol Charleston, West Virginia 25305
	Veterans Education & Training Department of Education 1900 Washington Street, East Charleston, West Virginia 25305	
WISCONSIN	Educational Approval Council Department of Public Instruction 4802 Sheboygan Avenue Madison, Wisconsin 53702	Attorney General of Wisconsin Department of Justice Madison, Wisconsin 53702	Wisconsin Council of Independent Education 174 West Wisconsin Avenue Milwaukee, Wisconsin 53203
WYOMING	Licensing & Certification Services Unit State Department of Education Capitol Building Cheyenne, Wyoming 82001	State Examiner and Administrator Consumer Credit Code State Supreme Court Building Cheyenne, Wyoming 82001
	Veterans Education Capitol Building, Room 317 Cheyenne, Wyoming 82001	

APPENDIX E: RESEARCH STUDIES

To date there have been half a dozen important studies of private vocational schools and their students. We here summarize their findings.

1. The Specialty Oriented Student (SOS) Research Program, University of Maryland. Created by Dr. Kenneth Hoyt in 1962, it is a continuing program now headquartered at University of Maryland. Hoyt studied 76 private schools and collected data from 4,887 students and graduates. The following summary of his findings was printed in the September 1972 issue of the *Compass*, the journal of the Association of Independent Colleges and Schools (business schools):

> . . . on every major evaluative point, a clear majority of those former students, dropouts as well as graduates, gave a favorable report concerning the school they attended. Almost eight in ten completed training, over eight in ten found directly training-related employment, and over eight in ten reported those things they had learned in training helped them do better work on the jobs they found. Over six in ten reported their first job met or exceeded their expectations, almost six in ten reported that if they had it to do again, they would return to the same school and take the same training, and almost six in ten reported they could not have been hired for their jobs had they not taken this training. Over half rate their training program as "very high" or "above average" more than six months after they left school for employment. There is not a single point of evaluation where even a simple majority of this large sample of former students gave a negative view of the training they had received.

Hoyt told us, "The students we talked to like the schools."

2. The second major study was published in October 1966. Commonly called the Kincaid-Podesta study, it was produced by the Stanford Research Institute under contract to the U.S. Office of Education and is entitled "Supply and Demand Factors Affecting Vocational Education Planning."

The researchers fanned out into *one* California county, Santa Clara, and inventoried the proprietary schools they found there. They started with the Yellow Pages and were astounded, as we were, to find such large numbers of private schools. They visited 55 schools and interviewed 1,009 students, many teachers, and 38 school directors. The summary has been widely quoted:

> While our exploratory study of proprietary schools has merely scratched the surface of the situation in one California county, we hope it stimulates interest in what appears to be a neglected aspect of research on vocational education. On the basis of enrollment data, it appears that proprietary schools may be making a more substantial contribution than had been suspected in instructional areas that are also in the public domain.

Kincaid-Podesta used student interviews to back up their conclusions.

> Students also commented on the individual attention that they received and the relaxed classroom atmosphere. Some students remarked that they felt free to ask questions since they were no longer threatened by the scorn of the instructor or the ridicule of classmates, as had been their experience in high school. Although the physical facilities in most schools were not as good as those of public schools, none of the students interviewed mentioned this in our discussions.

3. Dr. Harvey Belitsky, Research Economist at the Upjohn Institute for Employment Research in Washington, D.C., mailed questionnaires to a thousand private schools in late 1967, to determine "how (or even whether) private vocational schools could be widely utilized in the, training of disadvantaged persons." In 1969 he published his findings in a book, *Private Vocational Schools and Their Students: Limited Objectives, Unlimited Opportunities*. For those interested in proprietary education, the book is required reading.

In *Proprietary Education: A Search of the Literature*, Susan Johnson described the book this way:

> Belitsky's findings are most often the basis of other studies. In fact, the characteristics of proprietary schools that he defines as flexibility in operations, admissions and schedules, small class size, training in small achievement units, special course offerings, job-simulated training settings and instructor accountability for students, appear repeatedly in other studies.

4. The American Institutes for Research (AIR), under contract to the U.S. Office of Education, published its work in December 1972. It's called "A Comparative Study of Proprietary and Nonproprietary Vocational Training Programs." Unfortunately, the AIR study is often disregarded, because of a flaw in its basic setup. Here's what happened.

AIR created two samples of schools for comparison, calling one "proprietary" and the other "nonproprietary." From a preliminary group of 150 proprietary schools, 51 were eventually chosen as the most appropriate for study. The nonproprietary list finally numbered 14 schools. Some were community colleges. *Five* of them, however, were private, tax-exempt schools that, in the words of the study itself, "are in some ways more similar to the proprietary schools studied than to the nonproprietary schools." Over one-third of the "nonproprietary" sample, then, were in the wrong category.

Therefore, locked into the hundreds of pages of tables and statistics are significant differences between the proprietary sector and the nonproprietary. If the cross-eyed, skewed statistics were corrected, with all public schools in a horse race with the private schools, the picture would change. Instead of the dead heat reported in the study, we'd see a race that the private schools would win.

This flaw in the AIR study is well known and has caused the study to be shuffled aside. This is unfortunate, because the study was otherwise carefully prepared. These growth occupations were selected for comparison: secretarial, bookkeeping, medical secretarial, dental assisting, data processing and programming, electronic technology, and engineering technology.

Fifty-one proprietary school directors and 14 public school presidents were interviewed; 3,340 private school students and 3,610 public school students answered detailed questionnaires about their background and vocational training. Alumni from 1969–71 were traced and questioned about their jobs. In her review of the literature, Susan Johnson summarized what the study produced.

> The AIR study did not find significant differences anywhere. They found that both kinds of schools serve students who are very similar in sex, age, education, prior work experience and family background, though a somewhat higher percentage of minority students exists in nonproprietary schools. They conclude that proprietary schools are not in competition with nonproprietaries, but rather complement them. They cite the proprietaries specific training, short courses, and fast responses to changes in

industry and manpower demands and conclude that the profit motive of these schools has a positive impact on their quality and effectiveness.

They find few differences in educational facilities of the schools which appear "adequate" in both areas—while proprietaries seemed to have more favorable student-teacher ratios and more laboratory time. They found the teaching staffs of both kinds to be extremely similar and both kinds employ equally well-qualified teachers.

Other interesting findings of the AIR study:

■ Virtually all of the private schools provided placement services, as opposed to only 64 percent of the public schools.

■ School interviews indicated that proprietary school profit margins currently tend to be low.

■ Data about job placement was not easy to come by in either kind of school. One-third of the private schools had no usable data while only one-third of the public schools had any.

■ At least 80 percent of all students said their school provided good job training, practical skills emphasis, good teaching, and equipment needed for learning.

■ Financial worry was cited as the most common problem faced by both proprietary and nonproprietary school students.

■ About 90 percent of all students said that "learning the practical skills required for an occupation" was a source of satisfaction. "Correlations reveal positive relationships between deriving major satisfaction from learning practical skills and proprietary status, small school size. . . ."

■ About three-quarters of those who actively sought related jobs did in fact obtain them after graduation.

■ Accredited schools and chain schools surveyed are no more effective in placing graduates than unaccredited and nonchain schools.

■ It is possible to recover the costs of vocational training within three years with increased salary benefits accrued in all subgroups except proprietary computer.

The AIR study is most helpful in the area of proprietary school operations. It is filled with excellent observations about schools, students, and skills.

5. Dr. Wellford "Buzz" Wilms of the Center for Research and Development in Higher Education at the University of California, Berkeley, is directing the largest study of private and public vocational training to date. The Bibliography of this book contains the references to the published results of the first two stages of this three-stage research program.

The basic form of the study is very similar to that of the AIR study. Wilms received cooperation from fifty schools (twenty-nine proprietary and twenty-one public, mostly community colleges) in four cities, teaching six occupational fields. He was able to study about 4,800 students and graduates.

Once the data was gathered, Wilms fed it into the University of Chicago computer and came up with hundreds of little boxes of findings that are all but impenetrable to a layman. Midway in the first stage of the study, he realized that his significant finding was that disadvantaged people "tended" to go to proprietary schools. He wrote us at the time:

> The first stage of my study is done and the first draft is being typed now. I found really significant social and psychological differences between the public and proprietary kids and it looks like the public schools just aren't reaching the students that they're supposed to. We knew that all along, but didn't have it at least documented, that they tend to go to proprietaries.

The results of the second stage of the study, "The Effectiveness of Public and Proprietary Occupational Training," were presented at a briefing at the National Institute of Education in November 1974. These are the principal findings:

▪ With few exceptions, graduates of public schools had almost the same job success as graduates of proprietary schools.

▪ Proprietary schools recruited and seemed to hold the less-advantaged student better than the public schools. The proprietary school student was more likely to be a member of an ethnic minority group, to have lower educational status, and to demonstrate verbal skills inferior to those of his public school counterpart. Neither kind of school compensated for less-advantaged students' background.

▪ Women always earned less than men, and in all but one case ethnic minorities earned less than whites in the same jobs.

▪ Proprietary schools operated with fewer resources than public schools, but in most cases they targeted those resources on specific, short, intensive job training. The proprietaries paid their teachers 65 percent of comparable public school salaries and worked them harder. Consequently, average proprietary instructional costs were 35 percent less than public costs.

▪ There existed no relationship between the characteristics of public schools and success of their graduates.

▪ Limited associations existed between proprietary schools' characteristics and their graduates' later success. Graduates who earned the most generally went to proprietary schools that were moderately large with higher-paid teachers who spent fewer hours in class.

▪ Only two out of ten public school graduates in accounting got jobs as accountants. The rest became clerks or took unrelated jobs. Proprietary schools placed twice as many graduates in accounting and related jobs.

▪ There were no significant differences in the public and proprietary computer programmer graduates' earnings, although the public graduates got higher-level jobs more often. Twenty-seven out of 100 public graduates and 20 out of 100 proprietary graduates got programming and related jobs.

▪ Eighty percent of public and proprietary school students who trained as dental assistants got jobs as dental assistants.

▪ Most women from both sectors who trained for secretarial jobs got them, although a sizable proportion took clerk-typist jobs. Proprietary graduates got secretarial jobs more often than public graduates and they earned significantly more in the long run.

▪ Most women graduates, public and proprietary, who trained as cosmetologists became employed as cosmetologists.

▪ In electronics, 81 percent of the proprietary school graduates got jobs either as electronic technicians (22 percent) or related work such as radio and TV repair and craft apprenticing (59 percent).

▪ Generally, proprietary training costs much more than public school training.

At a November 1974 briefing in Washington, Wilms commented on the old question of "shadiness" in the proprietary sector: "Of 29 proprietary schools that we asked to join the study, only two turned us down. That's a pretty small percentage. No evidence was found that proprietary schools, which attract applicants with fewer educational skills, either exploited their students or used deceptive advertising. The concept of 'shadiness' is not borne out at all."

The study itself reports that out of twenty-nine private schools, *only one* went out of business in the two years of the study and only two were sold in that period. Wilms concluded that it was a stable industry.

As yet, Wilms has produced no data on attrition or dropout rates. However, he has said: ". . . our survey in Chicago in September, 1972 showed that although the proprietary and public postsecondary schools started with about the same number of secretarial and data processing enrollees, the proprietary schools graduated *4 to 6 times* as many as the public community colleges. This same pattern seems to hold in the other locations we are studying."

6. Connoisseurs of these research studies should obtain William Hyde's *Metropolitan Proprietary Schools: A Study of Functions and Economic Responsiveness*. Published in December, 1974, it is now available either through the Comparative Education Center at the University of Chicago, Chicago, Illinois 60637, or the Library, National Institute of Education, Washington, D.C. 20208.

From the Introduction:

As the nation examines its educational priorities and resources, it is crucial for future planning that we not assume that proprietary school sector to be simply a private version of public vocational education, but recognize that its functions and responses may be unique. To this end, we examine how the schools, as private, profit-motivated firms, respond to a number of factors, all of which have implications for their operations and eventual survival. In one or more situations we examine how labor market conditions alter the demand for proprietary school training, how a proprietary school responds to changing market conditions and adapts to changing technology, and how another school is affected by the recent and rapid expansion of a community college offering similar courses. Finally, we examine the mechanics of market structure and operations within a subsector (cosmetology) of the proprietary school industry.

Some findings:

▪ The single most distinguishing feature of *profitable* schools is their ownership: they are owned by single individuals or small groups of people. None of the most profitable schools in Hyde's sample was owned by a parent corporation ". . . single owners as a whole may have deeper knowledge of and commitment to a school's operations than a group of individuals."

▪ Profitable schools spend very little to enroll students—in Hyde's sample, less than $100 per student, including the costs of recruitment, advertising, salespeople, bookkeeping, etc.

▪ Profitable schools operate with very low physical assets (in the study, less than $20,000 worth of equipment) but maintain relatively high enrollments (131 students).

▪ Profitable schools have higher student/faculty ratios. "Instructional costs often account for 60 percent of operating costs and thus any school that can maintain large classes may reduce operating costs considerably."

Hyde observes that new regulations affecting private school operations may eventually do everyone a disservice. Concerning the "full disclosure" requirements:

Before we impose a serious burden upon proprietary schools or spend large sums of monies (which would be necessary to obtain and disseminate the information) to provide such a service, we ought to have some inkling of how much practical use will stem from such efforts.

Even if students did avail themselves of the information, would it make any difference in what training they eventually choose? By itself, the fact that only a small percentage of proprietary school graduates receive employment in the occupation for which they were trained hardly justifies drawing the conclusion that students should have more information. It may well be that an *equally* small percentage of students in any type of training actually obtain employment in that field. Many students choose to change vocations. In a study of changes in vocational choices by community-college students, fully half of the sample changed their vocational choices within an 18-month period. Assuming that a number of students do not wish to change their vocational choice, what option do they have if the "screening" or "pyramid-ing" is equally great for all occupations? Clearly the appropriate perspective is not that the schools fail because they provide for only a small percentage of the total, but that they are successful in providing greater *opportunities* than any other system. Al-though many people may not obtain the exact job they would like to have, acquiring training may be the only chance a num-ber of people have for obtaining any employment.

And finally, no thought has been given to who would be re-sponsible for collecting such data or who would bear the costs of collecting the data necessary to provide prospective students with the basis for an informed choice. It is assumed implicitly that the proprietary school will be the agent. Yet, knowing how sensitive the financial structures of proprietary schools are, it is questionable whether they could bear these costs. If faced with the choice of collecting the data to allow them to make employment claims or relinquishing all claims to any vocational relevance, many might well choose the latter or (if the rules are too penalistic) simply close down—providing prospective students with less rather than more information and fewer training options.

In short, the enthusiasm for providing prospective students with more complete information has not been accompanied by either a consideration of possible alternatives or of the costs of in-formation. Certainly little evidence of the likely effectiveness of such a policy has been offered. . . .

Certainly any experimentation must involve not just propri-etary schools but all schools offering similar training. As long as one of our goals is to serve the best interests of consumers by im-proving the flow of information when individuals make a decision concerning the purchase of education, we ought to require all institutions providing similar training to supply the same statistics. Compelling one institution to provide information which when presented by itself might appear damaging to the school but when presented in contrast to other institutions indicates superior per-formance is misleading to the student and unfair to the school. The dropout rate in proprietary schools, for example, has been cited as a "problem." More to the point, this is a problem for all post-compulsory schooling. Surely every proprietary school would like to lower its drop-out rate, but the quoted 23 percent completion rate of computer school students or the 57 percent completion rate of business school students can be claimed to be as much a "solution" as a "problem." One must keep in mind the fact that in some community colleges about 20 percent of those beginning data processing courses finish and only 23 percent of those in business programs (half the proprietary school completion rate).

Historically, proprietary schools have survived in the face of forces over which they have little control, and which rarely enter the planning of public institutions, by shifting resources to meet changes in market and technological conditions and in student interests and by careful internal decisions. In recent years these conventional forces that govern a proprietary school's operations have been joined by competition from community colleges and by increased interest from educators and government, neither of which is necessarily harmful to the industry. But we must recognize that, although the eventual "settlement" between community colleges and proprietary schools is unknown, proprietary schools contribute a degree of flexibility, responsiveness, and diversity not so evident in public schools and may provide many services more efficiently than other institutions. If we seek to offer meaningful choices in post-secondary education and with consideration for costs, proprietary schools have the potential of being an instrumental component in achieving that efficiency and diversification.

7. Each year the American Council on Education surveys the backgrounds, characteristics and attitudes of thousands of college freshmen to develop national profiles that will help educational policy-makers identify trends in the nation's student body. Proprietary schools and vocational students were not a part of the universe surveyed until 1974. The results of a preliminary investigation were published in July, 1975 by the Higher Education Research Institute, Inc. of Los Angeles: "The Proprietary Student: A Pilot Study." The study itself was written by research analyst C. E. Christian. It supports the notion held by school owners that their students are a rather special lot, distinct from their public community college counterparts. One of the findings: proprietary students tend to be more "liberated." In response to the statement, "Women should receive the same salary and opportunities for advancement as men in comparable positions," 93.2 percent of proprietary students agreed, compared with 89.8 percent of community college students.

Following is the summary that accompanied the study.

SUMMARY REPORT OF PROPRIETARY
SCHOOL SURVEY

Proprietary school students are more confident of their educational and career plans and more labor-market oriented than other college students, according to a survey of 1400 students entering 15 technical and business schools across the country.

The survey, conducted in conjunction with the 1974 Co-operative Institutional Research Program sponsored jointly by the American Council on Education and the University of California, Los Angeles, showed that proprietary students view themselves as less likely to change their field of study or career choice or to seek vocational counseling, and as more confident of finding a job in their preferred field.

In choosing a career, the market-oriented concepts of high earnings, available jobs, and career advancement are more important to proprietary students than to other college freshmen. Proprietary students have higher self-ratings on academic, artistic, and writing abilities, as well as cheerfulness, attractiveness, popularity, drive to achieve, self-confidence and understanding, than do community college students. High school grades are slightly higher for the students entering proprietary schools than for community college freshmen in the national comparison group.

Concern about financing college is less pronounced among proprietary students than among other college freshmen. They make greater use of federal aid programs to finance their education, including Basic Educational Opportunity Grants, Supplemental Opportunity Grants, and federally insured student loans.

Life goals are similar for proprietary and other college students, although the proprietary students place a slightly higher value on raising a family and being financially successful. The proprietary students and other college freshmen share the same views on social issues, as revealed by their similar political orientation, dating behavior, and peer-group identification.

The proprietary schools in the sample enroll more nontraditional students than other postsecondary educational institutions, including greater proportions of older students, blacks, women, and veterans. Proprietary students consider academic reputation, special educational programs, and financial aid offers more important factors in the selection of a school than do their classmates in the national normative comparison group of all college and university freshmen.

APPENDIX F: A SUMMARY OF DISTINCTIONS BETWEEN COMMUNITY COLLEGE TRAINING PROGRAMS AND PROPRIETARY SCHOOLS

COMMUNITY COLLEGES	PROPRIETARY SCHOOLS
Mission: to provide collegiate education for everyone in their own hometown	Mission: to provide intensive job-oriented training
Open, passive admissions; non-selective	Sales approach to admissions
Faculty-centered	Student-centered
Students commuting; hometown distractions	Possibility of residence away from home
Large enrollments, averaging in thousands	Small enrollments, averaging in hundreds
Small vocational programs, few graduates	Sufficient graduates to attract employers
Major problems with student morale	Major problems with student financial assistance
Skill training combined with General Studies	Intensive skill training
Survival dependent on political process (taxes)	Survival dependent on reputation in the marketplace
Lectures and theory dominate training	"Hands-on" training emphasized
Teaching theory (input) emphasized	Results of instruction (output) emphasized
Students with uncertain career goals	Students committed to training and job goals
Three admission dates in school year	Year round, regular admission points
Majority—70 percent—are two-year programs	Majority—60 percent—are 4–12-month programs
Instructors tend to be middle-aged; absent longer from a job situation	Mixture of young and older instructors

COMMUNITY COLLEGES	PROPRIETARY SCHOOLS
Instructors have academic credentials	Instructors have credentials from world of work
Faculty protected by unions and tenure	Teachers hired and fired on basis of teaching skill only
Teachers paid more and work less	Teachers work harder and are paid less
Teachers involved in committee work	Teachers have few extra duties
20–40 percent of students complete course	50–90 percent of students complete course
Passive job placement	Active job placement
No record kept of course completion and placement	Records kept to prove performance
Value-free learning environment	Work ethic emphasized; discipline-oriented learning environment
Duplicates atmosphere of middle-class high school	Simulates work environment
Political, bureaucratic constrictions inhibit change	Rapid response to student and labor markets
Schools have institutional image and identity problems	Schools have problems with public acceptance and their own low self-concept
Strong liberal arts program	Liberal arts rarely offered; usually only fair
Remedial programs given low status	Remedial programs emphasized; enable schools to accept wider range of students
Complex college registration process	Uncomplicated procedures and requirements
Revolving door: casual enrollment and dropping out	Contracts bind students and schools together

BIBLIOGRAPHY

This bibliography is intended not only as a listing of sources used in writing this book, but also as a comprehensive guide to written material about the proprietary schools.

SOURCES AND GUIDES

American Trade Schools Directory. Croner Publications, 211–05 Jamaica Avenue, Queens Village, New York 11428. A loose-leaf book containing a list of about 5,000 private and public trade, industrial, and vocational schools, updated by monthly supplement sheets. Cost for book and one-year supplement service is $20.00.

The American Legion. *Need a Lift?* Published annually by the American Legion, Department S.P.O. Box 1055, Indianapolis, Indiana 46202. Price 50¢. A fine guide to careers, loans, scholarships.

Bird, Caroline. *The Case Against College.* New York: David McKay and Co., 1975. An excellent resource for people contemplating not-college. Case studies, a national list of people and organizations that will help find alternative solutions.

B'Nai B'Rith Career and Counseling Services. *Resources: Recommendations for Adult Career Resources.* B'Nai B'Rith Career and Counseling Services, 1640 Rhode Island Avenue, N.W., Washington, D.C. 20036. An innovative compendium of sources for career information materials. The materials are reviewed and addresses given.

College Entrance Examination Board. *The New York Times Guide to Continuing Education in America.* New York: Quadrangle Books, 1972. A thick and forbidding book packed with information "for adults who would love to pick up their education where they left off."

Coyne, John and Hebert, Tom. *By Hand: A Guide to Schools and Careers in Crafts.* New York: E. P. Dutton, 1974.

Edfac Publishing Company. *Career School Directory.* Edfac Publishing Company, 5126 Galena Drive, Colorado Springs, Colorado 80907. A well-done directory of proprietary schools. Cost is $12.95. Includes only names and addresses, but the book has as many of those as you'll need.

Evers, Dora, and Feingold, Norman. *Your Future in Exotic Occupations.* New York: Richard Rosen Press, 1972. A good book to daydream with.

Lederer, Muriel. *The Guide to Career Education.* New York: Quadrangle Books, 1974. Four hundred pages of occupations and information. Deadly serious.

Porter, Lee. *Degrees for Sale.* New York: Arco Books, 1972. Discusses degree mills, honorary degrees, etc.

U.S. Department of Labor. *Occupational Outlook Handbook.* Washington, D.C.: Government Printing Office, biannually. Eight hundred pages of occupations and information.

U.S. Office of Education. *Directory of Post-secondary Schools with Occupational Programs, 1974.* Washington, D.C.: Government Printing Office. This is the first list of public and proprietary schools offering career programs ever attempted by the government.

MAGAZINE ARTICLES ABOUT
PROPRIETARY EDUCATION

Bird, Caroline, and Necel, Stephen. "College: Dumbest Investment of All." *Esquire*, September 1974, p. 102.

Burck, Charles G. "Schools Where Students Pay to Learn Paying Jobs." *Fortune*, December 1975, pp. 124–130.

Cross, Patricia K. "The New Learners." *Change*, February 1973, pp. 31–35.

"Learning for Earning." *Time*, July 31, 1972.

Levin, Henry M. "Vouchers and Social Equity." *Change*, October 1973, pp. 29–34.

Shoemaker, Ellwood A. "The Challenge of Proprietary Schools." *Change*, Summer 1973, pp. 71–72.

Spitzer, Dana L. "Unselling the College Myth." *Change*, February 1973, pp. 25–28.

Wilms, Wellford W. "A New Look at Proprietary Schools." *Change*, Summer 1973, pp. 6–8.

"Vocational Schools: Promises, Promises." *Newsweek*, March 13, 1972.

NEWSPAPER ARTICLES ABOUT
PROPRIETARY EDUCATION

"Brooke accuses many career schools of 'ripoff.'" *Boston Globe*, November 19, 1974.

"Career schools provide real service." Letters Department, *Boston Globe*, July 1, 1974 (evening).

"Colleges Shift to Hard Sell in Recruiting of Students." *New York Times*, March 31, 1974.

"Extensive revamping of Vocational Education Urged." *New York Times*, October 13, 1974.

"FTC called biased on career schools." *Boston Globe*, November 22, 1974.

"The Knowledge Hustlers." *Washington Post*, June 23–June 26, 1974.

"Spotlight Series." *Boston Globe*, March 26–April 18, 1974.

von Hoffman, Nicholas. "The Hallowed Halls vs. the Education Mongers." *Washington Post*, August 30, 1975.

MARKET SURVEYS FOR PROPRIETARY EDUCATION

Edubusiness, Inc. *The Proprietary Schools Market.* Edubusiness, Inc., 1970 (privately published).

Stanford Research Institute. *Proprietary Occupational Schools.* Menlo Park, California: Stanford Research Institute, 1973 (privately published).

JOURNAL ARTICLES

"Colleges Weigh Larger Role of Proprietaries." *Chronicle of Higher Education,* March 26, 1974.

Glenny, Lyman. "Pressures on Higher Education." *College and University Journal,* September 1973.

"Low Income Students Found Favoring Proprietary Schools for Job Training." *Chronicle of Higher Education,* February 25, 1974.

Nash, Robert, and Agne, Russell. "Career Education—The Final Impoverishment of Learning?" *Peabody Journal of Education,* April 1973, pp. 245–254.

"Student Demands for 'Practical' Education Are Forcing Major Changes in Curricula." *Chronicle of Higher Education,* November 26, 1973.

SPEECHES

Glenny, Lyman. "The Race for Students: Competitive Challenges in Post-secondary Education." Speech before 1973 NATTS Conference. Available from National Association of Trade and Technical Schools, Washington, D.C.

Nyquist, Ewald B. "Giving Things Trade and Technical Pride of Place." Speech before the 1972 NATTS Conference. *Congressional Record,* Senate, September 22, 1972. Nyquist is New York State Commissioner of Education.

Worthington, Robert M. "Career Education: An Alliance with Private Vocational Schools." Speech before the 1972 NATTS Conference. *Congressional Record,* House, January 6, 1973. Worthington was Associate Commissioner for Adult, Vocational and Technical Education, U.S. Office of Education.

GOVERNMENT DOCUMENTS

"Proprietary Vocational and Home Study Schools." Federal Trade Commission. Documents of Accrediting Commissions. File No. 215–38, Public Reference Room, FTC, Washington, D.C., 1974.

"Reducing Abuses in Proprietary Vocational Education," House, Committee on Government Operations, House Report No. 93–1649, Washington, D.C.: Government Printing Office, 1974.

"What Is the Role of Federal Assistance for Vocational Education?" General Accounting Office, Washington, D.C. Report and Analysis of Office of Education programs, January 1975.

PROPRIETARY SCHOOL RESEARCH

American Institutes for Research. *A Comparative Study of Proprietary and Non-proprietary Vocational Training Programs*. Palo Alto, Ca.: Author, 1972.

Belitsky, A. Harvey. *Proprietary Vocational Schools and Their Students*. Cambridge: Schenkman, 1969.

Christian, C. E. *The Proprietary Student: A Pilot Study*. Los Angeles, Ca.: Higher Education Research Institute, Inc., 1975.

Clark, Harold F. and Sloan, Harold S. *Classrooms on Main Street*. New York: Columbia University Press, 1966.

Erickson, E. W. et al. *Proprietary Business School and Community Colleges*. Washington, D.C.: Inner City Fund, Inc., 1972.

Foster, C. L. *Missouri Private Vocational Schools: A Better Life for More People*. Jefferson City, Missouri: The Missouri Advisory Council on Vocational Education, 1974.

Hoyt, K. B. "SOS: A Call to Action." *American Vocational Journal*, May 1968.

————. "The Specialty Oriented Student Research Program: An Illustration of Applied Computer Technology." *Educational Technology*, 1971.

————. "The Individual and His Choice of Vocational Education." In *Second Yearbook of the American Vocational Association*. Washington, D.C.: American Vocational Association, 1972.

Hyde, William D. *Metropolitan Proprietary Schools: A Study of Functions and Economic Responsiveness.* Washington, D.C.: National Institute of Education, 1974.

Irwin, J. Michael. *The Proprietary School: Assessing its Impact on the Collegiate Sector.* Ann Arbor, Mich.: Center for the Study of Higher Education, 1975.

Johnson, Susan E. *Proprietary Education: A Search of the Literature.* Berkeley, Ca.: Center for Research and Development in Higher Education, University of California, 1974.

Katz, H. H. *Independent Private School Industry in the State of Illinois.* Springfield, Ill.: State Advisory Council on Vocational Education, 1973.

Kincaid, H. and Podesta, E. *An Exploratory Survey of Proprietary Vocational Schools.* Palo Alto, Ca.: Stanford Research Institute, 1966.

Moses, Stanley. *The Learning Force: A More Comprehensive Framework for Educational Policy.* Syracuse, New York: Syracuse University, October, 1971. (ED 053 378)

Miller, J. and Hamilton, W. J. *The Independent Business School in American Education.* New York: McGraw-Hill, 1964.

Miller, J. H. et al. *Civilian Vocational School Study.* Silver Spring, Md.: Presearch, Inc. (Prepared for the Chief of Naval Operations).

Reigner, Charles G. *Beginnings of the Business School.* Baltimore: H. M. Rowe Company, 1962.

Trivett, David A. *Proprietary Schools and Post-secondary Education.* ERIC/Higher Education Research Report No. 2. Washington, D.C.: American Association for Higher Education, 1974.

Wilms, Wellford W. *The Effectiveness of Public and Proprietary Occupational Training.* Berkeley, Ca.: Center for Research and Development in Higher Education, November 1974.

———. "Proprietary and Public Vocational Students." *ERIC Research Currents.* Washington, D.C.: American Association for Higher Education, March 1974.

———. *Proprietary versus Public Vocational Training.* Berkeley, Ca.: Center for Research and Development in Higher Education, University of California, November 1973.

U.S. Congress. House Republican Task Force on Education and Training. *Report on Proprietary Vocational Schools.* Reported in *Congressional Record,* H.R., Vol. 116, August 12, 1970.

DISSERTATIONS AND THESES

Bond, Sheryl. "Postsecondary Education in Accredited Private Vocational Schools." ED.D. Thesis, Bloomington, Ind.: Indiana University, 1974.

Coyle, Edward James. "Programs of Accreditation for Private Business Schools." ED.D. Thesis, Norman, Okla.: University of Oklahoma, 1959.

Hamilton, William J. "The Regulation of Proprietary Schools in the United States." Ph.D. Thesis, Philadelphia, Pa.: University of Pennsylvania, 1958.

Johnson, Elouise L. "A Descriptive Survey of Teachers of Private and Technical Schools Associated with the National Association of Trade and Technical Schools." ED.D. Thesis, Washington, D.C.: George Washington University, 1967.

Klinger, Clyde E. "State Licensure and License Laws Applied to Private Business Schools in the United States." ED.D. Thesis, University Park, Pa.: Pennsylvania State University, 1958.

Painter, Donald Edward. "The Private EDP School and Accreditation." M.A. Thesis, Washington, D.C.: School of Government and Business Administration of the George Washington University, 1969.

Snare, John L. "An Economic Analysis of the Veterans' Education Program Below the College Level, 1945–1955." Ph.D. Thesis, Durham, N.C.: Duke University, 1971.

RELATED STUDIES

Bolino, August C. *Occupational Education as a Source of Economic Growth.* U.S. Department of Labor, Manpower Administration. Office of Research and Development, 1972.

Educational Testing Service. *Report on Educational Assistance Programs for Veterans.* Princeton, N.J.: Educational Testing Service, 1973.

Jencks, Christopher, et al. *Education Vouchers.* Cambridge: Center for the Study of Public Policy, 1970 (Chapter 6).

Kaufman, Jacob J., and Lewis, Morgan V. *The High School Diploma: Credential for Employment?* University Park, Pa.: Institute for Research on Human Problems, Pennsylvania State University, 1972.

Mayhew, Lewis B. *Higher Education for Occupations.* Atlanta: Southern Regional Education Board, 1974 (Chapter 2).

National Commission on the Financing of Post-secondary Education. *Financing Post-secondary Education in the United States.* Washington, D.C.: Government Printing Office, 1973.

Orlans, Harold. *Private Accreditation and Public Eligibility.* Lexington, Mass.: Lexington Books, 1975.

Panel on Youth of the President's Science Advisory Committee. *Youth: Transition to Adulthood.* Washington, D.C.: Government Printing Office, 1973.

Task Force on Work in America. *Work in America.* New York: Praeger Books, 1973.

COMMUNITY COLLEGES

Astin, Alexander W. "The Measured Effects of Higher Education." *The Annals of the American Academy of Political and Social Science,* November 1972, pp. 1–20.

Bender, Louis W. "Community Colleges Should Adopt Competitive Free Market Initiatives." *Community College Review,* Fall 1973, pp. 15–22.

Bushnell, David S., and Kievit, Mary Bach. "Community Colleges: What Is Our Job?" *Change,* April 1974, pp. 52–53.

Citizens' Task Force on Higher Education, State of Ohio. *Final Report to the General Assembly.* Columbus: Ohio Board of Regents, May 1974.

Corcoran, Thomas B. "The Coming Slums of Higher Education?" *Change,* September 1972, pp. 30–35.

Illinois Economic and Fiscal Commission. *The Illinois Public Junior College System: Program Review, 1973.* Springfield: Author, 1973.

Karabel, Jerome. "Community Colleges and Social Stratification." *Harvard Educational Review,* November 1972.

Miami-Dade Community College. *Final Report from the Ad Hoc Committee to Study Attrition at Miami-Dade Community College, North Campus.* Miami, May 1973 (mimeographed).

Pincus, Fred L. *Tracking in the Community Colleges.* Research Group One Report No. 18. Baltimore: Research Group One, 1974.

Roueche, John E. *A Modest Proposal: Students Can Learn.* San Francisco: Jossey-Bass, 1972.

Zwerling, Steven L., and Park, Dabney, Jr. "Curriculum Comprehensiveness and Tracking: The Community College's Commitment to Failure." *Community College Review*, Spring 1974, pp. 10–20.

CORRESPONDENCE EDUCATION

Alexander, William M. *Independent Study in Secondary Schools.* New York: Holt, Rinehart and Winston, Inc., 1967.

Erdos, Renee F. *Teaching by Correspondence.* London: Longman, Green & Co., 1967.

Glatter, Ron, and Wedell, E. G. *Study by Correspondence.* London: Longman Group Limited, 1971.

Gleason, Gerald T., ed. *The Theory and Nature of Independent Learning.* Scranton, Pa.: International Textbook Company, 1967.

Kempfer, Homer. *Private Home Study Schools in Illinois.* Springfield: State of Illinois Advisory Council on Vocational Education, 1973.

Lockmiller, David A. "Correspondence Education." *Encyclopaedia Britannica*, 1968, pp. 544–45.

MacKenzie, Ossian, and Christensen, Edward L., eds. *The Changing World of Correspondence Study.* University Park, Pa.: Pennsylvania State University Press, 1971.

MacKenzie, Ossian, et al. *Correspondence Instruction in the United States.* New York: McGraw-Hill, 1968.

Pugni, J. L. *Adult Education Through Home Study.* New York: ARCO, 1965.

Wedemeyer, Charles A., ed. *The Brandenburg Memorial Essays on Correspondence Instruction*, 2 volumes. Madison, Wis.: University of Wisconsin Press, 1963.

————, and Childs, Gayle B. *New Perspectives in University Correspondence Study.* Chicago: Center for Study of Liberal Education for Adults, 1961.

GENERAL WORKS

Arendt, Hannah. *The Human Condition*. New York: Garden City, Doubleday, 1959 (especially Chapters 3–4).

Barker, Roger C. *Ecological Psychology*. Stanford: Stanford University Press, 1968 (especially Chapter 7).

Berg, Ivar. *Education and Jobs: The Great Training Robbery*. Boston: Beacon Press, 1971 (especially Chapters 4 and 9).

Berger, Peter, ed. *The Human Shape of Work*. New York: Macmillan, 1964.

Callahan, Raymond E. *Education and the Cult of Efficiency*. A study of the Social Forces That Have Shaped the Administration of the Public Schools. Chicago: University of Chicago Press, 1962.

Cremin, Lawrence A. *The Transformation of the School*. New York: Random House/Vintage, 1961 (especially Chapters 1 and 2).

Foote, Nelson N., and Cottrell, Leonard S. *Identity and Interpersonal Competence*. Chicago: University of Chicago Press, 1955 (especially Chapter 4).

Goodman, Paul. *People or Personnel*. New York: Random House/Vintage, 1968 (especially Chapters 4 and 6).

Holland, John L. *The Psychology of Vocational Choice*. Waltham, Mass.: Blaisdell, 1966.

Hoyt, Kenneth B., et al. *Career Education: What It Is and How to Do It*. Salt Lake City: Olympus Publishing Co., 1972.

Marland, Sidney P. *Career Education: A Proposal for Reform*. New York: McGraw-Hill, 1974.

Mumford, Lewis. *The Myth of the Machine: The Pentagon of Power*. New York: Harcourt, Brace and Jovanovich, 1970 (especially Chapters 6 and 7).

Schumacher, E. F. *Small Is Beautiful*. New York: Harper Torch Books, 1973 (especially Chapters 5, Part I; 4, Part IV. Excellent introduction by Theodore Roszak).

■ 253